WORLD

HAU
BOOKS

www.haubooks.com

WORLD
AN ANTHROPOLOGICAL EXAMINATION

João de Pina-Cabral

The Malinowski Monographs Series

Hau Books
Chicago

The Malinowski Monographs Series (Volume 1)

The Malinowski Monographs showcase groundbreaking monographs that contribute to the emergence of new ethnographically-inspired theories. In tribute to the foundational, yet productively contentious, nature of the ethnographic imagination in anthropology, this series honors Bronislaw Malinowski, the coiner of the term "ethnographic theory." The series publishes short monographs that develop and critique key concepts in ethnographic theory (e.g., money, magic, belief, imagination, world, humor, love, etc.), and standard anthropological monographs—based on original research—that emphasize the analytical move from ethnography to theory.

Cover and layout design: Sheehan Moore

Typesetting: Prepress Plus (www.prepressplus.in)

ISBN: 978-0-9973675-0-8
LCCN: 2016961546

HAU Books
Chicago Distribution Center
11030 S. Langley
Chicago, IL 60628
www.haubooks.com

HAU Books is marketed and distributed by The University of Chicago Press.
www.press.uchicago.edu

Printed in the United States of America on acid-free paper.

Table of Contents

Preface

What do we mean when we refer to world? How does world relate to the human person? Are the two interdependent, and, if so, in what way? What is the world at hand for an ethnographer? Much has been said of worlds and worldviews, but are we really certain that we know what we mean when we use these words?

This book is centrally concerned with exploring the conditions of possibility of the ethnographic gesture and, by implication, with ethnographic theory and the debates that presently fire it. The important changes that have occurred over the past two decades concerning the way in which we relate human cognition with humanity's embodiedness strongly suggest that we are on the threshold of a new conceptualization of the human condition—a new anthropology—that breaks away from the sociocentric and representationalist constraints that plagued the social sciences throughout the twentieth century. This essay is a contribution toward that momentous change.

I myself have a long career as an ethnographer, and that is what, over the years, moved me to engage with theory. Consequently, most of what I have written here is directly informed by the three long-term ethnographic projects I have carried out over the decades (rural NW Portugal, 1986; urban Eurasians in south China, 2002a; naming systems in NE Brazil, with V. Silva 2013). All of them have been centrally engaged with contemporaneity, in contexts where modernity was the order of the day, and where globalization was everywhere present. Whether by chance or design, the fact is I was never allowed to entertain the primitivistic fancies that continue to enthrall so many of our colleagues.

This led me very early on to place a central focus on historicism as part of ethnography, on the one hand, and on its political significance, on the other. Having first encountered anthropology in South Africa during the period of apartheid and then moved to postrevolutionary Portugal, I was from the outset convinced of the political and moral worth of the ethnographic enterprise—not as a direct instrument of resistance against exploitation and oppression (as some of my teachers espoused), but as a necessary means for debunking hegemonic truths, among them racist and classist convictions and imperialist lies.

The ethnographic empiricism that has marked my intellectual path is something that I cherish and which I mean to continue to pursue in the future. Nevertheless, from the very beginning, I have been struck by the fact that ethnographic description cannot be undertaken without the support of comparative analysis and of anthropological (and, more broadly, social scientific) theoretical elaboration. There is something dishonest—or, better phrased, unfortunate—about writing ethnography as if (a) one could dispense with theory or (b) one were the first ethnographer to visit "my people." In particular, one is struck by the transparent delusion of those among our colleagues who manage to convince themselves that they no longer need to engage honestly with the history of the discipline! Over the years, I have systematically pursued these convictions and today I find myself writing a book that in many ways traces the paths where that constant engagement with theoretical and ethnographic history has led me.

The starting point here was to make sense of the notion of world. The concept became central to anthropology ever since Paul Veyne's study of the attitudes of classical Greeks toward their myths impacted our discipline ([1983] 1988). But, in the mid-2000s, it became apparent that serious confusions were being espoused. We needed to go back to the drawing board. This was particularly evident the moment anthropological thinking came to be influenced by neurophenomenology and the philosophers who propose radical embodied cognition. One could perceive there the glimpse of a sophisticated new path out of the fin-de-siècle idealist disposition, and the corresponding self-serving paternalism, that besieged anthropology during the 1990s and 2000s. Suddenly, the poststructuralist efforts of our teachers in Oxford in the late 1970s came to appear increasingly relevant.

Thus, when I took up Donald Davidson in the late 1990s, the idea was to find a path from his epistemologically clear waters toward the more murky waters of phenomenology that I would inevitably have to navigate if I wanted to study personhood, presence, and transcendence. Supported by his advice

(Davidson 2005), at no point did I worry about mixing different inspirations or picking and choosing concepts and arguments from diverse sources, so long as they stood well together. My goal was clear: to produce a minimal realist anthropological account that both safeguards the ethnographic task and illuminates the human condition.

It was not until I started moving from chapter to chapter that some of the central arguments of the book emerged. As the title suggests, the starting point was an examination of world as it is to be found in the work of our contemporary colleagues (chapter 1, "World"). That led directly to an encounter with the challenge of transcendence, as it continues to be one of the more contentious sides of our discipline. It became apparent that, although many of us chose to ignore it, contemporary anthropology remains deeply indebted to Evans-Pritchard's struggles with faith, augury, and witchcraft at midcentury. Thus, I was led to his inspiration in R. G. Collingwood's thought and to the Ontological Proof of God's existence (chapter 2, "Transcendence"). Transcendence raises the issue of imagination. Sartre and Evan Thompson were the inspirations for a move beyond representationalist approaches, in search of the limits of imagination (chapter 3, "Imagination"). In turn, that implied a revisitation of Wittgenstein's impact on my Oxford teachers in the 1970s and on the work of the contemporary philosophers who are exploring radical embodied cognition (chapter 4, "Person"). Finally, the argument came together in an attempt to show that personhood and world correspond but that metaphysical pluralism is the abiding condition (chapter 5, "Worldview"). In the course of the narrative, some discussions and concepts are reencountered time and again as they become increasingly clarified. This is the case, for example, with the central differentiation between intentionality and propositionality, with personal ontogeny, with personhood and presence, with cohabitation, with ontological weight, with retentivity, with the ethnographic gesture, and with relation and relatedness.

In writing the book, I was obliged to dialogue with concepts and arguments originating in very many and very diverse disciplines (neuropsychology, phenomenology, critical philosophy, analytical philosophy, developmental psychology, physics, human geography, political science, etc.). There is nothing surprising about this, as social anthropology has ever been open to broad intellectual inspiration—indeed, this is one of the more appealing facets of our disciplinary tradition. It is notably the case during moments, such as our present one, when we need to break with the established grooves of received wisdom in order to address some central quandary. The result is that this book is punctuated by words and arguments that many readers may find unfamiliar. The reader should not stop reading upon encountering an unfamiliar concept, as I have made a point of proposing definitions for all of the central concepts explored in the book. For reasons of narrative economy, however, these definitions are not always to be found at the point of first encounter with the concept.

In attempting to achieve an anthropology of person and world, I have unearthed three central aspects of each of them that respond in broad terms to the way in which our analysis of *sociality* has evolved:

(i)   the world embraces humans as a *source* due to their capacity to address it intentionally (i.e., with purpose), thus initiating worlding;

(ii) as, in becoming persons, humans acquire a presence, they start confronting the world perspectivally as a *domain*, so the world encompasses them dyadically;

(iii) and, finally, with the rise of propositional thinking, the world is divided by symbols into a myriad of intrinsically plural entities. Relations emerge out of the containment imposed by the *limits* of propositionality.

Transcendence is our privilege as persons; it is what allows us to see the world as creation, a world which includes us. Yet, owing to this very personal transcendence, metaphysical pluralism is not reducible. From an anthropological perspective, the ambivalence of world that Heidegger identified (its uncertainty, its fuzziness, its indeterminacy) *cannot and should not* be resolved; it remains with us as a challenge, for it is a central conditioning feature of the emergence of persons in world. In his own distinct mode of speaking, Davidson called it "the anomaly" (2004: 121). Ethnography—an examination of humans carried out by persons in ontogeny—must learn to operate within that condition, frustrating as it may at times be.

I hope, thus, to have contributed toward creating the space of possibility for an ethnographic theory for the twenty-first century that remains essentially realist and within the parameters of the broader scientific project, but that opens up new pathways for the continued conceptual incorporation of ever-new ethnographic evidence. The anthropology here proposed is not one that belongs to Greeks or Trojans, but one that leaves itself open in human history to ever-widening levels of ecumenical incorporation. The beauty of ethnography as a scientific method is that it calls on its practitioners to remain fully, participatingly human; never to attempt to rise above our common human history, whatever it may come to be.

Acknowledgments

I have been blessed with friends who, as Cicero would have it, have dealt with me *cum benevolentia et caritate* (1884: VI, 20). Without their patience, their curiosity, and their contrary arguments, none of this would have come to light.

The idea of writing on world emerged from the debates I had with Christina Toren and Andre Gingrich at the time of our seminar on "The Challenge of Epistemology" (see Toren and Pina-Cabral 2011). The first attempt to present the main argument took place at a conference in honor of Andre in October 2012, at Eva-Maria Knoll's generous invitation, in a beautiful hall overlooking Vienna's autumnal Prater. Ulf Hannerz and Marcus Banks were there and their suggestions were precious.

Once he heard what I was writing about, Giovanni da Col, with his unwaveringly critical comments, became the primary mover of this project. That was a trust that I cherish, for in my already long career I have found that there are very few publishers with true vision. At the time, Glenn Bowman and Cecilia McCallum egged me on; they were important inspirations. But my own father's youthful fascination with Saint Anselm, and the dear company of both of their ghosts each time I pass by Canterbury Cathedral (for some weird twist of fate, I now live round the corner), contributed much to the writing of this chapter.

The third chapter, written subsequent to supervising Joana Gonçalo Oliveira's MA thesis on the late thinking of Rodney Needham, is a mark of the profound influence that the latter left on my comparative thinking throughout the decades. He knew I was grateful for his prickly intellectual generosity and I know that, if he were still alive, he would most likely reject vehemently what

I make of his arguments. In turn, I was privileged by having been able to count with the contribution of Joana's acute theoretical curiosity.

Chapter 4 has been essentially written for a very long time. I never published it, however, for I received an irritated letter of rejection from *L'Homme* that made me aware that, without the preparation of the chapters that now precede it, the argument would seem outlandish to the more conventional. It was originally written as the result of long and intense debates with Joan Bestard Camps as a response to our teaching together a class on kinship theory to his MA students. Whilst my opinions are strictly personal, his contribution to this debate and to the formation of my thinking is immense. Enric Porqueres i Gené shared skeptically some of these discussions in the bars and streets of balmy Barcelona. I am deeply grateful for their companionship and for their love of argument. In 2009, my stay as Tinker Professor in the Department of Anthropology of the University of Chicago and, later on, as Invited Professor at the EHESS in Paris (and my conversations with Stephan Palmié in Chicago and Philippe Descola in Paris) were influential to the shaping of these arguments as they developed through the series of papers on naming that I was then writing for my joint project with Susana Matos Viegas, "The Web of Territoriality." Later still, Catarina Fróis and Ann MacLarnon were also helpful critics. During our many treks and travels, Minnie Freudenthal and Manuel Ribeiro do Rosário were a constant source of argument and inspiration. Throughout all of this, I am most grateful of all to Monica Chan, for having always supported me unswervingly through thick and thin.

As I was drafting the lines of conclusion, I was informed of Hermínio Martins's sudden death. I dedicate this book to a man whose erudition was as vast as his interpretive charity.

Canterbury, January 2017

CHAPTER ONE

World

Anthropologists, historians, and qualitative sociologists often take recourse to the word *world* as if its meaning were self-evident. While, indeed, it might be argued that the broad enterprise of science is nothing but a study of world, the word remains highly ambivalent, often extending its meaning in a perilously polysemic fashion in the course of any single debate. When we describe some feature of the "world of the Nyakyusa" (Wilson 1951), which differs from that of other peoples, the meaning of the word is rather distant from that given to it by philosophers when they speak of "world-involving sentient activity" (Hutto and Myin 2013: 157); the same applies when we oppose home to world (Jackson 1995), or when we talk of social world, as Bourdieu so often did (e.g., 1991). How do these meanings combine? Is world still a useful category for ethnographers?

Of late, as it happens, the category has been playing a rather crucial role in anthropological debates. Tim Ingold, for instance, predicates one of his seminal arguments with the statement, "People do not import their ideas, plans or mental representations into the world, since the very world . . . is the homeland of their thoughts' (1995: 76). Here, we can assume that Ingold means by world something akin to Martin Heidegger's "the manifestness of beings as such as a whole" ([1929/30] 1995: 304), in short, everything that there is. So, the meaning of the word would differ from a more socially localized one, as in "the world of the Nyakyusa." And yet that leaves out the main perplexity posed by Ingold's sentence: there being many ways of deciding what there is, which one should his reader adopt?

These perplexities have haunted the social sciences for a very long time. Twentieth-century anthropologists ranged from those who espoused more or less unsophisticated forms of realism to those who adopted semiotic idealisms. On the one hand, for example, there was Max Gluckman's positivism or Marvin Harris' materialism; on the other, there was the kind of idealism that James Boon and David Schneider argued for in the 1970s when they proposed "liberating" kinship as a "cultural semantic field" from "sociofunctional prerequisites," granting it "an autonomous integrity analyzable in its own right" (Boon and Schneider 1974: 814). There is a dichotomist propensity at work in anthropological theory that makes it somehow safer to adopt either one or the other extreme. In midcentury England, this was largely represented by Evans-Pritchard's radical rejection of the Durkheimian positivism of his predecessors in his 1949 Marett Lecture, "Social anthropology: Past and present" (1962), and was long instanced in the Oxford versus Cambridge divide. But the dichotomist propensity continued: once more, in the 1980s, American postmodernist interpretivism reengaged it; and then, in the 2000s, perspectivism brought it back all over again. To opt for a starting point such as Roy Wagner's "man invents his own realities" (1975: ix) is to engage a dangerous truism, for whilst in one sense this is a verifiable observation, in another sense it leads us profoundly astray, pushing to secondary level the central fact that our existence (and all human communication) is predicated on the inhabiting of a largely common world.

Over the past four decades, as I proceeded with my own ethnographic projects,[1] I could not help but feel that we had to overcome this dichotomist propensity, as it was both intellectually reductive and ethically unviable. This book constitutes an attempt to articulate the structure of the concept of world (cf. Frankfurt 2009: 2) as it is being used in contemporary anthropological debates with the primary aim of developing a theoretical approach toward the possibility of the ethnographic gesture. The book proposes a view concerning world that aims at overcoming the effects of the *all-or-nothing fallacy* that so often dominates anthropological theorization, that is, "the fallacy of reasoning from the fact that there is nothing we might not be wrong about to the conclusion that we might be wrong about everything" (Davidson 2001: 45).

---

1.   See www.pina-cabral.org for a review of these projects.

Our inquiry here is different from Martin Heidegger's question in his famous lecture course of 1929/30 (1995): "what is world?" It differs in that we do not ask about the essence of world or its entities; rather, we aim to lay out the conditions of possibility for the ethnographic gesture. Our inquiry is about "the world which is present at hand" to the ethnographer. As Foucault put it concerning Kant's *Anthropology from a pragmatic point of view*, our aim is rather "not the description of what man is but what he can make of himself" ([1961] 2008: 52).

Thus, as ethnographers, we do not ask "is there world?" but, in the wake of Wittgenstein's inspiration, we ask "what world are we engaging?" This book, therefore, examines the everyday blurred concept of world that is a permanent component of all human engagement. Our starting point is that, for the persons ethnographers engage with, there is world; persons live with the assumption of world. This being the case, world is an evidence for ethnographers and what we are called to do as anthropologists is to see how world works out for us—whether or not there "actually" is world. As it happens, in any case, one is bound to agree with Sean Gaston—who has written a history of the concept of world since Kant—that it is pointless to try to avoid the experience that humans have of being "*in media res*, a finding oneself in the midst, in the middle of a relation to an indefinite and ungraspable beginning and end" (2013: 161) After all, this too was Kant's founding concern in his *Anthropology*.

Therefore, and since we are not metaphysicians but anthropologists, it would be pointless for me to deny world, because the evidence of its role in human sociality is such that we would be denying our vocation. And as to the worthiness of the anthropological endeavor, that is, I am afraid, a judgment that we must answer historically rather than metaphysically. The worthiness of anthropology (and of ethnographic methodology) can only be assessed by what it has allowed us to see over the years about the world we live in, the world amidst which we cannot but be. Therefore, we cannot grant much authority on that matter to metaphysicians when they deny world (e.g., Gabriel 2015). Finally, most of these philosophical debates on world start and finish with language. Since all of us are persons, there is nothing surprising about that. But it does mean that we allow ourselves to fall into anthropocentrism, and that is something that our very ethical constitution as humans does not recommend that we do.

As humans, we are also animals, and the world in the midst of which we cannot but find ourselves has a lot to do with the world of the animal that we also continue to be—that *we are*, note, not were. So, we have to see that, language being ours, we have means to inscribe things in the world that our coevals of other species do not, but we broadly share with them many of these things, for animals too are in the midst of world. Here we must agree with today's vital materialists (e.g., Bennett 2010 or Connolly 2011) that our very humanity obliges us to de-anthropocentrify. In short, even although it will always be developed within language, an anthropological examination of world cannot be bound by the limits of language, for the world as a condition antedates historically and remains beyond language.

Therefore, while this book is concerned with the world of persons, we cannot discard or reduce the significance of what Heidegger calls "the comparative examination" ([1929/1930] 1995: 176–78). In fact, his three theses—that a stone has no world, that an animal is poor in world, and that a human is world forming—help us focus on an important characteristic of some of the debates that have been firing of late the interdisciplinary understanding of human existence. They must be understood as a broad formulation of the principal levels of differentiation in the relation with world.

In the wake of Bruno Latour, there are many who question not only that humans are the only world-forming agents but also that stones have no world. People such as Jane Bennett have argued convincingly in favor of the need "to undo the conceit that humanity is the sole or ultimate well-spring of agency" (2010: 30). Similarly, William Connolly sustains that we live in an "immanent world of becoming," and thus he decries what he calls "the anthropic exception," that is, the "radical break between humanity and other processes" (2011: 31). One is bound to agree broadly with these thinkers, but one has to admit that Heidegger's theses—while they cannot be taken on board today in the precise way they were phrased—do outline three broad conditions of differentiation before the world that impose themselves. These conditions of differentiation must be seen as levels of emergence in the sense that Jagdish Hattiangadi (2005) has memorably proposed. Thus, I find it impossible to follow Bennett's diktat that we must "bracket the question of the human" (2010: ix), for that is precisely what anthropology cannot do, since human personhood is a level of emergence: that is, it gives rise to a stable whole that, once it has arisen, can be seen as self-perpetuating in the sense that it can only be understood to the extent that it interacts with itself (Hattiangadi 2005: 88).

It is hardly a matter of "placing humans at the ontological centre or hierarchical apex" (Bennett 2010: 11), but it is a matter of understanding the specific characteristics of human emergence as a self-perpetuating facet of the world.

To do that we have to engage with the nature of personhood, since only persons can engage in propositional thinking and, therefore, address the world as world. Ours is not a generic human condition; it is the condition of historically specific persons in ontogeny.[2] Our world is not only human; it is personal—and there is a specificity to that which is irreducible in the sense that Hattiangadi proposes when he claims that "though a whole is always composed of its parts, sometimes the types of things that constitute the parts cannot be fully described in all causally relevant respects without describing how they interact with the types of things that are wholes *as wholes* that are composed out of them" (2005: 89).

In short, as the human world operates conjointly at all three levels of emergence (material, animal, and personal), we have to be attentive to the "ambivalent character of the concept of world," the standpoint from which Heidegger starts his questioning ([1929/30] 1995: 177ff.). In consequence, that is also the essential point of departure to what follows. Much like Heidegger and Davidson (2004: 121), we do not aim to abolish the ambivalence of the "anomaly"; rather, we aim to contribute toward its further unveiling. This book proposes an outlook on world that allows both for the universalist hopes of the anthropological endeavor within the broader project of science and for the particularistic demands of ethnographic practice.

A MINIMALIST REALISM

Of late, anthropological theory has been oscillating between two alternative options concerning world forming. There are those who follow a metaphysical path in proposing to reenchant the world, with all of the rhetorical charm that goes with such excesses (Viveiros de Castro [2009] 2014; Kohn 2013); there are others, such as myself, who have opted to stick to the more pedestrian path of building a scientific analysis of what it is to be human in the world, for which you have to assume that all humans share common paths of humanity *and* of animality, and that only within these paths does it make sense to be a social scientist at all. Social analysis is carried out by persons in ontogeny, and it is to be received by persons in ontogeny. Verisimilitude, therefore, is an indispensable feature of all successful sociological or anthropological description, as any social

---

2. For the history of the concept of personal ontogeny, see Toren (1990, 1993, 1999, 2002, 2012).

scientist who has had to defend a Ph.D. thesis well knows. And verisimilitude depends on assuming the background of a common human world. This approach is, no doubt, less exciting from a rhetorical point of view because it obliges us to the constant exercise of critical attention implied in the fact that we are always part of what we observe and that there are insuperable limits to certainty.

As such, this book proposes a realism that is minimalist to the extent that it sees persons as capable of engaging the world in very diverse manners (cf. Lynch 1998). Humans are part of the world and respond to its affordances like the members of other species,[3] but they do so in a particular way. Like other animals, we too can only make meaning in a social way, but unlike them, we develop propositional (symbolic) thinking. This means that we are capable of contemplating our position vis-à-vis world. Yet we do so only in as much as we develop personhood.

We cannot, therefore, discuss world without considering "for whom." But, as we will demonstrate, contrary to the belief of those who succumb to the all-or-nothing fallacy, this minimal realist position is perfectly compatible with a single-world ontology based on a nonrepresentational approach to cognition of the kind espoused by Donald Davidson in his late writings, where he develops further his notion of "anomalous monism" inspired by Spinoza's thought (cf. 2005: 295–314). Anthropologists would do well to pay greater attention to Davidson's interpretivist rereading of W. V. Quine's critique of understanding, for it provides a ready escape route for many of the quandaries concerning mind, knowledge, and belief which have haunted anthropological theory since Evans-Pritchard's days and which were brought to a skeptical paroxysm in Rodney Needham's *Belief, language, and experience* (1972).

Essentially, Davidson's view is that "*there is a single ontology,* but more than one way of describing and explaining the items in the ontology" (2004: 121, our emphasis). He describes the emergent properties resulting from personal constitution in history as an "anomaly"—that is, although "mental entities are identical, taken one at a time, with physical entities," "there are no strictly law-like correlations" between the two (ibid.). Taken in its broadest definition, this

---

3.   Cf. Davidson: "It may be that not even plants could survive in our world if they did not to some extent react in ways we find similar to events and objects that we find similar. This clearly is true of animals; and of course it becomes more obvious the more like us the animal is" (2001: 202).

"anomaly," to use Davidson's quaint expression, is common to all animals, but its effects are again significantly potentiated by the emergence of human propositional (symbolic) thinking.[4] We must steer off our propensity to indulge in the all-or-nothing fallacy: humans are not only social, they are also persons who can appreciate that their own selves are part of the world—to that extent they are world forming. Thus, for a minimal realist, the relation between personhood and world is fundamental.

For some, like Connolly, this emphasis on the "anomaly" is incorrect: "The line between agency and cause is historically linked to Cartesian and Kantian contrasts between human beings invested with the powers of free will and nonhuman force-fields susceptible to explanation through nonagentic causes. But the powers of self-organization expressed to varying degrees in open systems of different types translate that first disjunction into a matter of degree" (Connolly 2011: 173). One is obliged to agree with him concerning the mind/body duality. Indeed humans share with other species the intentional forms of thinking. But one cannot follow him concerning the possibility to conceive of the person as separate from the world (here called "presence"), which is a function of propositional, human-specific thinking (cf. Hutto and Myin 2013). Broadly defined, Heidegger's "poorer" world of animals corresponds to a level of emergence, but the personal condition of humans corresponds to yet another. There is a historical supervenience of one on the other, for the animal condition supervenes on materiality and the personal condition on animality. As Hattiangadi put it, "Looking at a new entity as emergent is to focus on its novelty against the background history of the substrate that precedes it" (2005: 94). Emergence in this sense occurs in world but involves a change of aspect of world for the entities that emerge.

My hope in writing this book is that, from such a historicist perspective, we can bypass the all-or-nothing fallacy and the dichotomistic propensity of anthropological epistemology, which ontologist idealism again rehashed over the past decade, and develop the bases for *a truly ecumenist anthropological theory*. By that I mean one that works toward a common anthropological field of debate, one which all humans can access should they so desire.

---

4.   As will be clarified further in chapter 3, "propositional" is here being used in a sense approximate to the meaning given to "symbolic" by the older Peirce (Short 2007; cf. Hutto and Myin 2013)

THE WORD

Today, the more general acceptation of the word *world* is "what exists," that is, everything. According to the *Oxford English Dictionary*, however, the main reference is to the planet Earth. The etymological root of the word lies in the Old English word *woruld*, meaning "human existence, the affairs of life"; itself derived from the Proto-Germanic **weraldiz*, a combination of the words for "man" (**veraz*; related to Latin *vir*) and "age" (**aldiz*, meaning age, generation), thus implying "the age of man." Further to be considered is that both the Latin *mundus* and the Greek *kosmos* bore etymologically connotations of order, cleanliness, and neatness.

It is important to realize that the etymological connotations we have just briefly outlined have not lost their relevance today. For example, when people claim that the most pressing problem of our time is humanity's relation to a world that can no longer be taken as infinitely robust and inexhaustible, what meaning are they placing on the word? In this context, the limited meaning of planet Earth is not sufficient by any means but the meaning "all that exists" also falls short. On the other hand, the further implications that emerge from the etymology, concerning humanity's dwelling place and an ordered context for human habitation, are decidedly at stake. There are lessons to be learned from the word's polysemy and, as we will see, world's ambivalence will eventually turn out to be impossible to cast aside.

However, owing to the importance of the legacy of Christianity in the development of the scientific tradition in Western Europe, the word has absorbed into itself the notion of man's fallen condition. As such, the world—that which presently exists—has come to be opposed to that which is yet to occur: Christ's second coming. This range of meanings is condensed in the notion of *mundane*; a notion that conjoins in a millenarian fashion two very separate but metonymically related meanings: (a) everyday humdrum existence and (b) that which is not divine, spiritual, heavenly, and is therefore assumed to be shallow, false, doubtful, even irregular (as when, in French, the vice squad is called *police mondaine*). The conjoining of the two carries within itself a world-denying implication that facilitates the dualist strains in European thinking and is best represented by Descartes' radical philosophical restart—his *cogito ergo sum* declaration—that is so fundamental to the development of the modern scientific tradition. A somewhat different type of dualism concerning the deception of the senses also plays a central role in the Buddhist traditions and has remained globally very influential. In fact, historically, it constituted a major source of tension with China's Confucian school, which is probably the least world deny-ing of the major philosophical traditions.

Therefore, for contemporary anthropologists, after the profound epistemolog-ical changes that took place in mid-twentieth-century philosophy, the best way of going about discovering what is world is surely to see how it presents itself in peo-ple's historically situated lives. Note, we did not write, "what meaning the word has for the people we study," as ethnographers are prone to put it, for that is only part of the issue. A small shift in meaning is being performed here that should not be silenced. Davidson and the late Wittgenstein are surely correct when they state that triangulation with world is an indispensable component of all acts of human communication. Therefore, our research concerning world cannot be lim-ited to the collecting of the meanings of the word world, the category world, or even less the belief world. World exists and is immanent (in the sense of imposing itself—Connolly 2011), so world is anterior to language and is a condition for it, both ontogenetically and phylogenetically. Thus, "the accessibility of beings" is an intrinsic condition of all human communication (Heidegger [1929/30] 1995: 269), including when the latter deals with world, such as our present discussion.

We are bound to cast aside the dualist suspicions concerning the world's reality that characterized both the Christian and the Buddhist traditions, and which were based on a systematic distrust of the senses, for they were victims of the all-or-nothing fallacy. We follow Davidson in claiming that, "If words and thoughts are, in the most basic cases, necessarily about the sorts of objects and events that commonly cause them, there is no room for Cartesian doubts about the independent existence of such objects and events" (2001: 45; see Godlove 1996). If, in this way, we reject the duality between shape and substance, then all our communication is based on an always-anterior existence of world: "We do not first form concepts and then discover what they apply to; rather, in the basic cases, the application determines the content of the concept" (Davidson 2001: 196). Therefore, we must never abstract from history: *irreversibility* and *unpredictability* are constitutive characteristics of the human condition in this world of becoming (cf. Arendt 1958: 233).

BASIC MIND AND SCAFFOLDED MIND

Today, we are pressed to avoid the twentieth-century proneness to entertain a metaphysics of society, to consider sociality in an abstract fashion as something that exists in terms of the species or of groupness aside from personhood. Human sociality remains ever bound to the interactions of singular embodied persons. Furthermore, as George Lakoff and Mark Johnson (1999) have argued for category formation, and Rodney Needham (1987) has discovered for duality, our own body experience (of containment and of handedness, respectively) is constitutive of our most basic mental properties. For an ethnographer, therefore, to study the varied ways in which humans are "at home in the world" is to study the particular conditions of their existence as specific human persons who encounter each other conjointly in space-times that are common to them to the extent that they are historically specific, that is, space-times that transport a history of human sociality within which each participant of the company came into being.[5]

Inhabiting the world as persons is not only to be of the world or to be directed at the world, as in the philosophical meaning of the word *intentionality*. For persons who have entered into language (in the broader sense of the term), as opposed to the other animals, inhabiting the world is confronting the world formatively, in the sense of thinking *propositionally*. Thus, we must be mindful of the distinction that Daniel Hutto sets up between intentional thinking, which humans share with other species (*basic mind*), and propositional thinking in language, which is specific to humans (*scaffolded mind*):

> The very possibility of conceptual meaning, even in the case of phenomenality, requires an intersubjective space. Acknowledging this entails no denial of the existence of nonconceptual, noncontentful experiences with phenomenal properties associated with basic minds. . . . Our facility with concepts about such experiences is parasitic on a more basic literacy in making ordinary claims about public, worldly items. . . . The acquisition of such conceptual abilities depends on being able to have and share basic experiences with others. (Hutto and Myin 2013: 173)

In short, persons inhabit the world in both intentional and propositional ways, which means that they are in permanent ontogenesis—that is, they work reflexively at the fabrication of their own singularity.

Note that we are not limiting propositional thinking to the boundaries of "conscious/linguistic" thinking, an error that has dogged anthropological theory

---

5. I find Ingold's "dwelling perspective" an interesting formulation of what may be involved here (1995: 75–77).

throughout the past century. The world feeds back on humans the ontogenetic actions of earlier humans in ways that they cannot foresee—the notion of *scaffolding of mind* is, in this regard, usefully evocative of what humans do in the course of their lives. The notion originated in studies of skill acquisition (including language acquisition—Gibson 1979) and is dependent on the concept of *affordances*. These are defined as relations between an animal's purposiveness and the environment's features, giving rise to meaning (see Chemero 2003). In speaking of scaffolded mind, we are generalizing the proposition that learning is essentially a process not of imitation but of participation in tasks in a world where affordances are shared.[6]

Humans invest their meanings in the world (they reify meaning) and then interact with these reifications—theirs and other people's. Even if I am alone, I permanently interact with the traces of others; I encounter the traces of earlier persons as affordances with which I engage in my own processes of meaning creation: in this way, being-in-the-world turns out to be always being-with-others, as Heidegger insisted. In their sensorial immediacy, these affordances both provide alternatives to meaning and shape meaning, in that they communicate their properties by relation to available routines (Lupton 2015: 623). Indeed, the very development of problem solving and skill acquisition in children is a process of scaffolding, to the extent that adults provide the child with pathways for problem solving (see Wood, Bruner, and Ross 1976: 90).[7]

Yet, even although the world feeds back on humans the meanings they invested in it, the ambiguity of world will never vanish. We can only create meaning because we know that things might not be; meaning is veridical and, to that extent, it is fuzzy—for it is based in constant error assessment. Two important corollaries can be taken from this: first, we are subject to the *indeterminacy of interpretation*, that is, no meaning will ever be fixed or permanently determinable; second, we are subject to *underdetermination*, that is, there will never be certainty in knowing. This is what Davidson meant when he claimed that he was a "monist" (there is one single ontology) but that his monism was anomalous,

---

6.   "Scaffolding supports higher-order thinking, which begins in socially mediated interactions and gradually becomes part of an individual's cognition" (Belland and Drake 2013: 904).

7.   This formulation covers many of the implications of Latour's concept of "interobjectivity" (1996), which proposes that, in human sociality as opposed to animal sociality, subjects and objects coexist in forming human/nonhuman collectives.

for world will ever remain indeterminate and underdetermined, that is, it will remain historically plural.

The person is born as a member of the human species but is not born fully human, as it is only in the course of ontogenesis that the person enters into humanity. We are neurologically equipped with a propensity to enter the world of human communication and to remain within it through memory—this constitutes primary intersubjectivity. But, in order to enter into the world of human communication (to acquire a scaffolded mind and engage in symbolic thinking), we have to be enticed into humanity by other humans who had already been enticed by others before them, and so on and so forth back to the gradual and discreet origins of the human species—this constitutes secondary intersubjectivity.

Primary intersubjectivity goes on occurring for the rest of our lives. "Nonverbal responding, quite generally, only involves the having of intentional—but not propositional—attitudes" (Hutto 2008: xiii). But, through the immersion in the complex communicational environments of early ontogeny and the relations of mutuality by means of which carers capture and are captured by children, young humans develop a secondary intersubjectivity that operates above primary intersubjectivity. It is by intersubjectively engaging in "unscripted conversational exchanges" (ibid.: 136)—leading to secondary intersubjectivity—that humans acquire the central propositional attitudes of belief and desire. Thus, children are driven away from infant solipsism by participating in complex communicational contexts where viewpoints clash and where they are subjected to a series of diverse unscripted narratives and explanations (in short, *company*). The very idea that it may be possible to inhabit the world in solitude is ludicrous— as Davidson famously put it, "the possibility of thought comes with company" (2001: 88). This sentence constitutes perhaps the central guideline to the arguments developed in this book.

As it happens, my own ethnography of personal naming among secondary school children in Bahia (NE Brazil) encouraged me to focus on the multiple processes of scaffolding of mind, strongly confirming the outlook on personhood briefly sketched above, to which we will return in the course of this book. Children assumed their personal names, played with them, and manipulated them (by means of small adaptations and recontextualizations, erasures, hypocoristics, diminutives, etc.—Pina-Cabral 2013b). All of this happened, however, in a context where their namers and primary carers were present (or had absented themselves with significant implications) and engaged in processes of personal surrogation with them—that is, relations of profound affective mutuality

(Pina-Cabral 2013c). The perspectival foci that structured the child's world—self, home, family, nation—emerged from a game of triangulations within an embodied world where new affordances were constantly offering themselves as invitations to action. As they embraced the world more broadly and interacted with others in ever-widening circles, children engaged the scaffolds (reifications) that were provided by the environment and the narrative contexts in which they were immersed (see Pina-Cabral 2010d and Belland and Drake 2013). Their docility toward the adoption of these scaffolds (together with the hegemonic relations they carried) was a condition for their own coming into personhood—what Radcliffe-Brown called their "consociation."[8] Deep historical recurrences, going way beyond anything the children themselves could consciously formulate, combined with shallow local specificities as invitations for action; engagement with the world at large combined with a deeply felt sense of local closure. Children could only revolt (and that they did) to the extent that they had already entered into the scaffolded interactions of human sociality.

AT HOME IN THE WORLD

If we want to explore what world can be to humans, then perhaps the best starting point is to choose an ethnographic study by an anthropologist who has set out to examine just that. My surprise is that since the days of Lévy-Bruhl so few philosophers have chosen to avail themselves of this rich lode of evidence. Out of a number of possible examples, I have chosen to focus on Michael Jackson's phenomenologically inspired study of the Warlpiri Aboriginal people of Australia. Called *At home in the world* (1995), the book is an attempt to theorize the concept of home by overcoming the obvious and much-noted sedentarist implications that the concept carries in most contemporary scientific thinking, and that owes a lot to the long-term history of Western Europe (see Pina-Cabral 1989). As Jackson puts it in the synopsis of his book, "Ours is an era of uprootedness, with fewer and fewer people living out their lives

---

8. Radcliffe-Brown ends his classical essay on joking relationships with a reference to a debate he was then having with Marcel Mauss concerning the latter's *Essai sur le don*: "The joking relationship is in some ways the exact opposite of a contractual relation," he sustains, as it is based not on contractual binomiality but on continuity and fusion (Radcliffe-Brown [1940] 1952: 102–3). There is no reciprocity between the partners; there is a fusion of interests, not a matching of interests.

where they are born. At such a time, in such a world, what does it mean to be 'at home'?" (1995, back page). In fact, as he proceeds to explore the ways in which the Warlpiri produce and inhabit what we might choose to call their home, he is forced to give us a varied and increasingly complex set of suggestions concerning what world is, both to him and to them.

After all, it is not possible to debate home without placing it in world, for two main reasons: one is that home is that which is not world; the other is that home is perhaps the central feature of any person's world. These two contrasting meanings actually constitute boundary markers for a complex continuum of contexts where the word *world* seems to most of us to come in handy. This latter aspect is especially significant, and Jackson does manage to produce a verisimilitudinous account of it in his book. Furthermore, his insights can be available both to most trained anthropologists and to the Warlpiri themselves, with whom he debated the book before publishing it. His study, therefore, is not out of history; it is very much part of what world is becoming. Much as was the case when I worked in coastal Bahia (Pina-Cabral and Silva 2013: ch. 9), and is the case with most ethnographers these days, there were no sharp linguistic barriers between Jackson and his subjects. Yes, there were profound linguistic differences that Jackson does indeed explore, but both he and the Warlpiri had a significant take on each other's linguistic universes anterior to their actual (historical) encounter.

As this ethnographic case exemplifies, there are subtle veins of meaning that go from one usage of *world* to another, both creating semantic overlap and inducing difference. They lead us from one aspect to the other, much like a salesman who wants to sell a car goes through the various features of the vehicle without ever losing touch of the notion that *this* is the vehicle that we must want (not just this kind of wheel, or this kind of motor, or this kind of paint, etc.). Thus, we continue to refer to world in spite of its essential ambivalence, as Heidegger noted, but also because of it. The ambivalence becomes a margin for worlding to occur.

So Jackson tells us that "I had learned that for the Warlpiri, as for other Aboriginal people, the world was originally lifeless and featureless. It had been given form, instilled with life, and charged with meaning by totemic ancestors" (1995: 57). Here we meet up with the old paradox of the world-before-the-world: if for the Warlpiri such a world had no meaning, was it world? For the purposes of the present discussion, however, the more relevant question is: What is at stake for the Warlpiri when the notion of world is so generically used? In this case, from the context, we can assume that Jackson's sentence refers to an environment that embraces humans and reaches beyond their existence—what we might call a *cosmos*. And yet we know that the Warlpiri are aware that there are places in the world where there are no Warlpiri-kind totemic ancestors, so it is legitimate to ask them: Who formed the world of non-Warlpiri peoples? In short, a universalist meaning of world (the cosmos) and a localized meaning (a specifically sociocultural meaning, as in "the world of the Nyakyusa") are somehow made to merge as a result of Jackson's ethnographic mediation, both for him and for the Warlpiri.

A few pages earlier, musing about his African experiences among the Kuranko of Sierra Leone, Jackson had told us, "I wondered if any person is ever free to begin anew, to walk out into the world as if for the first time" (ibid.: 51). Of course, the answer to his question turns out to be negative because all persons are rooted in anteriority and there is no exit from history. But for our present purposes, there is a noteworthy difference between this "world" here and the one discussed in the paragraph above. Here, world is the opposite of home; it is the contrasting outside that accounts for the presence of self and home and whose manifestation is the planet Earth and the bodies within it, in their material diversity.

In this second instance, world now integrates two parts that are hierarchically complementary: world plus home. In short, another set of meanings emerges that assumes that world is fundamentally perspectival: this second vector of world results from postulating a perspectival home or self that opposes it. Such a meaning is inscribed in our historically acquired proclivities as anthropologists, owing to the role that the notion of mundanity plays in Christian theology. But there is a case for arguing that this polarization between "world outside" and "self/home within" is so pervasive in the ethnographic record that it can be considered as a constant of human experience: as Godfrey Lienhardt argued, "One can lay too much one-sided stress on the collectivist orientation of African ideas of the person. . . . The recognition of the importance of an inner, mysterious *individual* activity, comparable to what is meant by speaking in English of 'what goes on inside' a person is attested by many proverbs' (1985: 145, original emphasis). I chose this example because of Lienhardt's emphasis on "mysterious"—on the evanescent nature of the perspectival centre that the person constitutes.

This connects with the way Jackson proceeds:

> At that moment, sitting there with Zack and Nugget, Pincher and Francine [his partner], I think I knew what it means to be at home in the world. It is to

experience a complete consonance between one's own body and the body of the earth. Between self and other. It little matters whether the other is a landscape, a loved one, a house, or an action. Things flow. There seems to be no resistance between oneself and the world. The relationship is all. (1995: 110)

As he experiences a merging of embodiment and propositional thinking, Jackson is forced to qualify world by reference to "the body of the earth," and this is no passing matter, since the groundedness of being is precisely what he is trying to get at in this passage. Self/home are now integrally and materially part of world, and this implies cosmic universality once again: "In shared bodily needs, in patterns of attachment and loss, in the imperatives of reciprocity, in the *habitus* of the planet, we [that is, all persons] are involved in a common heritage" (ibid.: 118).

In the wake of Merleau-Ponty, Jackson comes to see that the very possibility of anthropology and ethnography is dependent on this "*habitus* of the planet," not contrary to it.

The possibility of anthropology is born when the other recognizes my humanity, and on the strength of this recognition incorporates me into his world, giving me food and shelter, bestowing upon me a name, placing upon me the same obligations he places upon his own kinsmen and neighbours. I am literally incorporated in his world, and it is on the basis of this incorporation and my reciprocal response to it that I begin to gain a knowledge of that world. Anthropology should never forget that its project unfolds within the universal constraints of hospitality. (Jackson 1995: 119)

There could be no better ethnographic instantiation of what lies behind Davidson's principle of "interpretive charity." According to the latter, in order to manage to interpret a speaker, we have "to read some of [our] own standards of truth into the patterns of sentences held true by the speaker. The point of the principle is to make the speaker intelligible, since too great deviations from consistency and correctness leave no common ground on which to judge either conformity or difference" (Davidson 2001: 148) This implies what we have always known, as it were intuitively: that ethnography is only possible because the world of the ethnographer and the world of the native are largely common.

Note, for instance, the way in which Jackson lays out in this sentence the central paths for the possibility of the ethnographic gesture: food, shelter, name, relatedness. Personhood, both in its organic (food, shelter) and its social specificity (name, relatedness), is a boundary condition for world and it is universal in its diversity. So a third vector of meaning of world appears to emerge: one that opposes the visceral groundedness of personhood to propositional thinking (within language). This conjoining is the quandary that Ingold tries to address in the sentence I quoted earlier: "People do not import their ideas, plans or mental representations into the world, since the very world . . . is the homeland of their thoughts."

In Jackson's engagement with the Warlpiri, then, we witness the various implications of world coming together in a set of three principal vectors of opposition: (a) *the cosmic vector*—the universally embracing cosmos as opposed to the locally conceived culturally constructed worlds; (b) *the perspectival vector*—the encompassing world as opposed to the central but evanescent reference point of home or self; and (c) *the propositional vector*—the world as embodied materiality as opposed to propositional thinking.

These vectors manifest themselves in three formally distinct modes of world (see diagram 1):

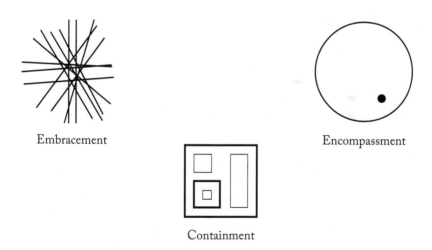

Embracement   Encompassment

Containment

Diagram 1. The three modes of world.

(i)   wider and vaguer levels of cosmic *embracement* operate as sources of experience for more locally defined and more clearly structured worlds;

(ii) world *encompasses* self, home, or *heimat* in such a way that these perspectival domains both contrast with it and are a constituent part of it;

(iii) world materially limits our sense of internal existence (our "arena of presence and action"—see Johnston 2010) in that it *contains* it,[9] preventing its
spreading and situating it.

Embracement, encompassment, and containment are distinct but related processes, and in everyday experience *the three modes of world* combine in a process
of becoming through which world constantly unfurls and multiplies (*world
worlds*, as Heidegger famously put it). It is a movement of (i) totality versus
singularity; (ii) encompassment versus identification; and (iii) exteriority versus
interiority, which never stops being vaguely aporetic because totality, encompassment, and exteriority never disappear before singularity, identification, and
interiority. Even as world becomes worlds, world remains.

Thus, for example, in a sentence like the following by Glenn Bowman writing about Jerusalem as a pilgrimage site, we see the three vectors evolving in
such a way that world unfolds into a number of worlds while remaining present
as world, in as much as it is the condition of possibility both for the distinct
pilgrimages and for the author's ethnographic study of them:

> The centrality of the [biblical] text meant that it was the reference point by
> which religious Christians judged the world through which they moved, but the
> proliferation of meanings accreted around it as it variously developed through
> the historical spread of the Christian faith meant that the worlds constituted in
> its terms were very different—even when, as in the case of Holy Land pilgrim-
> ages, those worlds were nominally the same. (1991: 100)

Other pilgrims too go around those very same streets and react to the very
same texts. The sharing of a space and a text imposes itself on the pilgrim at
the very moment they are postulating a divergent perspective from pilgrims of
other kinds. The evidence of the embracing world challenges the completeness
of the job of ethnic or religious identification. Alterity[10] remains irreducible and
identification incomplete.

---

9.   See Lakoff and Johnson's notion of bodily containment (1999).

10. A reviewer argued that Emmanuel Levinas' thought (much as Heidegger's) is
     too divergent from our guiding inspiration in Donald Davidson's philosophical
     insights for it to be a useful reference. On first approach, this may indeed appear
     to be the case. To the contrary, however, the late thinking of Davidson (2005) is
     amply compatible with Levinas' use of the concept of "alterity as anterior," which so

At this point we must be reminded of Davidson's injunction that there can only be communication between two speakers when they can triangulate it with the world: that is, the "*habitus* of the planet" is a condition of possibility for humans to mutually understand each other (both at the level of person-to-person understanding and at the level of culture-to-culture understanding), but it is also what divides us. Confronted with the desert's unresponsiveness to human presence, Jackson experienced a moment of doubt: "In the desert, I had become convinced that it is not in the nature of human consciousness to enter the world of nature. The truth of nature does not participate in the truth of human consciousness" (1995: 116). The reference to the desert here is not a passing one; it is essential to what he is telling us, that the desert is a specific environment that shapes human experience. In this momentary confrontation with the desert, the reduction of mind to consciousness again calls our attention to the unresolved, aporetic side of the third mode identified above: human mind (propositional, reflexive mind) and world interpenetrate without ever fully meeting, that is the major implication for anthropology of the theory of the indeterminacy of interpretation (see Feleppa 1988). Persons are of the world but they confront the world. "Some balance must be possible between the world into which we are thrown without our asking and the world we imagine we might bring into being by dint of what we say and do" (Jackson 1995: 123). This is what Jackson calls "the existential struggle," and it is the principal object of his book—the conditions of presence.

When he speaks of "disengaging from the world about us" in order "to be in touch with ourselves" (ibid.), or when he claims that the sound of traffic outside is "a world away," he is using the more general cosmic implications of the word. But then, speaking of a moment of great personal intensity, he says,

> It was not unlike the experience of watching someone you love dying—the same sense of the world falling away, of oneself falling away from the world, and of all one's awareness condensed by pain into a black hole. At such times, the world at large is diminished and loses its hold, eclipsed by the viscerally immediate world of oneself. It is always a shock, going outdoors again after a birth or a death, to find that the world has not changed along with you, that it has gone on unaffected and indifferent. (1995: 135)

inspired the discussion of ethical issues and the role of the person in sociality in this book (cf. Levinas 1961).

Here we find a kind of logical *non sequitur*: "the world falling away from us" is held to be the same as "us falling away from the world." In fact, the error is only apparent, because the "world at large" and the "visceral world" cannot quite come to separate from each other; they are held together by the fact that sociality and intentional thinking are preconditions for propositional (reflexive) thinking. The world embraces us to the extent that it places us—not in space, not in time, but in existence. There is, then, something external in world, for there is no way out of world, we are contained by it; but the world is also an openness, as we are recurrently confronted by the indeterminate relations between words and world and our condition is not only to inhabit world but also to inhabit language. In sum, persons are world forming.

There would, then, be three aspects to world that Jackson is manipulating without ever being willing to separate them, for he sees them as mutually constitutive: (a) *the cosmic world*; (b) the *perspectival world*; and (c) *the propositional world*. The central conclusion we take from our examination, however, is that personhood—the fact that humans are propositionally thinking embodied creatures—is what holds together the complex dynamic between world and worlds, the world's ambivalence.

GLOBALIZATION

Let us now take another example from a different tradition of anthropological thinking: Ulf Hannerz's reflections concerning the present situation of anthropology and his own personal trajectory within it. *Anthropology's world: Life in a twenty-first-century discipline* (2010) takes a very different perspective on world from Jackson's book, as it is less concerned with how people studied by anthropologists inhabit world, and more with anthropology as a mode of inhabiting world. The focus is shifted toward the condition of being an anthropologist in a world that is becoming more . . . global. While never referring to Henri Lefebvre's concept of *mondialisation*, Hannerz also explores the way in which his condition as an anthropologist in the second half of the twentieth century was affected by this "shift from the nation-state to the world scale" (Elden 2004: 232–35), this process by which a new political and economic order emerged that followed on from the nation and the city, imposing new forms of domination, repression, and hegemony.

Hannerz's was the curiously contradictory life of someone who, never having left his own Swedish academic base (for he retired from the same department where he carried out his undergraduate studies),[11] worked and dialogued with colleagues and informants all over the world and had a worldwide academic impact. However, he notes, his "cosmopolitan" condition, is two-faced: on one side, the worried face of someone who contemplates humanity as a whole and its evolving political turmoil (the scale of Lefebvre's *mondial*); and, on the other side, the satisfied face of the one who looks out on the fascinating diversity of meanings and meaningful forms in the human world (Hannerz 2010: 93).

There is an affinity between the two faces, Hannerz suggests, which is potentiated by anthropology's main challenge, as he sees it, of "making the world transparent." (ibid.: 87) Now, transparency is a project of mediation between the two faces of the cosmopolitan observer: the globalized condition can only remain humanly pleasing to the extent that pluralism survives. "The world of anthropology keeps changing" (ibid.: 1), Hannerz claims: for anthropologists, the global and the cosmopolitan are two manifestations of facing the contradictoriness of world's becoming.

In fact, in the very first page of his book, Hannerz outlines the nature of the aporia that confronts him as he looks back at his life as a fieldworker. As it happens, he brings out the same three vectors that emerged from Jackson's study: the *cosmic* vector—"anthropology's world is the wider outside world"; the *perspectival* vector—"anthropology is a social world in itself"; and the *propositional* vector—"it is a world anthropologists are inclined to think of as made up of a multitude of 'fields'" (ibid.).

As the book evolves, we see Hannerz turning time and again to a central quandary concerning the very definition of his discipline. In Sweden his decision to become an anthropologist in the 1960s had involved a political conviction. That is why he had wanted to carry out research in Nigeria. The period was one of decolonization, and the young Hannerz's burning wish, which turned him into a social scientist, was to understand that process and contribute actively toward it. He saw as ethically problematic the internally turned *volkskunde* (folklore) type of academic engagement being carried out in the department next door. As he puts it, he wanted to be an "expatriate researcher," not someone

---

11. I was privileged to be part of the fascinating retirement symposium that his colleagues organized, which brought out very vividly his lifework and its curiously understated creativity.

turned in onto the historicist preoccupations of a national/nationalist type of research engagement. So the opposition between away and home fieldwork engagements was formative.

However, as things evolved in the 1980s and 1990s, neocolonialism turned into neoimperialism, and the face that contemplated the global order (the *mondial*) became sadder and sadder. Hannerz's experiences in Nigeria, when he finally managed to get there, were particularly distressing. At the same time, anthropology's other face also changed radically. There were departments of anthropology in most places where previously anthropologists had been expatriates, and a new "anthropology at home" emerged that was as cosmopolitan as Hannerz's own "away anthropology." It could hardly be classified in the same bag as the earlier nationalist-driven research that he had avoided in the 1960s. By the early twenty-first century, studying international reporters, Hannerz himself was going everywhere, from interviewing a neighbour of his in Stockholm to Washington, Johannesburg, Jerusalem, or Tokyo. Thus, he calls for the need to retain the "awayness" of the anthropology of the past that he most cherishes, by preventing the new cosmopolitan anthropology from becoming at the global level what folklore had been at the national level. His aim is to retain "our part as anthropologists as helpers of a worldwide transparency, as men and women in the middle" (ibid.: 91).

It is worth confronting here the quotes of two anthropologists of the earlier generation that inspire him. In 1988, Clifford Geertz had declared that "the next necessary thing is to enlarge the possibility of intelligible discourse between people quite different from one another . . . and yet contained in a world where, tumbled as they are into endless connection, it is increasingly difficult to get out of each other's way" (quoted in ibid.: 88–89). Hannerz then quotes Fei Xiaodong, who, in 1992, claims that people "shaped by different cultures with different attitudes towards life are crowded into a small world in which they must live in complete and absolute interdependence" (quoted in ibid.: 100).

This sense that, faced with the world's increasing smallness, there is a burning need to build on the world's plurality is what drives Hannerz's efforts at passing on anthropology to the next century. Between the *cosmic* and the *perspectival* modes of world, anthropology would be a kind of *propositional* mediator that turns interiority into exteriority and vice versa, thus preventing the global order from destroying the conditions for its own cosmopolitanism. Anthropology would be a task carried out by persons who convert the very means that turn

them into persons (i.e., propositionally thinking beings) into an instrument for
the production of ever-wider bird's-eye-view effects.[12]

A PLURALITY OF WORLDS

A number of arguments have emerged of late—some more coherent than others—claiming that there are "worlds," or, better still, that there is "a plurality
of ontologies."[13] The simpler form of the argument may be summarized in the
following terms:

> Rather than using our own analytical concepts to make sense of a given eth-
> nography (explanation, interpretation), we use the ethnography to rethink our
> analytical concepts. Rather than asking why the Nuer should think that twins are
> birds, we should be asking how we need to think of twins and birds (and all their
> relevant corollaries, such as humanity, siblinghood, animality, flight or what have
> you) in order to arrive at a position from which the claim that twins are birds
> no longer registers as an absurdity. What must twins be, what must birds be, et
> cetera? (Holbraad 2010: 184)

Thus formulated, the argument is immediately problematic owing to its ahis-
toricism and to the assumption that "us" is a geopolitically recognizable vantage
point. One wonders how the author accounts historically for the fact that he
reads ethnographies and why Nuer ethnography is his chosen example. How did
Evans-Pritchard actually manage to fall through the trappings of "our" world to
enter into "the Nuer world," only to come out again at the end? One must try
very hard not to remember that Collingwood's theory of history ([1946] 1994)
was quite as influential to Evans-Pritchard's formulations concerning the Nuer
as were the Nuer themselves.

---

12. As Heidegger puts it in his quaint language: "World is brought before Dasein
    through Dasein itself" (1998: 122).
13. Perhaps this is no more than "a certain (and thus unavoidably fading) moment
    in the recent history of the discipline, where a vaguely defined cohort of mostly
    Cambridge-associated scholars found it exciting to experiment with the nature
    of ethnographic description and anthropological theorizing in a certain way," as
    Morten Pedersen puts it (2012).

There are, however, other versions of the argument. These claim that we must "not see ethnography as a kind of translation from one worldview to another," that "all ontologies are 'groundless' in the sense that no one is the True Ontology" (Paleček and Risjord 2013: 10, 16). In their essay, Martin Paleček and Mark Risjord revisit Davidson's injunction that we ought to reject the dualism between scheme and content, attempting to adapt his nonrepresentationalism to anthropology (Davidson 1984: 183–98). This is a laudable exercise. Unfortunately, together with most of their colleagues of this inspiration, the authors' use of the word *ontology* depends on a shift in meaning concerning world that bedevils all their successive arguments. Contrary to what the authors believe, the adoption of ontological monism does not imply the claim that one can have access to the one-and-only True Ontology. Ontological monism does not postulate that truth lies beyond the realm of human experience but rather that truth is a foundational feature of thinking: "Without the idea of truth we would not be thinking creatures, nor would we understand what it is for someone else to be a thinking creature" (Davidson 2005: 16).

That apart, we have a problem: in anthropology, referring to ethnography as translation in the old Evans-Pritchardian manner has come to be such a familiar trope that we have stopped wondering whether that is really a useful metaphor (cf. Beidelman 1971; Pina-Cabral 1992). What do ethnographers do precisely? Now, skeptical relativism is buried so deep into the tissue of our anthropological language that we find it hard to give an account of ethnography that bypasses the problems raised by representationalist theories of thinking (see Chemero 2009). Paleček and Risjord are correct in trying to go beyond this, but they proceed to argue that "Davidson's later work can be used to scaffold the inference from a rejection of the scheme–content distinction to a pluralism of ontology" (2013: 16). Yet this is an incorrect assumption: Davidson is absolutely explicit about the fact that there is only one single ontology (there is only one world), and his dialogue with Spinoza at the end of his life is precisely an elaboration on that idea (2005: 295–314). To attempt to salvage the metaphysical nature of Viveiros de Castro's perspectivism (his *cannibal metaphysics*—[2009] 2014) by twisting Davidson's positions is plainly a misguided step.

The discussion, however, cannot simply be left at that. From the indubitable observation that there is evidence for the existence of distinct "webs of interpretation" that apply in different historical contexts, Paleček and Risjord conclude that ontologies exist and are incommensurable. According to them, ontologies are "the product of human interpretive interactions with one another and with their environments. These interactions are often very different, constituting different ontologies. They are incommensurable in the sense that no one way of engaging the environment is right or wrong in metaphysical terms" (Paleček and Risjord 2013: 16). I honestly can see no difference between this definition of the word *ontology* and the meaning traditionally attributed to the anthropological concept of worldview, apart from the fact, of course, that the word *ontology* is tinted with a spirit of idealism (a metaphysical association) and the word *worldview* is not (because it presumes its own plural, implying that, if there are differing perspectives, then there is one world).

This matter of incommensurability, in fact, has a very long history, particularly by reference to Thomas S. Kuhn's argument about scientific revolutions. In his later life, Kuhn himself (1962, 1983) took to criticizing the excessively relativist interpretations of his argument. In his survey of the debate, Philip Kitcher finds that Kuhn's earlier claims of incommensurability were interpreted too literally and that "we can revert to the idea that full communication across the revolutionary divide is possible and that rival claimants can appeal to a shared body of observational evidence" (Kitcher 1982: 690). The conceptual incommensurability that divides scientific paradigms turns out to be just like that which divides languages that are subject to translation—but always only partly due to the limits imposed by the indeterminacy of all communication. Kitcher's reading of the late Kuhn's take on incommensurability carefully avoids the all-or-nothing fallacy, arguing that most of Kuhn's readers go too readily to irrationalist conclusions that are essentially politically conservative and are, in any case, unnecessary in order to interpret the historical evidence presented by scientific revolutions.

In the same line, I espouse Davidson's claim that there are no radically incompatible human worlds because all human persons are endowed with the possibility of developing intelligent communication with all other persons (bar exceptional circumstances: e.g., insanity, drunkenness, extreme fear, etc., and I am not limiting myself to linguistic communication). Since all our thinking is based on intentional thinking as much as on propositional thinking, radical ontological breaks are inconceivable. We are historically part of the world. To claim otherwise would be tantamount to saying that ethnography is an impossibility since, in order to learn what other persons think, we first have to engage with them as human and, more than that, as humans cohabiting a recognizable world, as we saw Jackson arguing earlier. Without the triangulation made possible by world, there is no place for communication.[14]

Paleček and Risjord formulate this part of Davidson's thought in the following terms: "Insofar as we are not able to separate our knowledge of the object from the object itself, we are not able to separate our knowledge of ourselves from the knowledge of others. The interpreter becomes a crucial aspect of what it means to have thoughts" (2013: 12). From this, then, they proceed: "The ethnographer is engaging not just an individual in one-on-one communication but a whole interpretive community" (ibid.: 14). Surely that is an important point—quite as important as its symmetrical counterpart: the critique of *ethnographic exceptionalism*. That is, in engaging the ethnographer, the peoples of the world who were being subjected to imperialism throughout the modern era were not only engaging an individual in a one-on-one communication, but were engaging the full force of imperial globalization.

Now, it would seem that, if there are "interpretive communities," there are worldviews, that is, that which differentiates interpretive communities in the face of others (we will return to this argument in chapter 5). Of course, it may well be argued that these interpretive communities should not be seen as "views," for that would be to cede to representationalism and to an unjustifiably strong form of realism. Descola has recently produced a formulation of our relation to world where he tries to argue just this (to have his cake and eat it, so to speak). He adopts a kind of minimalist realism similar to the one I have been defending here, but then he appends to it a critique of the notion of worldview:

> There can be no multiple worlds because it is highly probable that the potential qualities and relations afforded to human cognition and enactment are the same everywhere until some have been detected and actualized, others ignored. But once this worlding process has been achieved, the result is not a world-view, i.e., one version among others of the same transcendental reality; the result is a world in its own right, a system of partially actualized properties, saturated with meaning and replete with agency, but partially overlapping with other similar

---

14. There is in this argument no claim that the borders of humanity with other animals are precise, nor that human proneness to communication cannot elicit forms of communication with animals that often approximate interhuman communication. As Heidegger (1998) would have it, intentional thinking in both humans and animals presupposes world, but a *poor* world: it has less of world .

systems that have been differently actualized and instituted by different persons. (Descola 2010: 339)

Here, we agree with Descola concerning the minimal realism but not concerning the worldview issue, since he unwittingly engages in the all-or-nothing fallacy. He is assuming (à la Paleček and Risjord) that the alternative to a multiple ontologies posture is a one-and-only True Ontology posture. To deny that when human persons share worldviews they are essentially engaging a historically common world is to deny history and feeds into the primitivist strain in anthropological thinking that carries out what Eugen Hammel long ago used to criticize as "one-village-one-vote comparativism" (1984: 29–43). Furthermore, there is human exclusivism in this, because it is reducing world to propositional thinking (and to conscious categorical thinking at that). But world in humans is grounded in the sort of intentional thinking that we share with animals; scaffolded (symbolic) thinking only comes after and above that and, as we have argued already, it is in any case rooted in our common human embodiment. Too many decades of unchallenged interpretivism have led anthropologists to assume implicitly that thought is primarily systemic in a culturalist sort of way and, therefore, that worlds = cultures.

But the ethnographer in the field is not engaging an interpretive community; she is engaging singular humans or, if we want to see it in time, a number of singular persons. Now that is of the essence, for it is due to her proneness to shared intentionality (cf. Tomasello 2008) that the ethnographer can achieve communication through interpretive charity, never through any sort of person-to-group communication. It is personhood that allows world to emerge (cf. Heidegger 1998: 123). In short, I may communicate with a number of different persons at the same time, but I can only communicate with them because they are singular humans (persons in ontogeny) like myself. To forget that is to allow ourselves to slip back into a Durkheimian type of sociocentrism.

We are here faced with another version of the quandary that the anthropology of kinship has been intensely addressing for a number of years:[15] there is a constant dynamic oscillation between singularity and duality in the dividual person. The unquestioned use of the word *individual* by authors such as Paleček and Risjord actually carries implications of which they might not be aware,

---

15. See Mariott (1976); Strathern (1988); Sahlins (2011a, 2011b); Pina-Cabral (2013b, 2013c).

for it assumes too casually the unitariness of personhood.[16] That unitariness is precisely what gives credence to ethnographic exceptionalism (i.e., the image of the lone ethnographer faced with the whole of the tribe in front of her tape recorder and then coming back to "us" speaking out the words of the tribe and not of the persons in it—explaining why twins can be birds or why blood is beer to jaguars, to use the more tired examples). But what we have learned from the long history of the debate about personhood and kinship is that singularity and plurality imply each other in relations of mutuality (Strathern 1988: 11–14; Pina-Cabral 2013c).

Therefore, the ethnographer who is carrying out her task is permanently oscillating between plurality and singularity in a process of ontogeny—she can only access interpretive communities because she engages singular communicators, and she can only engage the latter because she is willing to enter into their interpretive communities. Again, we are faced with the hegemonic strength of the all-or-nothing fallacy. There is no matter of True Ontology as much as there is no matter in denying the veridicality of all ontologies. The notion of a truth that can exist outside of human interaction in history is absurd. Truth is a feature of mind and "mind is a function of the whole person constituted over time in intersubjective relations with others in the environing world" (Toren 2002: 122).

For this reason, we cannot concur fully with thinkers like Jagdish Hattiangadi or Daniel Siegel, whose interest in psychology and psychotherapy leads them to treat mind in general as the relevant emergent entity. For anthropologists, whose concern with humanity is necessarily more holistic, the emergence is seen as occurring not in general, but in each historically singular animal and in each historically singular person, as Christina Toren insists. In humans, mind is a historically determinable occurrence: the ontogeny of each person is the moment of emergence of a new level of supervening—the "anomaly" occurs each time a person enters personal ontogeny. World, therefore, is a function not of mind in general, but of its occurrence in particular animals and persons.

CONCLUSION

In conclusion, yes, there is only one world but, yes, there are differences between the world of animals and the world of humans and, within the later, between

---

16.   An aspect that Maurice Bloch's "blob" (2012) also does not manage to bypass.

interpretive communities. If these differences were truly incommensurable, then there would be no ethnography.[17] But the contrary is also the case: as no communication can happen outside the indeterminacy of meaning, the question of commensurability is always relative from the start.

Having examined the way in which the word *world* is used by anthropologists, we conclude that the meanings attributed to it reflect a basic tension that operates along three main aspects: for each embodied person, (iii) the world in its limited materiality opposes itself to *propositional* thinking owing to (ii) the constant constitution of *perspectival* domains (home/self); in turn, the evanescent nature of these allows for (i) a constant play between the world as an embracing *source* and the world as a locally produced context. Personhood (propositionally thinking human beings historically engaged in sociality) is what allows for the three aspects of world to come together in a broad experience of world.

As phenomenology has taught us, human experience is social before it is rational. The world is one because, in personhood, alterity is anterior. In all of its plurality, the world cannot escape from history, that is, all those untold determinations that accumulate in each single act of any singular person. There is freedom in personhood to the extent that propositional thought institutes its own processes of determination that supervene on animal intentionality and on material determination. World, therefore, like persons, will ever waver in the unstable terrain that lies between singularity and plurality; it is one and it is many. Chapter 2 will examine the structural conditions of world and argue that ethnography, in order to capture them, has to engage transcendence.

17. As Godlove puts it: "Systematic religious conceptual contrast must be largely theoretical in nature, and relatively limited in scope" (1996: 5).

CHAPTER TWO

Transcendence

Insofar as human beings exist at all,
they already find themselves transposed in their existence
into other human beings, even if there are factically
no other human beings in the vicinity.

– Martin Heidegger ([1929/30] 1995: 205)

In their descriptions of people's lived worlds, ethnographers are expected to clarify what beings there are for the people they study (their ontology) and how these beings interrelate meaningfully within world (their metaphysics). The starting point of this chapter, therefore, is that metaphysical concerns are never absent from any ethnographic description that aims to "take seriously" the experiences described.[1] I now move to address the metaphysical implications of the process of worlding (cf. Tsing 2011), the human disposition that opens up the space of interaction where the "holism of the mental" operates

---

1. See the debate between Viveiros de Castro (2011) and Matei Candea (2011). As we will see later on, however, my own take on "taking seriously" rejects the possibility of ontological incommensurability in the ethnographic gesture. Thus, it emphasizes the creative nature of the ethnographic analysis and focuses preferably on the verisimilitude of the narrative.

(Davidson 2001).[2] Concomitantly, I argue that transcendence is not to be seen as a feature of this or that culture or ontology. Rather, it is a recurrent feature of human experience, as it is a function of the very process of constitution of human persons in ontogeny by means of what Lévy-Bruhl called "participation." The chapter starts by setting these discussions within the history of twentieth-century anthropology in order to make sense of where we have come from. In particular, it argues for the continued relevance of a tradition that finds its roots in R. G. Collingwood's rendering of the Ontological Proof of God's existence, developed by Saint Anselm of Canterbury in the late eleventh century.

THE ENCHANTMENT OF WORLD

Most of the founders of our discipline at the turn of the twentieth century—people like McLennan, Lubbock, Tylor, or Frazer—were "great believers in laws of social evolution and in the necessary interdependence of institutions, and all . . . agnostic and hostile to religion" (Evans-Pritchard 1962: 35). As Max Weber (1948) might have put it, they were enthusiastically engaged in the modernist project of disenchanting the world. This was not the case, however, with those who followed them after the 1920s methodological revolution led by Malinowski.

While the evolutionist fathers of the discipline were prone to disparage religion and magic as forms of thinking that science would dismantle, and thus considered the beliefs of "primitives" to be somehow inferior to their own, this was *not* the generalized approach on the part of the trained ethnographers who were making their way in the profession in the British Empire or the United States after the 1920s. It is, for instance, arguable that the impact of the work of Edward Burnett Tylor, John Lubbock, Robert Marett, or James Frazer on the interwar generation of anthropologists was far lesser than that of the work of the great missionary and administrator ethnographers of the turn of the century. In any case, this was certainly Max Gluckman's opinion concerning the lasting impact of Henri-Alexandre Junod in Southern African ethnography (1962: 7–9);

2.   Here I am not using the word "holism" in the fashion it is most commonly encountered in anthropological literature. Donald Davidson's expression "holism of the mental" describes the participations that exist among all our thoughts and that tend to be figured into structures, without ever fully achieving an overarching structure.

and the cases of Bruno Gutman (1926; see Steiner 1999a) in Kenya, Elsdon Best among the Maori, or R. S. Rattray among the Ashanti should suffice as examples.

Contrary to their predecessors, those who followed in the steps of Malinowski vowed to be respectful toward the transcendental experiences they encountered in the field, refusing to treat them as somehow invalid, untrue, erroneous, or wrong-headed. The experiences of "enchantment" that they witnessed were taken to be genuine cases of transcendence.[3] There was a price to pay for ethnographic relativism, however, and that was the adoption of an agnostic posture toward the native opinions conveyed. Methodological relativism was taken dead seriously by such people as Audrey Richards, Ruth Benedict, Raymond Firth, or Marcel Griaule—to give a few random examples. You will be hard pressed to find one single professionally respected anthropologist from the 1920s onward who disparages the genuine spirituality of the transcendental experiences (the "beliefs") they describe in their ethnographies (even Lévy-Bruhl came to that opinion at the end of his life—[1949] 1998). In fact, they despised people like Tylor and Frazer for doing just that. The effort to show the reasonableness of native "beliefs" was hardly exclusive to anthropologists who admitted to being Christian believers, such as Evans-Pritchard, Godfrey Lienhardt, or Mary Douglas, and it included even people who were explicitly inspired by materialist views, such as Max Gluckman or Meyer Fortes.

While Christian affiliation was indeed not predominant among professional ethnographers after the 1920s, (a) they were all deeply attentive to and respectful about the transcendental experiences they described, "taking them seriously" at all times, and (b) many of them were, in more or less private fashion, engaged in some form of personal spiritual quest, often non-Christian: Steiner's Judaism, Leach's Humanism, Srinivas' and Madan's Hinduism, Needham's Buddhism, Lienhardt's or Douglas' Catholicism, Turnbull's alternative spiritualist engagements . . . to quote just a few examples. In the American case, in fact, the matter was made even more complex owing to the readiness of many of the North American Amerindianists to be adopted and initiated by the tribal peoples they studied. In many such instances, this involved deeply felt life-long engagements

---

3.   I use transcendence here to refer to that which is beyond the ordinary range of perception. The usual examples are the experience of the sacred or of the otherworldly, but the presence of my own personhood is also transcendent. As Heidegger argues, Dasein transcends: "Although it exists in the midst of being and enhanced by being, Dasein as existing has always already surpassed nature." (1998: 109).

with Indian forms of spirituality (see Kan 2001). The same can be said of Afro-American religion in the more impressive cases, such as Pierre Verger, Zora Neale Hurston (e.g., [1935] 1990), Edison Carneiro, and Ruth Landes (e.g., [1947] 1994).[4]

Post-Malinowskian methodological agnosticism was made possible owing to a conjugation of two oppositional axes: firstly, the adoption of an ontological separation between mind and matter; and, secondly, a strict differentiation between collective and individual belief. Ethnographic relativism relied on a kind of bargain: you believed the native's experience for so long as you accepted not to confront it with your own. It is only thus that Evans-Pritchard ([1973] 1976), for example, could cope with the paradox of being certain that witches such as the Azande conceive of them do not exist (in material reality), yet he himself witnessed one passing in the middle of the night, because he had completely immersed himself in a collective world where it was reasonable to witness such things.

However, as Evans-Pritchard precisely meant to show by this aporetic example, methodological agnosticism, handy as it was, placed the anthropologist in a singularly problematic condition, for it meant that he or she accepted the life of the spirit but abdicated from granting it real existence—it was a sort of borrowed enchantment, to coin a phrase. Ethnographic relativism was no more than a suspension of disbelief and, to use Heidegger's expression (see Wrathall and Lambeth 2011), it left anthropologists in a situation of suspension, for either they were *godless*—when god alone might have provided the link with transcendence—or they were *godforsaken*—finding that their "faith" was a challenge too difficult to bear. The problem was especially acute for those who, like Evans-Pritchard, refused the bargain as somehow reductive. This is how I can make sense of his often-quoted statement that it was the Nuer who convinced him to convert to Catholicism ([1973] 1976: 245). What the Nuer taught him was that the life of the spirit is true to the extent that transcendence is a genuine facet of the human condition; the particular form you choose for it then is not really as important, as it is a matter of personal circumstance.

Yet the choice had tragic implications, for in accepting a God, you were not only accepting a "belief-system," you were also engaging yourself in a morality,

---

4.   Indeed, in all of these cases, their careers were marred by prejudice. Landes, in particular, suffered for many decades from the boycott imposed by Herskovits owing to his homophobic prejudice (Cole 2003).

a form of life, and that was a very heavy burden to bear for people whose lives were immersed in the complexities of modernity, as were most twentieth-century anthropologists. This was probably what Evans-Pritchard meant when he so often regretted that he was such a "bad Catholic."[5] The anthropologist-believer inhabited both sides of the equation: he or she was a scientist *and* a "primitive" at the same time, as Franz Baermann Steiner comments about himself.[6] The anthropologist who refused to be godless was transformed into a walking contradiction—he or she was godforsaken.

These terms are borrowed from Heidegger's late writings, where he debates our contemporary metaphysical condition. There, he argues that these are the two metaphysical options in the "age of choice" (Wrathall and Lambeth 2011: 171; cf. Heidegger 1999). For twentieth-century anthropologists of religion, methodological relativism promoted such a schismogenic condition. While the mind/matter polarity allowed for a temporary intellectual respite, ultimately it did not resolve the paradox posed by having to make transcendence compatible with a scientifically conceived material world. While Evans-Pritchard (1962) accuses most of the anthropologists of his day of being godless, and thus incapable of coping with the fact that religion is a human inevitability, I believe it is reasonable to argue that his own extreme anti-intellectualist option was a manifestation of godforsakenness: a despair at the impending loss of the sacred. Ultimately, the two responses were of a kind.

From the perspective of Christian proselytism (cf. Larsen 2014) it may indeed look like anthropologists who were not practicing Christians were somehow blind to spiritual matters. But here is where some knowledge of the history of anthropological theory may help. The paradoxes produced by the mind/body opposition and its conjugation with sociocentrism have posed themselves from the beginning. Evans-Pritchard's first essay against what he called the "English intellectualist school" dated to 1933, eleven years before his conversion. Ever since 1972 (Needham 1972), in any case, we have been explicitly advised that there are serious intellectual problems with the representationist and collectivist assumptions that characterized midcentury anthropological

---

5.   The lifestyle choices implied in religious adherence placed him in constant contradiction with himself, and that is what ultimately caused his life to be so tragic (cf. Larsen 2014). As a matter of fact, Steiner (1999a) struggled with similar problems, albeit for different reasons.

6.   Humorously but also tragically, in light of his own transethnic love life (Steiner 1999a: 40, 47–48, 59).

relativism—among both believers and nonbelievers. The debate concerning the nature of "belief/faith" has been long and fecund in anthropology and it remains probably yet unfinished.[7]

If there is one discipline that, from the beginning, did not accept whole-heartedly the scientivistic project of disenchanting the world, anthropology is it. Since the 1980s, however, and with increasing intensity of late, we have witnessed a tendency to explicitly criticize methodological agnosticism and to call for a reenchantment of world (Turner's anthropology of experience and Taussig's works were probably some of the primary signs of this). This movement accompanies a generalized dissatisfaction in the discipline—which found its moment of awareness around the millennium (see Jenkins 2000)—with the way in which irrationality is pervasive and beyond control in the global world we inhabit today: politically, economically, ecologically. This disenchantment with our world is accompanied by a call for a reenchantment of "other" worlds, leading to a new approach to the ethnographic task.

Like Evans-Pritchard himself, the anthropologists of today defend that the experiences they describe (e.g., shamanism) are genuinely transcendental—their "cannibal metaphysics" are presented as fully valid human experiences (Viveiros de Castro 2009). Yet a significant change has come about in that, instead of attempting to find the reason in apparent unreason, there is a taste for emphasizing the "strangeness," otherworldliness, or transcendence of the objects of study. Much like their forebears, these ethnographers and their readers purport to inhabit a spiritless world, yet the presentation of their ethnographic material emphasizes its genuine transcendental nature. Some have called this disposition "the ontological turn," and it is often (but as we will see not always) presented as a form of pluralism of worlds resulting from a postulation of ontological incommensurability between them (Pedersen 2012). What came to pass was a revival of older and more transcendentalist categories, such as animism, totemism, and shamanism, accompanied by a ferocious critique of some of the more trusty tools of ethnographic analysis, such as methodological holism or worldview analysis. Whilst Lévi-Straussian modes of structuralist analysis were taken on

---

7.   To cite only the high points: Gellner (1974); Pouillon (1982); Ruel ([1982] 2002); Veyne ([1983] 1988); Needham (1985); Tambiah (1990); Latour (1991); Sabbatucci (2000); Robbins (2007). Furthermore, it must be seen as related to the debate on "the decline of magic" (see Thomas [1971] 1991) and on "superstition" (see Pina-Cabral 2014a).

board in a silenced manner, Latourian naturalism made big inroads under the guise of "animism" (e.g., Descola 2005; Kohn 2013).

However, the revisitation by these contemporaries of such concepts as animism, totemism, shaman, soul, or spirit does not imply the adoption of the attitudes of distancing that characterized the founding masters of our discipline: same words, different intentions. Contrary to the midcentury interpretivists whose towering figure was Evans-Pritchard, our contemporary colleagues instinctively reject the metaphysical divide between mind and matter that made possible the flowering of the anthropology of religion sixty years ago. In order to achieve this, some choose to adopt forms of ontological pluralism, others argue for an animistic reenchantment of the world. This chapter sustains that we have to avoid both of these options since, as was argued above, the practice of anthropology demands that we postulate a single ontology.

Rather, as Evans-Pritchard already suggested in his courageous defense of Lévy-Bruhl in the 1930s, we must attend to the process by which the ontogeny of partible persons takes place in sociality (Evans-Pritchard [1934] 1970; see also Mills 2013). If we do so, we can account for transcendence whilst abandoning the mind/matter polarity, thus finally bypassing the tragic choice between godlessness and godforsakenness that haunted twentieth-century anthropology and which Evans-Pritchard grapples with in his Aquinas Lecture of 1959 (1962).

MIDCENTURY INTERPRETIVISM

The young E. E. Evans-Pritchard, then Professor of Sociology at King Fuad I University in Cairo,[8] published three short papers where he laid down the theoretical foundations for what was going to be his life's work: "The intellectualist (English) interpretation of magic" (1933); "Lévy-Bruhl's theory of primitive mentality" ([1934] 1970); and "Science and sentiment: An exposition and criticism of the writings of Pareto" (1936). However, his lasting influence in the discipline was not established until ten years later. His first ethnographic monograph, *Witchcraft, oracles and magic among the Azande* ([1937] 1976), only became a classic of the discipline in the postwar period (see Douglas 1970: xiii).

---

8. A post held earlier on by another of Malinowski's *personae non gratae*, A. M. Hocart.

Together with Franz Baermann Steiner (1999a, 1999b), he had a major impact on a group of young anthropologists who came to write their theses in
Oxford immediately at the end of the war and who were going to shape the discipline globally (Mary Douglas herself, Louis Dumont, M. N. Srinivas, Paul and
Laura Bohannan, Julian Pitt-Rivers, Godfrey Lienhardt, Thomas Beidelman,
Ian Cunnison, John Peristiany, Rodney Needham, John K. Campbell, etc.). Owing to them, Evans-Pritchard's interpretivist turn in the early 1950s and his
favored metaphor for ethnography as "translation of cultures" (cf. Beidelman
1971) became the foundation for most anthropological approaches to metaphysical matters on both sides of the Atlantic during the second half of the
twentieth century.[9] The Azande granary (see figure 1) or the Nuer twins were
going to become familiar theoretical mnemonics for practically all trained anthropologists thereafter.

Figure 1. The Azande granary (Evans-Pritchard, Sudan, 1927–30, Pitt Rivers Museum
Photographic Collection).

The son of an Anglican priest, Evans-Pritchard had undertaken by then a deeply emotional conversion to Catholicism (in 1944—Larsen 2014: 91), and his religious struggles played no small part in his anthropological thinking. Although
both Steiner (a practicing Orthodox Jew) and Evans-Pritchard were careful in

---

9.   Joan Bestard Camps called my attention to the fact that, whilst this was certainly
      the case in English-speaking environments, in Spanish-speaking countries the
      influence of Ortega y Gasset played a similar role.

keeping their religious options away from their academic works, it is not irrelevant that they were both deeply engaged "believers." Indeed, many of their students in Oxford who were to have a significant impact in discussing matters of religion were also religiously affiliated (e.g., Godfrey Lienhardt, M. N. Srinivas, Mary Douglas, Rodney Needham, Eva Gillies, and many more—see Larsen 2014). For such people, the border between the two metaphysical conditions that methodological relativism imposed (that of science and that of faith) required painful policing.

Judging from his later writings, we might surmise that Evans-Pritchard had been dissatisfied with Durkheimian structural functionalism from the very beginning. His theoretical inspiration is rather to be sought in the works that Mauss and Lévy-Bruhl were publishing in the interwar period and, in turn, his work and that of his colleagues directly affected their syntheses.[10] The fact is that it was only in 1949/50—at a time when he was President of the Royal Anthropological Institute, Radcliffe-Brown having retired, and Malinowski having died—that he felt empowered enough to write his first theoretical manifesto ("Social anthropology: Past and present," the 1950 Marett Lecture—1962). He was bold in his criticism: "I believe we shall not hear much more of sociological laws . . . and that that will be much to the benefit of anthropology" (ibid.: 44). In fact, he had never been happy with the sociological positivism of the Durkheimian school. He actually wonders whether there is "an entity which can be labelled 'society' and that such an entity has something called a 'structure', which can be further described as a set of functionally interdependent institutions or sets of social relations. These are analogies from biological science and, if they had their uses, they have also proved to be highly dangerous" (ibid.: 55).

Evans-Pritchard's Marett Lecture, his Aquinas Lecture, and his 1961 essay on "Anthropology and history" (ibid.) can be read together as proposing an interpretivist approach to anthropology that was deeply at odds with the previous anthropological status quo and was at the root of the distancing that eventually took place between himself, Meyer Fortes, and Max Gluckman. But it should be stressed that the differences between these men were not merely theoretical, as they had deep political and philosophical roots. Evans-Pritchard's new

10. In his reply to Evans-Pritchard, Lévy-Bruhl (1952) declares that he regrets that when he wrote his books, he did not have the quality data that was later available as a result of the work of ethnographers of a newer generation. I imagine that the confrontation with such work, and particularly Maurice Leenhardt's, would be one of the main reasons for his change of mind at the end of his life.

approach was politically conservative and philosophically based on the meth-odology of history proposed by R. G. Collingwood (see ibid.: 51), whose lec-tures he had attended in Oxford in the 1920s when he was a student of Robert Marett at Exeter College and clearly had never forgotten.[11] Evans-Pritchard was a brilliant ethnographic writer whose empiricist creed led him to leave out of his writings any reference to his theoretical moorings. In his own words, "Perhaps I should regard myself first as an ethnographer and secondly as a so-cial anthropologist, because I believe that a proper understanding of the eth-nographic facts must come before any really scientific analysis" (1963: 24). As a result, his profound theoretical debt to Collingwood's idealism has remained largely unnoticed in anthropological milieus.[12]

The founding stone of Collingwood's philosophy of history is that the logic of nature and the logic of mind are radically distinct (Collingwood [1946] 1994). This explains largely Evans-Pritchard's conviction that "fundamentally there never were any real grounds for dispute between what natural science teaches about the nature of the physical world and what the Churches teach about faith and morals" (1962: 43). The only access to human action, Collingwood sustained, is through reflexive thinking. So, in order to get to know human action, you have to position yourself in the role of the knower as it were by proxy. The ethnographer, therefore, has to place himself in the position of "the primitives" he studies so as to get to know what they know.[13] This is one of the reasons why, in his methodological writings, Evans-Pritchard emphasizes so much the need to actually experience physically the life and tools of the people one studies (e.g., [1973] 1976: 243). And, in order to give "us" access to the knowledge thus obtained about "them," the ethnographer has to "translate." In

---

11. See also Peter Winch's comments on Collingwood: "There is a certain respect, indeed, in which Collingwood pays insufficient attention to the manner in which a way of thinking and the historical situation to which it belongs form one indivisible whole" (Winch [1958] 2008: 123) This can be seen to apply to all the long line of subsequent anthropological interpretivisms that (whether they know it or not) find their original source in Evans-Pritchard's reading of Collingwood's philosophy of history. I want to thank Tim Jenkins for having called my attention to Evans-Pritchard's dependence on R. G. Collingwood's idealist methodology of history.

12. Mary Douglas, for instance, comments explicitly that he promoted "a virtual silence of his intellectual debts" (1980: 29).

13. As we will further develop later, these primitivist theses depend, of course, on an implicit representationalist theory of mind that has become naturalized in most anthropological discourse (see Pina-Cabral 2010a, 2011, and 2013c).

this process, however, one comes to achieve some greater knowledge of oneself. As Collingwood put it, "To know something without knowing that one knows it is only a half-knowing, and to know that one knows is to know oneself" ([1946] 1994: 204). Thus, the study of "the primitives" was a part of the larger history of humankind for, again in Collingwood's words, "the historical process is a process in which man creates for himself this or that kind of human nature by re-creating in his own thought the past to which he is heir" (ibid.: 226).

Human nature ("man's essence") is created by humans in the process of existence by the thinking of history. Thus, when they bring the experiences of the "primitives" into history, anthropologists are actually shaping human nature. The myriad historical and anthropological monographs being written are nothing but "chapters in a single historical work," the process of emergence of human essence (ibid.: 27). This metaphysical circularity between essence and existence is profoundly connected with Collingwood's particular interpretation of the Ontological Proof, which we will discuss later on in this chapter.

A surprising characteristic of this approach is that it is based on a deep distrust of the cognitive capacities of all humans—what I call for the sake of this argument anti-intellectualism. In Collingwood's formulation: "It is only by fits and starts, in a flickering and dubious manner, that human beings are rational at all" (ibid.: 227). Humans are not essentially driven by ostension: to the contrary, there are a whole lot of "social restraints on perception," which it is the ethnographer's task to identify.[14] As an ethnographer, therefore, Evans-Pritchard did not despise the primitives for thinking in logically unsatisfactory ways or for failing to take the correct conclusions from their experience, since he believed that "no one is mainly controlled by reason anywhere or at any epoch" (in Douglas 1980: 33). Many of the readings of Evans-Pritchard's work on the Azande fail to see that he was attempting to explain how religious thought operates; he was not validating it as being rational or truthful.

For both Collingwood and Evans-Pritchard, "Scientific thought is a very specialized experience that only takes place in very specialized conditions" (ibid.: 31). In fact, the ethnographer's main task as an interpreter of culture was precisely to explain "how a metaphysical system could compel belief by a variety of self-validating procedures" (ibid.: xviii). Thus, Douglas describes the main challenge that Evans-Pritchard addresses in *Witchcraft, oracles and magic*, as the

---

14. This is how Mary Douglas explains the nature of the project that Evans-Pritchard set himself when writing *Witchcraft, oracles and magic* (1970: xvii).

need to explain "how a people can use an acceptable idiom to present their political system to themselves without worrying about how little it corresponds to the facts" (Douglas 1970: xvii). This concurs perfectly with Collingwood's preoccupation to explain how modes of thinking that rely on mutually exclusive absolute presuppositions can survive perfectly well next to each other.

As it happens, however, this anti-intellectualism is at the root of Evans-Pritchard's personal religious options, and, in this sense, his theoretical views as a social anthropologist cannot be separated from his political and religious conservatism. We must not forget that the Catholicism he opted for at the time of the war was not the Catholicism that we are familiar with today and that was largely molded by the Second Vatican Council in the 1960s. He opted for the Ultramontane Catholicism of his day rather than the bland Protestantism of his own father's faith. Protestantism's reliance on the Bible as the source of belief was, in his eyes, eroded by historical criticism; whilst, on the contrary, the Catholic reliance on papal infallibility and the authority of the church left it safe beyond the realms of reason. His option, therefore, must be seen as an anti-intellectualist declaration very much in the line of Collingwood's idealism: "As Comte long ago most clearly saw, . . . Protestantism shades into Deism and Deism into agnosticism, and . . . the choice is all or nothing, a choice which allows of no compromise between a Church which has stood its ground and made no concessions, and no religion at all" (Evans-Pritchard 1962: 45).

A POLYDIVINISTIC AGE

When we read the work of our more recent colleagues in the light of those of an earlier generation, however, it becomes evident that the divide between the godless (those who deny the sacred) and the godforsaken (those who insist on awaiting a new coming) has shifted its ground. Authors such as Eduardo Viveiros de Castro (2009) are engaging in genuine metaphysics, even as they do so by proxy. If my assessment is correct, anthropology is presently undergoing a further and perhaps even more profound paradigmatic change than in the 1920s. Heidegger calls this change "the passing of the last god," when he claims that we are searching for a way of being human which is newly "open to transient and particular but intense manifestations of a plurality of sacreds" (Wrathall and Lambeth 2011: 163), where the anxiety about transcendental inaccessibility that characterized the twentieth century and tortured people like Evans-Pritchard no longer applies.

When Márcio Goldman (2003) states that he actually could hear the drums of the dead being called by the shaman, he does not share the sense of paradox that accompanies Evans-Pritchard's similar declaration about seeing a witch passing in the Azande night sky. The main difference is that contemporary anthropologists no longer rely on the kind of "fideistic" type of belief (see Sabbatucci 2000) that Rodney Needham (1972) deconstructed in his book about Evans-Pritchard's concept of belief. To put it in another way, Goldman no longer feels he has to "believe in" in order to "believe that" (see Ruel [1982] 2002)—being and understanding are seen as related but separate.[15]

In truth, this change in aspect (or, better still, this ontological transformation) did not come about unannounced. This form of ethnographic engagement with magic and the metaphysical that preserves their transcendence independently of the ethnographer's own declared belief system has been emerging in anthropology over the past decades, making its presence felt in some of the more well-read ethnographic experiments. One of its most excessive and at the same time most poignant reminders is Michael Taussig's *The magic of the state* (1997), that weirdly fascinating book. This is how he starts it:

> How naturally we entify and give life to such. Take the case of God, the economy, and the state, abstract entities we credit with Being, species of things awesome with life-force of their own, transcendent over mere mortals. Clearly they are fetishes, invented wholes of materialized artifice into whose woeful insufficiency of being we have placed soulstuff. (1997: 3)

It would seem, then, that his materialist background was going to drive him to reject transcendence, but then he proceeds:

> I hope to clarify matters somewhat, and not only for myself, by thinking about the magic of the state in a European Elsewhere—*your metaphor, my literality*—as related to a free spirit who frequented those parts, a sunny place, she said, from

---

15. In fact, the problem with some of Viveiros de Castro's recent comments on this matter (cf. 2011) is precisely that he continues to pitch his arguments against a notion of belief that does not take into account the fact that anthropological understanding about what belief is has evolved significantly over the decades.

where oil flows out, cars, ammo, and videos flow in, and where a crucial quality of being is granted the state of the whole by virtue of death, casting an aura of magic over the mountain at its center. (1997: 4, my emphasis)

Rather than contrasted, therefore, literality and metaphor are somehow being combined. Two decades ago, when these pages were published, we took them to be an instance of creative writing; and that they are. But since then it has become clear that, buried inside Taussig's metaphysical ranting, there was the emergence of a whole new way for anthropology to overcome its uncomfortably dichotomic metaphysical condition: Heidegger's "passing of the last god" (1999). We have given up on Evans-Pritchard's hope of finding the advent of a "world-grounding being" in Ultramontane Catholicism, but we have not given up on transcendence. Rather, to the contrary, anthropologists have chosen to become open to the experience of transcendence in a plurality of divine fashions: we are "polydivinistic" to the extent that we learn to foster "whatever practices we have left to us for receptivity to the sacred" (Heidegger's words—Wrathall and Lambeth 2011: 178).

In line with this, Taussig concludes his book by claiming that the main role of anthropology is to bring such a conscience to actualization: that is, "the storing in modernity of what are *taken to be* pre-modern practices such as spirit possession and magic" (1997: 198, again my emphasis), and this for the sake of "profane illumination." We assume that if these magical practices "are taken to be," then it is because they are not really—or is it modernity that no longer "is"? Thus, Taussig's search for an immanent transcendence—for grounding the world's strangeness in its own processes of becoming—relies on a kind of withholding of disbelief; it relies on a vicarious experience, assessed via the polydivinism of the Other: the strange Maria Lionza, the erotically charged goddess of the Venezuelan Other. Taussig remains "modern," he preserves his "Westernness," and so the true experience of transcendence can only be achieved by proxy.

And indeed, this is a condition very akin to that which Eduardo Viveiros de Castro has been elaborating over the years[16] when writing about Amerindian multinaturalism (2009: ch. 3) inspired by Lévi-Strauss' *Mythologiques*—the old master's extensive survey of the mythical corpus of the whole of the American

---

16. Deleuze claims that "transcendence is always a product of immanence" (2001: 31) We agree. The issue is the nature of the anthropological account we give of that emergence.

continent. The Amerindian world, Viveiros de Castro claims, is "a world of immanent alterity, where the human retains its primordiality" (ibid.: 28). That is, contrary to "us"/ "Westerners," for whom the transcendental manifests itself as utterly nonhuman, Amerindians experience "nature as variation" by means of a game of dislocation that Viveiros de Castro calls "perspectivism," and that consists in treating all existing things as centers of intentionality (ibid.: 12). Whilst "we" have many cultures but one nature, "they" have many natures but one culture, since the focus of the perspective (personhood) is open to all beings.

When he crosses the boundary of his embodiment as human, the shaman "adopts the perspective of the subjectivities of other species, so as to manage the relations between the latter and humans" (ibid.: 25). This disposition is based on considering that nonhuman agents (other species) see themselves and their own behavior much like we humans see our own. According to Viveiros de Castro, this involves a radical relocation of the notion of personhood that frees it from humanity, in that personhood becomes anterior and logically superior to humanity. So, both personhood and perspective cease to be seen as the distinct property of this or that species. Rather, they are treated as a matter of degree, that is, they are the capacity to occupy a point of view (ibid.: 22). For the Amerindians, "Between the formal subjectivity of the souls and the substantial materiality of the organisms, there is a central ground which is the body as a bundle of affects and capacities, and which is the origin of the perspectives" (ibid.: 40).

All this is very fascinating and takes anthropological theory to realms of theoretical sophistication which it has rarely attained since the days of Evans-Pritchard and Lévy-Bruhl. Viveiros de Castro asks us to "take seriously" Amerindian multinaturalism; and that, of course, we must do, to the extent that we must learn its lessons. But its lessons will never be ahistorical; they will never remain purely virtual or textual. They are our contemporary lessons and they are not about the ontological appositeness of such an ontology for, whether they happen to be Amerindian or not, anthropologists *qua*[17] anthropologists are not about to become convicted multinaturalists. I need hardly stress that anthropologists are not really expected to adopt Amerindian forms of myth making. Of course not; the lessons anthropologists have to learn from reading the *Mythologiques* are about how to overcome the inadequacies of previous anthropological modes of thinking so as to account for Amerindian metaphysics.

---

17. And here, Heidegger's discussion of the "as" (*qua*) is much to the point (1995: 353ff.).

To follow Collingwood's suggestion, we are making ourselves by making all of these ontologies part of our history (not only the Amerindian ones, but also that of the Buddha, that of Plato, that of Saint Anselm of Canterbury, etc.). No human experience should remain strange to us; we must think through them all in our efforts to give body to our increasingly ecumenical condition.

Still, in order to do that, we have to trace a path that makes them all humanly possible and, therefore, available. We do not have to find the coherence among them, the compatibility that will unite them all, nor do we need to close the boundaries of the species; we just have to make such experiences verisimilitudinous. That is the task of ethnography, first, and of anthropological comparativism, later. But it remains unavoidable that, faced with such a variety of "regimes of veridiction" (Descola 2014), we are left with having to propose a metaregime of veridiction. In short, we are ontologically responsible for the awareness of the existence of a plurality of ontologies.

Now, as argued in the first chapter, that can only be done satisfactorily by refusing to see meaning and reason as dissociated from historically rooted human experience. It would all be easy if it were a matter of narratives, as when Viveiros de Castro claims that: "If there is one thing that it falls to anthropology to accomplish, it is not to explicate the worlds of others but rather to multiply our world, people it with 'all those expressed, which do not exist apart from their expressions'" (2011: 137). But the problem is that we are not faced with having to determine how worlds *are* (note the plural) according to this or that "expression"; we have to account for how meaning is made by persons in world. The reason for this is that triangulating human expression with world is the only means anyone (ethnographer or not) has of having access to the meaning of others.

Furthermore, the matter would be simpler if indeed we were dealing with collectively defined ontologies, that is, "cultures." But cultures (and their component elements) cannot be observed as such; they are the product of the analytical efforts of the ethnographer. Viveiros de Castro claims:

> Anthropology's mission, as a social science, is to describe the forms which, and the conditions under which, truth and falsity are articulated according to the different ontologies that are presupposed by each culture (a culture here being taken as analogous to a scientific theory, which requires its own ontology—that is, its own field of objects and processes—in order for the theory to generate relevant truths). (2011: 143)

Not only is he assuming an all-or-nothing theory of truth in the above passage, but he is assuming that cultures offer themselves for our observation (a) as cultures (which is not the case, the job of the ethnographer is analytical) and (b) as narrative structures, like a scientific theory. This, of course, is not the case. Viveiros de Castro had to approach the Araweté before *he* produced a metaphysics of the world he inhabited with them. He is the author of their ontology. It all becomes even more complex, of course, when we are dealing with fully contemporary urban contexts, where a history of anthropological debate is already part of what is being studied, as Matei Candea noted (2011). There, it is simply impossible not to distrust the disposition for proposing ontological barriers which anthropology inherited from nineteenth-century primitivism.

Faced, then, with the need to "take seriously" ethnographic material, transcendence, in particular, becomes a challenge for the anthropologist, for the very words we use to convey it betray us horribly, owing to their profound ontological implications. Words such as "god," "soul," or "spirit" should never be used without considerable reserve. See, for example, the confusions that have characterized the anthropological adoption of the word *soul* when applied to Chinese traditional contexts (Pina-Cabral 2002a: 120–25). Lévi-Strauss and Viveiros de Castro, of all people, are fully aware of this, even as they use these terms. Such words have the same effect as "modern" and "nonmodern" in Taussig's writing: they reconstitute the ontological barrier (the *summa divisio*) through the back door. If, however, we give up on single-world ontology, adopting a form of culturalist agnosticism, we are back in a situation of godforsakenness.

There is, nevertheless, a lesson that we must take from the work of the Amerindianists: the lesson of becoming. That is, the observation that, whatever our ontology comes to be, it cannot be about fixed entities but it must be about transformation. It cannot be about simple repetition or symmetry, but it must be about movement of essence, about broken symmetry (cf. Lévi-Strauss [1958] 1963). As it happens, we are strongly encouraged to go that way by a radically different authority: that of contemporary physics (see Lederman and Hill 2004). As Marc Kirschner, John Gerhart, and Tim Mitchison propose, "There is no guarantee that the capacities of human knowledge in an undesigned world will ever mesh entirely with the crooked ways of the world itself"—that is, indeterminacy rules (2000: 81). In short, we have no reason to worry about the epistemological break, since the notion that it is possible to know the world in a fully determinate manner never even arises.

If, then, we find that the postulation of a single external source of transcendental truth—such as implicit in the Traditions of the Book—is no longer
available to us, as it prevents us from making sense of too many other humanly
desirable worlds, but we find that Amerindian multinaturalism, or Greek poly-
theism, are equally unavailable, then where are we going to search for the original ground to the experience of transcendence that we no longer wish to treat as
being somehow inchoate, primitive, or false, as did McLennan, Lubbock, Tylor,
Westermarck, or Frazer in their day?

ANIMIST TRANSCENDENCE

This was an issue that troubled Evans-Pritchard his life through. In a methodological paper written in 1973, he asks: "In writing about the beliefs of primitive
peoples does it matter one way or the other whether one accords them validity
or regards them as fallacious?" ([1973] 1976: 244). His decided conclusion is
that it matters, but then he despairs over the fact that he cannot really believe in
witches but yet he did learn a lot about God from the Nuer. If indeed "witches"
and "God" were mere representations, empirically encountered cultural items,
they should have had the same truth status. It is a problem to which, he exclaims, he has no answer. His anthropological agnosticism is godforsaken.[18]

As it happens, a similar quandary remains very present in the works of
Philippe Descola, one of the most congenial anthropological accounts of world
that has emerged over the past two decades (see, e.g., Descola 2014). His is a
minimalist realist account that is diversified by the claim that humans exist
within distinct "ontological filters." He suggests that "'what is the case for us' is
not a complete and self-contained world waiting to be represented according to
different viewpoints, but, *most probably*, a vast amount of qualities and relations
that can be actualized or not by humans according to how ontological filters
discriminate between environmental affordances" (ibid.: 272–73, my emphasis).
Unfortunately, this position also fails to advance our contemporary puzzlement
with transcendence. First, one can see that Descola is going over ground that
Evans-Pritchard had already covered in his interpretivist turn, but, second, one is
struck by the "most probably" clause. This clause is a declaration of "withholding

---

18. In that sense his personal (not anthropological) option for Roman Catholicism can
be seen as a deeply courageous response to metaphysical despair.

of disbelief," a declaration of agnosticism (to speak perhaps less metaphorically than it might at first seem), and thus a recognition of godforsakenness.

According to Descola, human worlds can be composed according to "ontological filters" or "framing devices." These are "systems of differences in the ways humans inhabit the world" and there can be four of them: animism, totemism, analogism, and naturalism, in that order (ibid.: 273–74). Irrespective of the patently heuristic value of the differences that Descola identifies, readers have to ask themselves where does he place himself when he proposes them. For where he places himself is where "we" are placed (we being his anthropologically informed assumed audience, whether we are Portuguese, as is the present case, Chinese, Amerindian, or whatever). Thus, Descola sees human difference when faced with world in a kind of continuum where animism is the farthest away from the description and naturalism/us is the closest. This is why the apparently discreet escape valve in the above sentence—the agnostic clause—turns out to be so relevant. Naturalism is our own ontology but we can only really know it exists because we contrast it with that which is least "ours": "Naturalism inverts the ontological premises of animism" (ibid.: 277).

Again, independently of the genuine heuristic appositeness of Descola's quadriculation of world, this account shares with that of Viveiros de Castro (and both of them with the Ur-myth: Lévi-Strauss's *Mythologiques*) what I have been calling over the years a "primitivist disposition."[19] That is, the notion that collective Others do it otherwise and anthropologists are not collectively part of those who otherwise it. In short, anthropologists are postulated as being collectively and ontologically external to the human realities they describe—the latter, of course, being also described as eminently collective. I call this disposition primitivist not only because of its historical roots in the nineteenth-century evolutionistic history of our discipline, but principally because it associates essentiality with primordiality (things that are most simple, are also considered to be more essential, and, therefore, anterior).

Descola, for example, concludes his most recent account by stating that in order "to take stock of the fact that worlds are differently composed," we have to "understand how they are composed without automatic recourse to our own mode of composition" (ibid.: 279). Thus, to take recourse to a metaphor, each collectivity of humans is fitted into its respective ontological shelf, but no one is about to

---

19. All this is made painfully clear in an interview that Lévi-Strauss (1998) gave to Viveiros de Castro and that has been published in Portuguese in *Mana*.

account for the whole bookshelf. This kind of agnosticism, therefore, amounts in the end to a form of culturalist idealism to the extent that it forgets we do not import representations into the world, because we are always already part of it. In metaphysical terms, indeed, we are essentially back where Collingwood left us.

Faced with the godforsakenness of such positions, it is no wonder that a number of colleagues are attempting to open ontological doors for "the passing of the last god." Many, in the wake of the work of Bruno Latour, are trying to postulate the bookshelf by radically and openly embracing transcendence (cf. Bennett 2010 or Connolly 2011). This, I insist, is quite as honest a theoretical option as the forms of agnosticism that Evans-Pritchard, Descola, and Viveiros de Castro espouse. William Connolly's defense of what he calls "immanent naturalism," which has received so much critical attention of late, is a case in point (Connolly 2001). Again, we are dealing with an author who, like Michael Taussig, takes the literal implications of his engagement with transcendence by regularly slipping from philosophical analysis into poetry.

In anthropology, the most creative postulation of this position is perhaps to be found in Eduardo Kohn's book *How forests think: Toward an anthropology beyond the human* (2013). He starts by manifesting his impatience with our contemporary quandary: "The recognition of multiple realities only sidesteps the question: can anthropology make general claims about the way the world *is?*" (ibid.: 10, original emphasis). In order to resolve it, he proceeds to develop a creative and highly idiosyncratic reading of Peircian semiotics. He proposes to go beyond the human in order to "situate distinctively human ways of being in the world as both emergent from and in continuity with a broader living semiotic realm" (ibid.: 16). He sees life as causally producing thought. (Incidentally, for him too, stones do not think—which Connolly and Bennett would strongly dispute.) Thus, he attempts to reunite thinking and understanding.

So far so good, but then he claims that "if thoughts exist beyond the human, then we humans are not the only selves in the world" (ibid.: 72). In this way, he proposes to generalize animism: "If thoughts are alive and if that which lives thinks, then perhaps the living world is enchanted" (ibid.). Thus, like Taussig, Viveiros de Castro, and so many anthropologists before them, Kohn wants to safeguard the genuine "strangeness" (and this seems to be one of his favorite words) of the way in which the world presents itself to the Ecuadorean Runa among whom he lived. However, he is going one step further in his attempt not to dissolve, deny, or diminish the genuine mystery of what the forest and its beings communicate to the Runa. He is looking for transcendence in immanence.

I must refer the reader to Kohn's book for the complexity of his argument and the masterful way in which he intersperses dense ethnographic analysis with complex semiotic theory. For the purposes of the present argument, however, it is sufficient to note that the coherence of his theoretical proposition depends on the manipulation of the meaning of two central words: *self* and *representation*. Kohn refuses to distinguish "representation" from "presentation" or "reference";[20] neither does he make the distinction between intentionality and propositionality (basic thought v. scaffolded thought).[21] In this way, he attributes reflexivity to forms of intentionality that, patently, do not possess it. So he confuses intentionality (being directed at the world, possessing a *telos*) with propositionality (the capacity to engage the world reflexively, which can only be acquired through access to language). Thus, for him, since all life demonstrates intentionality, all life thinks, and, since thinking is representing, all life manifests self: *ergo*, "Dogs . . . are selves because they think" (ibid.: 73).

Kohn defines self as "a form that is reconstituted and propagated over the generations in ways that exhibit increasingly better fits to the worlds around it" (ibid.: 55). Now, as it happens, he is not the first to attempt to extend the meaning of self beyond consciousness in order to describe more generally life's concern to exist or to carry on being. Francisco Varela and his associates have been using the notion of a "primitive feeling of self" to describe "a kind of primitive self-awareness or animation of the body" (Thompson 2007: 161). They are, however, careful to dissociate such a use from a representationalist view of mind, such as Kohn adheres to, precisely in order to avoid the sort of abusive generalizations he engages upon.[22]

There is, furthermore, a problem of conceptual economy, so to speak, in this option to define selfhood in such a deeply unconventional manner, so as to apply it to both persons and nonpersons: the original reason that the Freudians gave for adopting and divulging the concept in the first place was to refer to an entity that reflects upon its own existence. The reflexivity of self was self's definitional distinction throughout the twentieth century. Some of us, such as myself, may

---

20. See Thompson (2007: 288): "A re-presentational experience constitutes its object precisely as both phenomenally absent in its bodily being and as mentally evoked or brought forth."

21. See Hutto and Myin (2013). This is further developed in chapter 3 below.

22. In Thompson's words, "[It] seems unlikely that minimal autopoietic selfhood involves phenomenal selfhood or subjectivity, in the sense of a prereflective self-awareness constitutive of a phenomenal first-person perspective" (ibid.: 163).

have doubts about the concept, in particular concerning the way it lends itself to forms of reification of thought that fail to understand that self is essentially a positionality (an arena of presence and action, as Johnston [2010] puts it) and that tend to confuse selfhood with soul (see Givens 2012). But the problem is that this is precisely what Kohn's animism aims to do: he wants to reanimate the world and, in doing this, explain transcendence as a product of immanence.

As it happens, Kohn is indeed pointing in the right direction in attempting to resolve the quandary of transcendence; unfortunately, his animism stands or falls on what amounts to little more than a metaphor between how humans think and how semiosis operates in nonhuman life.

THE ONTOLOGICAL PROOF

At this point, we might usefully go back to the roots of Evans-Pritchard's thought in Collingwood's philosophy of history and its reliance on a very particular interpretation of a philosophical form of proof that is generally known as the Ontological Proof of God's existence (henceforward OP). Collingwood is hardly the only modern thinker to have entertained it, as a number of his more distinguished contemporaries, such as Bertrand Russell and Kurt Gödel, seem to have been equally fascinated by the implications of the proof (Southern 1990: 128). Collingwood argues convincingly that, of all of medieval philosophy, the OP is perhaps the most valuable legacy to modernity. Descartes, Spinoza, Hegel, are some of those who explicitly took recourse to it. Indeed, as Collingwood puts it, Kant constitutes "perhaps the only occasion on which anyone has rejected it who really understood what it meant" ([1933] 2005: 126). Whilst, in its simplest form, the argument may appear to the uninitiated as almost puerile, we are well advised to look beyond that first reaction if we take the history of philosophy as our guide. As Anselm's biographer notes, whether or not we find the argument logically convincing (and we have Gödel as an authority on that, no less!), it surely has "some hidden source of life," for it continues to challenge us today (Southern 1990: 132).

Anselm (1033–1109) was a Benedictine monk of Italian origin who, in 1093, became the second archbishop of Canterbury after the Norman Conquest.[23] While his life in the monastery at Bec, in Normandy, as a thinker and

---

23. I am indebted to R. W. Southern's exemplary personal and intellectual biography of Saint Anselm (1990)

intellectual leader, had been deeply contemplative, his time as archbishop was troubled by serious political conflicts with the king. Like so many English ecclesiastic leaders after him (Saint Thomas à Becket and Sir/Saint Thomas More being perhaps the more tragic examples), he found his allegiance to the pope conflicted with his allegiance to the king and he was forced into exile more than once. As he was a devout adherent of the Benedictine monastic ideal, Anselm's tenure as archbishop was characterized both by to a reinforcement of the rights and independence of the monastic community at Canterbury and by a continuation of his predecessor's work of rebuilding the cathedral, which had burnt down in 1067. We owe to him much of the eastern part of today's building (Southern 1990: 326–27).

Anselm was a devout and orthodox Christian believer, inspiring himself in the Augustinian theological tradition. His starting point is that, since thinking creatures were created by God, it should be possible for them to find within themselves, by contemplation, God's own traces (Connolly and D'Oro in Collingwood [1933] 2005: xi). Thus, he dedicated himself to the discovery of how "the reality of God's existence is bound up with the very nature of human understanding" (Evans 1989: 106). As a result, his arguments are not dependent on authority; they are based on the examination of the sense impressions and on self-knowledge, and aim to be self-authenticating (Southern 1990: 122). Thus he called his first treatise *Monologion*, precisely "because in it he alone speaks and argues with himself"—explains Eadmer, his disciple and biographer (ibid.: 116). Apparently, the proof of God's existence formed itself in Anselm's mind one day at Bec, during Matins, as *Deo gratias* was being sung, and he proceeded to expound it in his second treatise, *Proslogion* (Anselm 1998: 82–105). The two works were composed between 1076 and 1078. In what follows, I will also take recourse to his essay called *De veritate*, probably written three or four years later, where he expounds what we might call today his epistemological assumptions (Southern 1990: 172).

The OP hinges on a definition of God that Anselm possibly found in Seneca (that-than-which-nothing-greater-can-be-thought), but which he places in a radically new context (ibid.: 129–30). He essentially attempts to prove that the nonexistence of God is logically indefensible. The following is the argument in his own words: even one who denies the existence of God (the Fool, as Anselm calls him, following Psalm 13: 1)

is forced to agree that something-than-which-nothing-greater-can-be-thought exists in the mind . . . [but] surely it cannot exist in the mind alone. For if it exists solely in the mind, it can be thought to exist in reality also, which is greater. If then that-than-which-a-greater-cannot-be-thought exists in the mind alone, this same that-than-which-a-greater-*cannot*-be-thought is that-than-which-a-greater-*can*-be-thought. But this is obviously impossible. Therefore, there is absolutely no doubt that something-than-which-a-greater-cannot-be-thought exists both in mind and reality. (Anselm 1998: 87–88, original emphasis)

He concludes, it is not possible to deny God's existence without entering into self-contradiction. And note, this is not a mere play on words, since the argument is logically coherent. What the OP does not tell us about is the nature of its subject matter, which Anselm proceeds to develop in the rest of his oeuvre. Once we distance ourselves from his particular conception of what God is, the OP becomes a powerful argument concerning how essence (a being's beingness) and existence (a being's occurrence) are in fact related. It is in this sense that Spinoza uses it in the first sentence of his *Ethics*, when he cites it indirectly in order to present his obscure but increasingly influential definition of God (*Deus sive natura*): "By that which is self-caused, I mean that of which the essence involves existence, or that of which the nature is only conceivable as existent" (Spinoza [1677] 2013: I, definition 1)

And this is where Collingwood takes up the argument. For people like himself, Russell, or Gödel, what is at stake in the ontological argument is not the nature of any specific God. For them, the OP does not prove the existence of the Christian God. What it proves is that, in matters of metaphysics, essence and existence must be thought of as ultimately inseparable—there is no pure *ens rationis*, thought is never free of objective or ontological reference (Collingwood [1933] 2005: 127 and 124). Collingwood's recourse to this argument in his *Philosophical method* prefaces his denial of philosophical skepticism in that it proves that thought "affords an instance of something which cannot be conceived except as actual, something whose essence involves existence" (ibid.: 131) Similarly, Evans-Pritchard's point about his learning about God (his Ultramontane Catholic God) from the Nuer suggests that his belief in God did not depend on any particular theological argument or specific theological faith; it was something that he found when he was forced to immerse himself in human interaction—something the Nuer demanded of him, as opposed to the Azande (Evans-Pritchard [1973] 1976). Rather, he concluded, people do not live by reason. As he put it: "No one is mainly controlled by reason anywhere or at any epoch" (cited in Douglas 1980: 33). The Absolute—or transcendence, to speak more generally—is implicit in human experience; we find it within ourselves through meditation, for it is there in us before we have even started to reason about the world.

ANSELM'S INSIGHT

Now, only a few years after he discovered the OP, Saint Anselm attempted an explanation of how he saw essence as implying existence by relation to the human person. His argument is particularly fascinating for anthropologists today because it sits on a notion of personhood that is radically distinct from the individualist take that twentieth-century anthropology mostly assumed and which dates to the Enlightenment. Anselm operated with a notion of the human person that is a reflection of God's person and he explains one by reference to the other. For him, the Trinitarian God is a partible person, so the dividuality of persons is an intrinsic part of his anthropology, so to speak.

In fact, the implications of this go deeper than mere theology, for they are patent in his letters to his friends. His engagement with his monastic condition was so deep and emotional that his letters to his monk friends evoke in us echoes of homosexuality—which, according to his biographer, is a deeply irrelevant and chronocentric reading (Southern 1990: 149–53). Moreover, this partibility carries with it broader implications, since he saw in the pleasures of friendship a foretaste of the pleasures of heaven. Thus, he postulates a joint soul as an essential characteristic of the monastic community and, therefore, for him, parting from his companions (as he had to do more than once in the latter part of his life, to his immense chagrin) was nothing less than a *scissura animae* (a breach of the soul).

In *De veritate* (Anselm 1998: 151–74), his influential essay on truth, Anselm grounds reason in belief. He grants precedence to belief over reason, thus working on a tradition of thinking grafted to the Platonic inspiration of Augustinian theology. In short, after having searched his soul in deep meditation, Anselm concludes that engagement with God is a precondition for cognition, not the other way round. Content and form coemerge; belief is a condition for reason, not its result. Anselm famously declared, "For I do not seek to understand so that I may believe; but I believe so that I may understand. For I believe this also, that 'unless I first believe, I shall not understand'" [Isa. 7: 9]' (ibid.: 87).

Following on Collingwood, we must ask ourselves whether we can capture today that which, in Anselm's insight, was so convincing that it continues to provoke our imagination. Sure enough, it might have been simpler to discard his insight, but that would have left us anthropologically impoverished. After all, when Emmanuel Levinas (1961) places alterity as anterior to identity, when Christina Toren (2002: 122) argues that "mind is a function of the whole person constituted over time in intersubjective relations with others in the environing world," or when developmental psychologists tell us that intersubjectivity is anterior to subjectivity (see Bråten [1998] 2006), are we not running surprisingly close to Anselm's insight? What we have come to discover of late is that personal ontogeny is launched before propositional thinking emerges. In other words, in order to have conscious thoughts, humans have had to be called into communication by other humans before them. Language use is associated to personhood and each human does not invent language individually each time; rather, the members of the human species predicate personhood on a previously existent history of language use. (Here language is being used in the broadest possible sense to include gestural communication as practiced by infants.)

Back in the twelfth century, Anselm wrought his arguments concerning truth and immanence by searching within himself for the origin of what allowed him to understand the world. Taking recourse to introspection, he found that the Other, which he called God, was buried deep within himself and was anterior to his own thought. He saw it as constituting the origin of his being (*fons et origo*—cause and source). And, much like him, we are also disposed today to place belief before understanding, in the sense that we are willing to accept that, for each one of us, personal ontogeny started before reason. In other words, so as to think reflexively (i.e., so as to engage in content-bearing propositional thinking), each human person has to have been previously inserted within a process of human communication. Levinas' observation that "human experience is social before it is rational" is probably the simplest way of capturing what is at stake here (Finkielkraut [1984] 1997: 10).

Thus, much like Anselm perceived nine centuries ago, for each one of us, definitions do impose themselves before reason. We do not first learn the structure of grammar and then the meaning of words—both happen at the same time. In our post-Darwinian age, each one of us is seen as a product not only of his or her own immediate microhistory (our personal ontogeny) but also of the history of our species (human phylogeny).[24] As we are all called into humanity

---

24. Evolution is human history. Ingold states this in a somewhat different manner: "History is but the continuation of an evolutionary process by another name" (1995:77).

by other humans, communication is indeed a condition for existence as a world-forming person and not the other way round. Sociality is anterior to personhood (see chapter 5).

As it happens, there is a further interesting lesson concealed within Anselm's words. The Latin sentence used by him to translate the Prophet Isaiah's words is *nisi credidero, non intelligam*,[25] that is, "unless I first believe, I shall not understand." Yet, in the modern Latin Vulgate, the sentence is rendered as *si non credideritis non permanebitis*, which the King James' translators versed as: "If ye will not believe, surely ye shall not be established." What, then, is the relation between understanding and being established in a land (in the sense of being a legitimate dweller, which is the meaning that modern translations give to Isaiah's original prophecy)? In the different biblical renditions the passage is translated in many differing ways, but curiously always bearing the same semantic slippage between inhabiting and being believed: "If you are not firm in faith, you will not be firm at all" (English Standard Version);[26] "If you do not stand firm in your faith, you will not stand at all" (New International Version);[27] "If you do not have faith, you shall not be believed" (Moeller Haus Publisher, based on the Qumran Dead Sea Scrolls).[28] Ultimately, however, we are learning here a lesson about the relation between dwelling and understanding that is at the crux of our present debate. Understanding—because it happens to persons—implies a sharing of place and there is no anterior moment in which one was ever alone within one's reason before facing the reason of others.

Far from me to try to engage in biblical exegesis or in the history of scholastic philosophy, my aim here is merely to note that, as is often the case in the etymology of individual words, in this web of related translations we meet up with a series of transformations that associate understanding to dwelling (being convincing, being firm, residing, dwelling permanently, setting up roots in a land, being legitimately established as owner of a land). What links understanding to dwelling is that both imply a rootedness in a shared placed (iii—the configured environment) and in the wider world (i—the embracing cosmos), combining to produce the social legitimacy of the agent (ii—the perspectival role of home). Anthropologists have been exploring this insight for quite a while. For example,

---

25. http://www.thelatinlibrary.com/anselmproslogion.html.

26. http://www.biblesociety.org.uk/the-bible/search-the-bible/ESV/Isa/7/.

27. http://www.biblegateway.com/passage/?search=Isaiah+7.

28. http://www.moellerhaus.com/7-8.htm.

in his discussion of "dwelling," Ingold explains that "human children, like the young of many other species, grow up in environments furnished by the work of previous generations, and as they do so they come literally to carry the forms of their dwelling in their bodies—in specific skills, sensibilities and dispositions" (1995: 77).

We conclude that to postulate an epistemological break between human content-bearing understanding and nature is to overlook the modes of operation of personal ontogeny and human phylogeny. If a condition for propositional thinking is to have entered thought by the hand of other humans within modes of dwelling that are never abstract but always historical, then the wider meaning of "world" will be necessarily tied up to the unicity and diversity of history in all of its complexity: cosmic history, sociogenetic history, phylogenetic history, and ontogenetic history—the cosmos, life and the social, the species, the person.

AGAINST REPRESENTATIONALISM

Reformulated in terms of our contemporary notions of personhood, Anselm's insight was that his own internal arena of presence and action (his self or ego, cf. Johnston 2010) did not preexist world (*origo*), neither did it produce world (*fons*); rather it was grounded upon a previously existent configured world. First he had to believe; only then could he engage in reasoning: existence preceded essence.

The central importance of this observation for anthropology is that it forces us to question our more established assumptions concerning the nature of the human mind. In default mode, anthropologists take cognition to be intellectual: content bearing, conscious, and linguistically shaped. Whoever counters these basic representationalist assumptions is just taken to be discombobulating. Anthropological folklore, for example, takes it as settled that "people think in languages." Multilinguals like myself are asked recurrently in what language do we dream, as if that question could make any sense. The reason people ask is that they take it for granted that if you dream in English, you think in English. I often have tried to explain that, yes, concepts and words specific to particular languages do play an important part in one's mental universe; but no, we do not "think in any one language in particular." In any case, my own experience is that my response always fails to register on my interlocutors; the intellectualist assumptions are too powerful, so they overrule. I am simply taken to be a confused person.

In the same way, the ethnographic task is assumed to be that of capturing people's concepts (normally represented in our texts by specific native words that we take out of context) and explaining them to our learned public so that they too can "think" them. These concepts that ethnographers learn are taken to be emic, that is, conscious, linguistic, representational. It is a constant surprise to me how unremittingly resistant anthropological commonplace has been to the challenges posed by people like Gregory Bateson or Rodney Needham, who crashed against the limitations of this view of mind various decades ago (Bateson 1972; Needham 1987: 233; see also 1972), or people in other disciplines such as Francisco Varela, Evan Thompson, and Eleanor Rosch (1991). In particular, more recently, the emergence of embodied cognition as an important actor in the philosophical scene has largely passed unnoticed (e.g. Clark and Chalmers 1998; Hutto 2008; Chemero 2009; Gallagher and Jacobson 2012; Hutto and Myin 2013). Recent efforts at providing an overview of cognition for anthropologists have once again indulged this representationalist tradition (cf. Bloch 2012). I am convinced, however, that it is high time that anthropologists took on board the growing consensus among philosophers and neuropsychologists that basic cognition is embodied, that is, it is not grounded on content-bearing representations.

As the supporters of radical embodied cognition have demonstrated, the assumptions of the representational view are simply not warranted in the face of our present knowledge (see Chemero 2009 or Thompson 2007: 267–311). In short, most thought processes are not of a linguistic kind, as assumed by the majority of anthropologists. This is not to say that there are no areas of mind where such content-bearing ideas exist supported by complex systems of reification, including, of course, language. But even in such processes the possibility of one's conscious access to one's own thought processes should not be taken for granted, as there is little evidence that we can have integral direct conscious recall of our own thought processes, even those that take recourse to images mediated by language and symbolic forms (see Frankfurt 2009). Indeterminacy operates not only between communicating persons, but also within single persons.

There is a way of circumventing this view of mind, if we accept that nonverbal responding in everyday contexts is not to be understood as "a property of content-bearing mental states or representations" (Hutto 2008: xii) Rather, "nonverbal animals and preverbal infants . . . are intentionally directed at aspects of their environment in ways that neither involve nor implicate truthconditional content" (ibid.). Over the past decade it has come to be increasingly patent that meaning is not merely in our heads (Chemero 2003). Rather, it is a function of the animal's relation with the surrounding environment, as it responds to affordances. These, in turn, are "animal-relative properties of the environment." In this sense, therefore, they are not *in* the environment, but *of* it (Lenarčič and Winter 2013). Scaffolded (symbolic) mind is characteristic of humans who "have appropriately mastered certain sophisticated linguistic constructions and practices" (Hutto 2008: xii), but it is based in the same processes of basic mind.

Anselm's insight, therefore, helps us make sense of the fact that our basic cognitive processes, those that lie at the root of the *shared intentionality* that started our ontogenesis as persons, are not representational processes (Tomasello 2008). Rather, they are a direct embodied engagement with the world, a worlding, as we will later qualify it. It is on the basis of such processes of intentionality that, through a participation in complex human communication (central to which is the learning of a human language), human beings start building their arenas of presence and action (their selves) and start accessing propositional thinking. But even then, our self could never possibly be a semiotic machine, operating through logically associated conscious representations, as representationalists would have it. Basic cognition goes on operating all the time; without it we could not be minimally proficient as living mammals.

In short, basic mind (i.e., most of our thinking) does not involve what anthropologists normally call "concepts": it is intentional, not conceptual. Neither does it follow the rules of some predetermined system of reasoning, some "logic," of the kind that Lévi-Strauss assumed in *The savage mind* (1966). The point is that, in order to achieve conscious, content-bearing thoughts, we previously have had to be grafted onto a *specific* world by means of basic mind. That is, "our primary worldly engagements are nonrepresentational and do not take the form of intellectual activity" (Hutto 2008: 51). Nevertheless, the world we inhabit (and, in particular, the contexts in which we are cared for as a child) is marked by the history of sociality in specific ways that constrain and mold our engagements with world and, consequently, with other human beings. Therefore, much like Anselm, later on in life, when we engage in reflexive self-analysis, we discover that those dispositions, this scaffolding of world, have always been there. In order to be able to think propositionally, we have had to depend on the tracks around world provided by nonrepresentational thought. We have had to believe so as to understand.

Now, all beliefs are propped on other beliefs—the condition Donald Davidson calls the *holism of the mental* (2001: 98–99). But it is important to realize that holism predates the existence of proper truth-conditional beliefs and coexists with them at all times. Mysteriously, it would seem, the world "worlds" (Heidegger [1929/30] 1995): it was present in us in all of its complexity even before we realized that we were present in it. God, indeed, would have been a useful way of mediating such a mystery. But, in science, we are short of Anselm's revealed God. Therefore, we become dependent on the notion that humans master intentional thinking before and as a condition for exercising propositional thinking, as the self only emerges in the course of personal ontogeny.

So now we ask: If the world was within us before we became persons, then, in precisely what way was it there? We emerge as persons in a world that is always historically specific. Therefore, the strict instructionalism of the representationalists also needs to be abandoned (see Hutto and Myin 2013: 49): it is not that we "learn a culture," "learn a religion," "learn a language"; it is rather that we find ourselves in a world where that cosmology or language is present. We do not think those things before we use them; we find ourselves using them before we reflect on what we are doing. Our houses, our streets, the rhythm of our days, our food, and so on, are immersed in historically shaped environments where the structuring of human action has happened long ago: as Jesse Prinz puts it, "The world is not a blooming, buzzing confusion; it is an orderly network of entities interacting in systematic ways" (in Hutto 2008: 110). Language is merely one of the many areas of reification of past human actions that surround us. That is one of the reasons why we are so often struck by epiphanies— suddenly we realize that the world is ordered; we are surprised to discover that there was meaning there, even before we postulated it. But the only reason we are surprised is because we had thought of ourselves as gods, as the originators of thought; we had cut ourselves off from human history.

In the same way, as ethnographers, we are puzzled when we find that our informants are often incapable of telling us what they believe in. There is that famous example of Malinowski slowly and painstakingly piecing together the local theory of human reproduction that none of his Kiriwina contemporaries had been capable of explaining to him (1932: 11–15). Can we honestly claim that, if he had to piece it together, then it is because it had not been there? No, we cannot afford to claim that, as it would sound the death knell of all subsequent ethnographies, our own ethnographies included.

If that, then, is the case, we are bound to agree that "culture"—that is, a semiotic system of representations—is probably not a useful way of describing what ethnographers are studying (cf. D. James, Plaice, and Toren 2013). Our subjects of study do not hold most of what we describe as conscious representations. And, contra Kohn, it makes even less sense to try to transform all forms of life into representational selves. Rather, the writing of ethnography consists of proposing an abstraction of the way people's world is shaped: it aims to inform about the way human action has reified itself into a specific local world, in the form of houses, objects, routes, names, languages, texts, gestures, rituals, and so on. Such things were going on all around our informants long before they even knew to distinguish them for what they are. Indeed, as Anselm discovered, each one of us had to have access to those things in order to develop propositional thinking, to come to be aware of our own selves.

TRANSCENDENCE AND PARTICIPATION

Have we, then, made any improvement in resolving anthropology's problems with transcendence? This is certainly the question that poses itself at this point, since to treat people's experience of transcendence as somehow erroneous amounts to a serious abdication of our capacity to account for the world humans inhabit. Today, this is a consensual assessment throughout our discipline. In what follows, therefore, we will go on to propose that a nonrepresentationalist view of mind may help us respond better to that challenge.[29]

We must first return to the notion of "participation," particularly as developed by Lucien Lévy-Bruhl in his late personal notes (published posthumously—[1949] 1998).[30] As Evans-Pritchard saw when he was a young lecturer in Cairo, this can be a very useful door toward understanding how transcendence is an inevitable part of personhood. In fact, the concept originated with Plato to refer to the way particulars "participate" in the "ideas/Forms." Aristotle, later, famously refuted it in his *Metaphysics*. The important shift in

---

29. This section follows on an argument already more extensively developed in Pina-Cabral (2014a).

30. Note, this concept of participation is not at all, of course, the same that Goodwin and Goodwin (2004) develop in their essay on the subject, where they make no reference to Lévy-Bruhl but rather cite Goffman's notion of Participation Status.

the meaning of the concept, however, occurred with Saint Thomas Aquinas, who held it to mean broadly "to receive partially what belongs to another in a universal way" (in Koterski 1992: 189). In the strongest sense, Aquinas uses it to describe how an effect shares in the perfection of its cause, not only in terms of its genuine composition (involving both its essence and its existence) but also in terms of imitation (i.e., the desire it experiences to return to its origin in God).

For Aquinas, as indeed for Lévy-Bruhl, participation is not merely a cognitive disposition; it also involves a sense of embodied copresence. Lévy-Bruhl takes the concept away from a Christian context and starts using it to refer to the way people ("primitives" at first, but later on in his life all persons) perceive themselves to be intrinsically involved in other people (i.e., to be part of them); indeed, both with other people and with certain objects (namely, in the light of Marcel Mauss' theory of the gift—[1925] 2016).

For Lévy-Bruhl, "participation" describes the fact that a person "frequently experiences participations between himself and this or that environing being or object, natural or supernatural, with which he is or comes to be in contact, and that, quite as frequently, he imagines similar participations between these beings and objects" ([1949] 1988: 52). Thus, in the ethnographic record, we encounter many examples that confirm that "individual beings or objects are only represented within a whole of which they are, if not the parts, at least integrating elements, composing elements (*les composants*), or reproductions" (ibid.: 22). Karsenti, his editor, further clarifies that what Lévy-Bruhl had observed was that "the beings and objects which are associated in collective representations only reach representation on the basis of a link that makes them always already participating in one another, so that one can claim that this link is felt even before these objects have been represented and related to each other as represented objects" (Karsenti 1998: xxiv).

As we can see from this sentence, throughout the twentieth century, notions like representation and belief operated a kind of silent compacting between personal dispositions (features of thought of each one of us) and collective dispositions (statistical tendencies observed among the mental dispositions of members of a group). However, to assume that personal mental processes (representations) and collectively shared dispositions (collective representations) are somehow phenomena of the same nature is to assume that groups have minds of the same nature as persons—a supposition that we are hardly entitled to make if we take embodied cognition seriously.

I am not the first, by any means, to return to the concept of participation. Stanley Tambiah, for example, makes a singularly valuable contribution to this discussion, which is informed already by the reading of Donald Davidson and other philosophers of the period (Tambiah 1990: 117–18). Whilst Marshall Sahlins stresses that participation is at the root of kinship (2001a, 2001b), Tambiah shows how it "emphasizes sensory and affective communication and the language of the emotions" (1990: 108). Thus, he claims, it is the basis of religious or magical phenomena (i.e., transcendental experience). This is how Tambiah redefines Lévy-Bruhl's concept: "Participation can be represented as occurring when persons, groups, animals, places, and natural phenomena are in a relation of contiguity, and translate that relation into one of existential immediacy and contact and shared affinities" (ibid.: 107). Unfortunately, once again, as in the case of Karsenti, Tambiah adopts the characteristic midcentury representationalist and sociocentric approach, where both groups and persons are held to hold "representations," and these are considered to be phenomena of the same nature. In the light of the critique of this model of mind that the theories of embodied cognition represent (see also Toren 2002), we are faced with the challenge of matching Lévy-Bruhl's profound insights concerning participation with contemporary approaches to cognition. To my mind, we can do this by proposing that his concept of participation synthesizes at least three major characteristics of the way humans respond to world as persons in ontogeny.

The first characteristic is the "mutuality of being"—that is, in Sahlins' recent formulation (2011a, 2011b), the way in which some persons are intrinsic to the existence of others. Persons are constituted multiply and relationally, all singularity being approximate and evanescent. Marilyn Strathern's concept of the "dividual person" helps us understand how plurality is anterior to singularity, always reimposing itself. Her connected notion of partibility describes objects and persons as mutually constituted and conceptually interconnected (Strathern 1984), and in many ways approaches Anselm's own conceptions of personal partibility molded in the three persons of God. This has significant implications in terms of kinship theory that seem not to have been taken into account so far by most anthropologists.

Indeed, mutuality leading to copresence in personal constitution means that persons inevitably form what mathematicians have been calling since the 1980s non-wellfounded sets. These are sets which contain themselves as members, thus forming an infinite sequence of sets each term of which is an element in the preceding set. Furthermore, this is the very quality that, according to Jagdish

Hattiangadi, allows for the emergence of entities: "Though a whole is always composed of its parts, sometimes the types of things that constitute the parts cannot be fully described in all causally relevant respects without describing how they interact with the types of things that are wholes *as wholes* that are composed out of them" (2005: 89, original emphasis). Propositionality must be seen as an emergent property that supervenes on intentionality. If we are to reconstitute kinship theory within anthropology, therefore, we must abandon the supposition that persons constitute groups that are wellfounded sets and work into our analysis the kind of circularity that results inevitably from the mutuality of being that is constitutive of personhood (cf. Moss 2014).

This leads us directly to an examination of the second characteristic of the relation between person and world. Here, we must rely on Rodney Needham's contributions toward the better understanding of the epistemology of everyday life inspired by the late work of Wittgenstein—namely, an approach to category formation that emphasizes the way in which concepts in natural languages are not subject to the rules of noncontradiction and the excluded middle, rather relying on a notion of opposition that remains ever incomplete and approximate, and on unmediated notions of causality.[31] The way in which cognition is essentially embodied is an facet of Needham's inquiry that has come to be fully confirmed, three decades later, by the work of neurophysiologists and philosophers of cognition, such as Andy Clark and David Chalmers (1998) and Anthony Chemero (2009), or of vision, such as Susanna Siegel (2012). In Needham's words: "The principle of opposition is reversible direction; and (directional) opposites are based on the spatial experience of the human body" (1987: 71–72). His argument concerning notions of causality similarly stresses the relationship between cognition and embodiment (Needham 1976). In fact, category formation will be approached by us in much the same way that fuzzy logic does when it exploits the tolerance for imprecision in dealing with complex problems of engineering (Pina-Cabral 2010a; Ross 2010).

The third characteristic concerns the nature of human communication and is a disposition that can be called *retentivity*. Here, we are inspired by the thought of W. V. Quine and Donald Davidson.[32] They argue that belief is essentially

---

31. On polythetic categories and causality, see Needham (1976); on opposition, see Needham (1987).

32. A further inspiration is the way Levinas uses "retention" as a part of personal constitution. Husserl, too, defines retention as the way in which a phase of a

veridical, that is, "to believe is to believe true" (Quine and Ullian 1978: 4). Therefore, a necessary condition for successful interpretation is that "the interpreter must so interpret as to make a speaker or agent largely correct about the world" (Davidson 2001: 152). However, whilst belief does depend formatively on people's assessment of what the case might be, one of the characteristics of humans is a proneness to favor belief coherence. Here again, we are in a graded situation rather than one dominated by clear-cut binary opposites. Concerning belief, therefore, the rule of the excluded middle also makes no sense.

Thus, ostensivity—that is, the association of heard words with things simultaneously observed—is indeed the boundary condition of belief, but it is often side-tracked by the need for belief coherence, giving rise to *retentivity*—that is, the tendency for beliefs to interconnect with each other, tending toward systematicity (without ever actually fully achieving it). As Quine puts it, "We form habits of building beliefs such as we form our other habits; only in habits of building beliefs there is less room for idiosyncrasy" (Quine and Ullian 1978: 59).

Retentivity consolidates over time in processes of collective coherence that, when identified by ethnographers, get called worldviews (see chapter 5). The experience of meaning is relational and holistic—there is no such thing as an individual belief, as all beliefs are dependent on other beliefs. This bears two significant implications. The first is that we prop our beliefs on each other, as Quine used to explain (cf. Quine and Ullian 1978), but we also maximize their correspondence both to the way the world is shaped and to what other people close to us readily respond to (the *habitus*), since mutuality is the rule and the borders between their minds and ours are constantly being fudged. Humans are prone toward favoring the maximization of meaning. This makes for psychic economy.

The second implication of retentivity is that persons are constituted initially through relations of participation that include not only the other persons around them, but also parts of the world. As Lévy-Bruhl had noted and then Mauss developed in the essay on the gift, participation also occurs between persons and things. Furthermore, personal ontogeny does not stop at childhood; it continues during the person's lifetime (and even after death in the more public cases). Personal ontogeny interacts with the scaffolding of the world since people are not only embodied but they also constitute arenas of presence and action

perceptual act remains in our consciousness not as a representation but as a presentation (cf. Ricoeur [1997] 2004).

(see Johnston 2010) in terms of the *habitus* within which they are constituted (see Mauss [1935] 2007). In short, retentivity and the constitution of world-views are unavoidably correlated with the process of personal ontogeny. We will return to this formulation at a later point in the argument.

As we have seen above, ever since Needham wrote his essay deconstruct-ing the notion of belief (1972), we have had to rethink the category, separating very clearly between, on the one hand, the propositional attitudes that are be-ing entertained—that is, what Malcolm Ruel ([1982] 2002) would have called "believing that"—and, on the other hand, the adherence to collective solidari-ties propped on the world implied in the entertaining of such propositional attitudes—that is, "believing in," or fideistic belief, to use Sabbatucci's favored expression (2000). My argument here is that, if we are willing to engage fron-tally with *mutuality of being, polythetic modes of thinking,* and *retentivity in belief,* we will realize that a proneness to experience transcendence is an inevitable product of the development of personal cognition.

Half a century ago, having thoroughly examined the literature then availa-ble, Gustav Jahoda critiqued those who continued to believe that education and the improvement of science would lead to a decrease in what was then called superstition. He concluded that "opinions of this kind are themselves irrational in nature," and that "the propensity can never be eradicated because, paradoxi-cally, it is an integral part of mechanisms without which humanity would be unable to survive" (Jahoda 1970: 142, 147). Jahoda is not all that distant from Frazer and Westermarck, half a century before him, much like Sahlins' discus-sions concerning mutuality of being are not all that distant from Lévy-Bruhl's concept of participation.[33]

Similarly, we are led to agree with Collingwood and his anthropological fol-lowers that it is a mistake to pretend that scientific rationalization can be the basis for a human form of life, since it is a technically specific form of engage-ment with the world that hardly satisfies the intellectual and emotional needs of human beings in sociality. Rather, scientific reason must be seen as the excep-tion—mediated by a series of methodological techniques that have been devel-oped precisely to help us sustain it. In his critique of Robin Horton's famous essays on African thought, Tambiah, quoting Alfred Schutz, similarly argues that "the activity of science is a circumscribed activity, undertaken in very special

---

33. As Sahlins indeed acknowledges (2011a: 10).

and restricted circumstances by partial selves of human beings, and . . . , therefore, this is a special ordering of reality, only one of several others" (Tambiah 1990: 103).

Furthermore, sociocentrism—that is, the modernist proneness to attribute to groups the characteristics of persons—prevented us from seeing that transcendence in human sociality is not something that humans learn, that is imposed on them by religious or magical norms. It is a disposition that they form in the course of their own personal ontogenesis and that they can hardly dispense with. Durkheim's foundational myth of society as expressed in the clan's dance around the fire in *The elementary forms of religious life* has continued to cast its primitivist shadows over us to this day. But he was wrong, as Evans-Pritchard clearly understood a long time ago.

What the Ontological Proof helps us to see today is that, if you withdraw everything, something still remains. When Descartes tried that same exercise (the *cogito*), he too found something there. But, imbued by the spirit of modern individualism, he could see nothing but himself. To the contrary, Anselm is uncertain of his own personal unicity; after all, he is only a person to the extent that God is a person and, like God, he too is dividual. What he finds is that he transcends; at the bottom of his being he finds a door to world beyond himself. What we find today is that, once the certainties of modernism have passed, we, too, look within our selves to horizons beyond ourselves. Our internal arenas of presence and action have open doors, for they are rooted in world. The world worlds within us, to put this in a more Heideggerian fashion. It would seem, then, that we will be much better off if we heed Anselm's sense of transcendence and Collingwood's corresponding anti-intellectualism.[34]

WORLDING

Let us now return to the relation between world and anthropology. Most uses of the word *world* carry with them the implication that world is somehow ordered. In fact, the very etymology of the Latin and Greek words points us in that

---

34. But curiously Mary Douglas did not, and that is one of the stranger features of her book on Evans-Pritchard (1980), where she undertakes to take away from his work precisely those aspects of his theoretical thinking that are more interesting to us today.

direction. Now if you make a quick mental experiment and ask yourself whether the "Nyakyusa/Ngonde world" was ordered (whether it did cohere in a structured manner), you have to answer in two apparently contradictory manners. On the one hand, yes it did: Nyakyusa persons worked hard at making their world cohere, and Monica Wilson (1951) managed to capture a good chunk of that. All of us work at living in reasonably ordered, predictable, meaningful environments. On the other hand, no it didn't. For example, it included bacteria, a feature the Nyakyusa did not account for, even although bacteria were certainly present in the margins of Lake Nyasa in the mid-twentieth century and they determined important aspects of Nyakyusa lives, as Wilson would easily confirm.

It is important that we should realize that this paradox is nothing but a product of our holding a representationalist theory of mind. Whilst a person's intentional engagement with world depends passively on the world being structured, the person's propositional engagement with world actively promotes structure (we might choose to call it, with Anna Tsing, "figuration"—2011), owing to the inevitability of retentivity. But the possibility of the emergence of the second assumes that the first is always already present. In short, the emergence of propositional thinking and personhood (i.e., the opening up of the arena of presence and action) is grounded on the kind of sociality that is characteristic of intentional thinking. Thus, *worlding* is a precondition for structuring to occur (for the building of cosmology, the configuring of a form of life) within the narrative forms of social engagement that take place among propositionally thinking humans in ontogenesis. As Tsing puts it, "The gift of worlding is its ability to make figures appear from the midst *and* to show them as no more than figures" (ibid.: 64, original emphasis).

The notion of worlding originates in Heidegger's work, as part of his use of the verb "to world."[35] All commentators seem to agree that his concept remains to the end rather vaguely defined, so that, by the time it is taken up by a person like Tsing (2011), to account for her study of scientific practice in a Latourian vein, or by Philippe Descola (2010, 2014), in his attempt to outline different modes of ontological positioning, it acquires necessarily different meanings and implications. In our own particular case, it seems important to show that the ethnographic gesture depends on the fact that *world worlds*: that is, world "is

---

35. Cf. *Being and time* (Heidegger [1953] 2010), and "The origin of the work of art" in *Off the beaten track* (Heidegger [1950] 2002).

more fully in being than all those tangible and perceptible things in the midst of which we take ourselves to be at home. . . . By the opening of a world, all things gain their lingering and hastening, their distance and proximity, their breath and their limits" (Heidegger [1950] 2002: 23). The ethnographic gesture is dependent on the fact that the world worlds; it offers itself to persons in ontogeny as a form of extension (space-time) where things are founded and order can be built. This is how the world comes to embrace us—it is aspect (i) of world, world as *source*.

In Emmanuel Levinas' formulation, intentional space is "above all an ambience made up of our possibilities of mobility, of distancing ourselves or approaching, therefore a non-homogeneous space with a top and a bottom, a right and a left entirely relative to the usual objects that solicit our possibilities of moving and turning" (1998: 36; see Caygill 2002: 21). For Levinas, human freedom as an affirmation of personhood is dependent on this anteriority because it transcends the propositionally structured ontologies. As such, "Unlike Platonic transcendence, this version of transcendence is traumatic, emerging from the foreign that lives in the same" (Caygill 2002: 28–29).

This is why transcendence both permanently challenges and affirms personhood. As will be further examined in chapter 5, personal ontogeny is a process of construction of singularity that is ever incomplete, a process of constitution of *presence* that is ever challenged by dividuality and time (see de Martino [1959] 2001: 97–98). Indeed, presence emerges from the purposiveness of intentionality, which is an orientation toward the future based on memory. In turn, the latter is an orientation toward the past. Thus, presence—as well as the relative freedom that it opens up—is permanently dynamic and tensional. In personal ontogeny, the arena of presence and action remains always evanescent and prone to transcendence—it is "beyond ontology, otherwise than being." In ontogeny, the postulation of personal presence is a discovery of oneself as other; to that extent, personal ontogeny is always an act of transcendence. The fact that it is permanently menaced and always incomplete, as demonstrated above, is what roots it in world.[36] As Heidegger put it, "The fundamental attunement of

---

36. "Arising within the structure of the *in* and *beyond,* this freedom for human beings is at once a liberation of self and the possibility of 'something binding.' It is this *simultaneous* loosening and binding of Dasein that Heidegger goes on to describe by the well-known phrase 'world never *is* but worlds'" (Gaston 2013: 83, original emphasis).

human Dasein [is] that which has the capacity to be at once there *and* not there" (1998: 88, original emphasis).

To my mind, then, transcendence must be seen as the very feature of thought that starts off both ordinary propositionality (as an open-ended effort, as a freedom), and self-constitution (the affirmation or challenge of presence). But it is also what allows for ethnographic approximation (the open-endedness, the freedom to de-ethnocentrify). If the world did not offer itself to persons in ontogeny as an extension (space-time) where things are founded and order can be built, the ethnographic gesture would be impossible (or, in any case, it would not de-ethnocentrify, as it would be trapped by ontology, by being). If persons (informant and analyst) were not prone to world (here used in the verb form), there would be no ethnography.

Methodologically, ethnographic analysis depends on the assumed expectation (the charity) that people in specific historically determined local contexts engage with a world which worlds, which can be holistically relational, and to which the ethnographer can eventually relate because she too is involved in worlding. In Anna Tsing's words, "Worlding as a tool asks how informants as well as analysts imagine the relationality of worlds that are self-consciously unfamiliar whether across cultures and continents or across kinds of beings and forms of data" (2011: 50). In that sense, I find myself closer to her interpretation of the word than to Descola's, for whom "there is another explanation for the very different ways, traditionally labelled 'cultural,' of giving accounts of the world in spite of a common biological equipment. Let us call 'worlding' this process of piecing together what is perceived in our environment" (2014: 272). I would consider that to be figuration, whilst "to world" is to experience the space and time for the holism of the mental to operate, producing figuration. Let it be noted, however, following Ernesto de Martino's lesson, that "worlding is simultaneously orienting and disorienting" ([1959] 2001: 63). If people's worlds were ontologically coherent, ethnographic fieldwork would *also* be impossible, as ethnographers would have no points of entry into another's world.

That means that most of what exists around humans (a) is not fully coherent (it is *underdetermined*), (b) must be interpreted in a number of different ways (it is *indeterminate*), and (c) is indeed *common* to the whole human species. Only owing to these three features can ethnographers learn to see the world from a new perspective when they "go out into the field"—even in contexts of considerable cultural distance, such as that met by Monica Wilson (1951) when she arrived on the shores of Lake Nyasa in the 1930s. These conditions are the

conditions of possibility of the ethnographic gesture, as indeed of all propositional thinking. What is truly brilliant in Quine's insight is that he taught us to
see that indeterminacy and underdetermination are not impediments to proper
understanding; rather, they are the conditions for human communication and
thought (see Quine and Ullian 1978).[37]

CONCLUSION

The previous chapter came to the conclusion that "world, like persons, will ever
waver in the unstable terrain that lies between singularity and plurality." Such
a statement assumes that there is an isomorphism between personhood and
world. We are now in a better condition to understand that this results from the
fact that the human condition is the condition of living embodied persons in
world. Human transcendence is the transcendence of propositional beings and
involves centrally the operation of symbolic thought. This, however, should not
distract us from the realization that there is "a deep continuity between life and
mind" (Thompson 2007: 149, 155). The living organism has to reach beyond its
present condition in order to maintain its identity across time. Human transcendence is a "richer" variety of the sort of intentional transcendence that is
characteristic of all life. The reason for this is that propositionality, as it emerges
in secondary intersubjectivity, opens up the way for the constitution of the arena
of presence and action, a matter we will examine further in coming chapters.

---

37. Witness a similar position being defended recently by Lloyd (2014) in a rather
useful discussion of translation.

CHAPTER THREE

Imagination

IN COLLABORATION WITH JOANA GONÇALO OLIVEIRA

> *DAUGHTER: So what? You tell us about a few strong presuppositions and great stochastic systems. And from that we should go on to imagine how the world is? But—*
> *FATHER: Oh, no. I also told you something about the limitations of imagining. So you should know that you cannot imagine the world as it* is. *(And why stress that little word [*is*]?)*
>
> – Gregory Bateson (1979: 205, original emphasis)

If the world does not simply offer itself diaphanously to our gaze, as Bateson tells his daughter, how do we imagine the world? The notion of imagination remains a central category in anthropological theorizing, not only in the way ethnographers are increasingly engaged with image analysis, but also in that we have by no means resolved the age-old question of knowing how humans in sociality share imaginative proclivities.

Therefore, in this chapter we ask: What does the history of anthropology tell us about human imagination? The ethnographic record suggests that human imagination is not boundless, otherwise how would ethnographic verisimilitude be so easily achieved? Yet, if there are limits to human imagination, what is their nature? In what way are we disposed to think in some form rather than another? Does it even make any sense to assume that the mind is absolutely free to associate? Would this not be tantamount to assuming a disembodied mind? Finally, as Bateson put it to his daughter, "And why stress that little word [*is*]?" We confront once again the old question: How do essence and existence interact?

According to Jean-Paul Sartre, who wrote a brilliant short essay on imagination in 1936, the reason why we stress "the little word" is because, on the whole, we continue to operate with a "naïve metaphysics of the image" (1936: 3). Inspired by Husserl's thought, Sartre introduces us to a new (post-Cartesian) way of approaching the topic that has become the assumed starting point for all the best thinking about imagination that has emerged in anthropology over the past decades. This is the case, for example, with Tim Ingold's seminal paper on "Building, dwelling, living," where he argues that imagination is the distinctive human feature that differentiates our way of being in the world from that of nonhuman animals. He claims that "human beings do not construct the world in a certain way by virtue of what they are, but by virtue of their own conceptions of the possibilities of being. And these possibilities are limited only by the power of the imagination" (2000: 177). If, then, there are limits to imagination as understood in this way, it would seem to be highly relevant to ask ourselves what they are. In this chapter, we look for guidance in Rodney Needham's claim that one may identify empirically *limits of imagination*.

This claim has not received the attention it deserves. One reason for that, we can speculate, is Needham's conviction that we cannot determine these limits abstractly from first principles and that they will not form a coherent monothetic class. For him, the only way of knowing what they are is to research them empirically through the comparativist use of the ethnographic record. This turns the process into a messy empirical inquiry, rather than a nicely appealing exercise of analytical imagination.

WHAT IS AN IMAGE?

Owing to the impact of Husserl's phenomenology, the conception of what a mental image is changed radically in the mid-twentieth century and, with that, should have changed our anthropological approach toward imagination. This is the main drive of Sartre's *L'imagination* (1936), where he attempts a history of the concept, focusing in particular on the period that extends from Descartes to Husserl. As the relation between image and imagination is not really straightforward, we must start by attempting to clarify it.

Sartre's central concern can be captured by means of a brief ethnographic example. In studying personal names in Bahia (NE Brazil), we found that persons approached their names not as fixed signs representing them individually, but as complexes of *reminiscences*. For example, as a response to being asked to draw a picture of the person who gave them their name, children freely associated: fostering grandmothers were associated to stoves, mothers were associated to suns and flowers, brothers to fancy clothing, fathers to cars and beer bottles, and so on (see Pina-Cabral 2013b). Furthermore, when we asked Bahians for "the meaning" (*significado*) of or "the reason" (*razão*) for their name, they searched freely for the associations that their names evoked and they readily expressed these, normally with a kind of narcissistic glee: Is it a saint's name, do I know the story? Is it an actor's name, do I know what roles he played? Is it a politician's name, a footballer's name, the name of my grandfather, the name of my grandmother's boss, and so on? Is it a "gentle" name? Is it a "posh" name? Is it a "gringo" name? Is it a "different" name (taken to be a positive feature)?

This being the case, one might have been led to think that personal names are marks of pastness; which they are, of course, but they are not at all only that. The very process of reminiscing—of evoking images that one retains from the past, that one "has stored within oneself," as the traditional European metaphor would have it—is accompanied by what we call *a destiny of openness*. That is, a process of imagination which is always open and permanently in gear. In short, reminiscing is transforming. And that is the reason for the narcissistic glee. In a culture, such as that of modern Brazil, where selfhood is a good that is openly cultivated, the opportunity of knowing more about "who you are" is welcomed with open arms. When the ethnographer felt free to give them some information about their name that they did not know (e.g., who Ruth was in the Bible or who Winston Churchill was), Bahians jumped at it with alacrity and one could witness them repositioning themselves in relation to these new reminiscences.

Personal names were being imagined in a way that evoked past images, but, in the process, they were being repositioned, changed, and transformed all the time. As the context of name use changed, so did the reminiscences. Each time you evoke an image, even silently to yourself, the image changes because it changes its position within the holism of the mental. Now, as Sartre taught us, names are signs when they serve to communicate, but the images these names evoke are actually acts of the mind, not passive representations. They are presentations, that is, intentional acts which occur in relation to a world that is always anterior.

According to Sartre, the principal difficulty in understanding what exactly it is to exist as an image results from a human proclivity to think of all modes of existence in terms of physical existence (reification), and so, as noted above, to adopt a "naïve metaphysics of the image."[1] The central challenge that posed itself for the modernists originated in Descartes' attempt to resolve the ambiguity that the image had in scholastic thinking, where it was seen as being half-material, half-spiritual (Sartre 1936: 7). He resolved it by declaring that matter and spirit are mutually exclusive: "The image, in as much as it is materially depicted in some part or other of your brain, could never be animated by thought (*la conscience*)" (ibid.).

For Descartes, therefore, although images are a matter of appearance, they have a kind of substantive existence in the brain; they are, in Sartre's formulations, *sensations renaissantes* (reborn sensations—ibid.: 57) or *reviviscences de la chose* (reviviscence of the thing—ibid.: 68). That is, for the Cartesian tradition, images are of the order of things, for they are imprints in the brain caused by perception; they are *re*-presentations. Images were interpreted as signs or schemes and, in turn, signs were thought to be constitutively images.

This idea of images was, in fact, dominant right until Husserl challenged it. Attempts on the part of philosophers such as Bergson to grant greater mobility to images as facts in the mind (*la conscience*) ultimately faltered owing to the mechanical conception of the image as a fixed response to material stimulation. This conception created a kind of fixity to thought that was clearly incompatible with the mutability of what humans do with images, that is, imagination. "From the moment one sees images as signs that have to be understood, immediately one is putting images outside thought" (Sartre 1936: 75).

There is, of course, no doubt to anyone that consciousness includes images. But we must find a way of freeing these from their Cartesian condition of mechanical manifestations of materiality, otherwise how can they change continuously in the face of new circumstances? Sartre asks, "What if images are never copies of objects? Perhaps they are nothing but protocols aimed at, in a way, making objects present" (ibid.: 59). Therefore, in the wake of Husserl, he claims we must avoid seeing images as inert supports of thought. Rather, images are

---

1.   A notion akin to what Lakoff and Johnson call "ontological metaphors" (cf. 1980: 25ff.).

the very process of thought. As all thought is thought of something, so objects out there in the world are correlative to thought (*conscience*) but they are not thought (ibid.: 122). Thus, Sartre concludes, "Images are acts, not things. To have an image is to be conscious *of* something" (ibid.: 136, his emphasis).

This view is in all ways compatible with the present state of affairs concerning imagery. Evan Thompson, for example, explains that "the visual experience is not the object of the imagining; the intentional object is the visualized object" (2007: 292). In the standard case of visual imagery what happens is nothing like the internal inspection of some sort of mental picture of the phenomenal world. Instead, "we mentally re-present an object by subjectively simulating or emulating a perceptual experience of that object" (ibid.: 297). Thus, he concludes with Sartre that "visualizing is not the inspection of a mental image, but rather the mental representation of what it is like, or was like, or would be like, to see something, given one's tacit knowledge of how things look, how that knowledge is organized, and one's sensorimotor skills" (ibid.: 298).

In short, we must get rid of the notion of imagetic representations that would somehow result from the impact of perception on the mind—"to imagine how the world is," as Bateson's daughter said. As Sartre would have it, "There is indeed a transcendental sphere of significations, but they are 'represented' not 'representations', and could never possibly be constituted by contents" (1936: 62).

Moving from Sartre's critique to today's concerns within anthropological debate, we are now in a position better to clarify what imagination can be held to mean for us. There are three principal features that have to be taken into account in defining it. The first is the matter we have been discussing: *image formation* and its condition as enactment, not as semiotic object of the mind. As we have seen, this applies to visual images, of course, but it applies equally to all other kinds of imaginings. Thus, the previously clear distinction between images (pictures in the mind) and concepts (meaning complexes, classes of objects) fades away. Thought is now seen as foundationally relational and based on an activity of transformation of circumstances that were always already given. Since thought is always about something, there is no such thing as an isolated thought, an isolated belief, an isolated image—there is no thought without world.

Furthermore, it is only by triangulating with world and by having a disposition for charity for the meanings of others that propositional thought can occur at all (cf. Davidson 2004; Pina-Cabral 2013a), which means that conscious thinking is an activity that can only be entertained by humans who have already entered into a linguistically shaped universe of communication (cf. Hutto 2008).

If, on the one hand, sociality both precedes personal ontogeny and is a precondition for it, on the other hand, it is only by studying persons in ontogeny that anthropologists can acquire any understanding of the strains, recurrences, and proclivities that shape human mental life.

The second feature of imagination is the matter of *transformation*. Since imagining is a form of enactment (not an imprint on the mind made by material perception—as per naïve ontology), it is dependent on the world as its condition of possibility. The notion that we have "pictures in the head" that remain fixed through time simply does not apply. Time being an essential feature of relating to world, and triangulation with the world being an indispensable feature of all communication (cf. Davidson 2004), mutability is constitutive of all imagination. We are led to conclude that images are constantly evolving in tandem with our own changing involvement with our material condition in world. There is yet more to say about this aspect, as we will see later on.

The third feature, finally, is *classification*. The constitution of classes of entities (concepts) is carried out through a process of image association, of imagination. As Davidson puts it, "To have a concept of a lion or of anything else is to have a network of interrelated concepts of the right sorts" (ibid.: 143). Thus, all thoughts are partly dependent both on their relations to all other thoughts (without which they could not exist) and on their relation to world (without which they would have no meaning). If images are fundamentally a revisiting of reactions to perceptual experience, they are, then, essentially associational and cannot be dissociated from the classificatory process of concept formation.

Here, then, we enter properly into the subject that most occupied Needham and that he stubbornly went on naming, using Durkheim's favored expression, collective representations. How is it that humans within sociality are prone to classify the world in similar fashions, sharing concepts and images? But perhaps this question is only possible to formulate at all because we inadvertently revert to our *métaphysique naïve*. To the contrary, we must remember that, if we place ourselves within such an individualist perspective, we will soon end up meeting the blank wall of interpersonal indeterminacy. And, contrary to many, we know that if "worlds" (as in another word for cultures) are incommensurable at group level, they would have to be very much more so at individual level, which would mean that there would be no way of producing collectively shared worlds—and much less of actually knowing that they exist. This is why we must opt for turning away from the case of a person thinking solipsistically and move toward the matter of communication; attempting to clarify how company is a precondition for thought.

Donald Davidson's primary contribution to this debate[2] is to encourage us to see that, in order to understand subjective thought, we have to depart from intersubjective communication in a real world. In such an account, sociality is foregrounded. Imagination is never absolutely private, even when we are working out our darkest secret thoughts. Thought is a by-product of sociality, which means that all imagination shares, to an extent, of the qualities of what used to be called "collective representation." But we can no longer entertain the naïve notion that a group has thoughts (images, representations). This means that, for us today, the recurrence in attitudes and concepts that ethnography encounters among any locally defined group of persons can only be seen as a process of reiterated approximation, not a form of mechanical repetition. Therefore, we are led to ask: What are the pathways of imagination as a social phenomenon? To what extent are we bound to move our imagination more in one direction than another? Can we find proclivities of the imagination by studying the ethnographic record?

RELAUNCHING COMPARATIVISM

A profound theoretical upheaval occurred in social anthropology from the mid-1970s to the mid-1980s, which was a response to a moment of doubt concerning the essential assumptions about human mind that dominated most of twentieth-century anthropology. This was occasioned by an intensive critical analysis of the late work of Ludwig Wittgenstein. The first person to brave that was Gregory Bateson (1972, 1979), in the course of his radical distancing from the dominant anthropological discourse in the United States. But the process was led further within social anthropology when both Rodney Needham and Edwin Ardener, albeit in different and contrasting manners, decided to undertake a deconstruction of Evans-Pritchard's 1950s interpretivism, which had been predominantly inspired by combining a Durkheimian analytic language inherited from Radcliffe-Brown with R. G. Collingwood's philosophy of history.[3]

---

2.   See, in particular, his brilliant 2001 essay "What thought requires", (2004: 135–50).

3.   For example, for a thorough rethink of Collingwood's notion of "translation," which was so central to Evans-Pritchard, see Edwin Ardener's still thought-provoking essay "Comprehending others" (2007).

This 1980s poststructuralist drive and its profound insights failed to be followed through by the next generation of anthropologists for a number of reasons, some institutional (the vagaries of departmental politics in Oxford), some personal (the early death of Ardener and the early retirement of Needham), but most important of all the fact that anthropological fashion in the late 1980s and 1990s, coming from the United States, turned the most visible debates of anthropology away from the process of questioning representation. Insightful analyses, such as Robert Feleppa's critical engagement with Quine's notion of indeterminacy of meaning (Feleppa 1988), were largely overlooked by "the semiotic turn." Moreover, in the 1990s, the Durkheimian terminological mold in which Needham's and Ardener's disquisitions were framed found little echo in colleagues who unwittingly associated this style with what they called "structural functionalism" and, thus, failed to engage meaningfully with the deep theoretical implications of what was being proposed. As it happens, in the case of Ardener, the esoteric nature of his formulations makes them exhausting reading still today.

The questioning that was being made at the time concerning the nature of representation, the nature of classification, and the constraints to imagination can now be picked up with new conviction. There is, however, an aspect to Needham's and Ardener's forays that is bound to lead to misunderstandings today. The Oxford poststructuralists were solidly grounded on the rich analytic terrain that they had inherited from a century and a half of ethnographically inspired social analysis. The universalist tone in which they set their arguments runs counter to the rhetoric preferences of those who, in the wake of the "semiotic turn," and then the "ontological turn," are not eager to think of humans as a unified category. To the contrary, together with a growing number of colleagues, we feel that it is high time to go back to a self-consciously comparativist study of the human condition and of the nature of scientific thinking that allows for anthropology to place itself at the center of its own history and for anthropologists to choose again to address anthropological questions informed by the constantly growing ethnographic canon. Not the canon of this or that anthropology (inevitably one of the four imperial traditions, cf. Hann 2005), but the canon that we are constantly rewriting from within the practice of an increasingly globalized anthropological debate (see Pina-Cabral 2005, 2006).

In Needham's late writings on imagination we find insights of central relevance to the debates that are going on today in anthropology concerning embodied mind and personhood. One preliminary comment, however, needs to be made. Needham's thought evolved very rapidly in the late 1970s and early 1980s but he continued to use the time-honored terminology of earlier anthropological schools. So, it seems necessary to start by clarifying that, in spite of freely taking recourse to terms like collective representation, image, archetype, system of classification, and so on, Needham had turned the corner of representationalism sometime in the early 1970s or even before that. Already in his introduction to *Primitive classification* he had complained that Durkheim and Mauss assume incorrectly that "conclusions derived from a study of collective representations . . . apply directly to cognitive operations" (1963: xxvi). He concludes his article on synthetic images (1978), that is, on the limits to freedom of imagination, with a quote from Wittgenstein that we do not hesitate to repeat here, for indeed it grounds all further arguments about mind, thinking, and belief:

> No supposition seems to me more natural than that there is no process in the brain correlated with associating or with thinking; so that it would be impossible to read off thought processes from brain-processes. I mean this: if I talk or write there is, I assume, a system of impulses going out from my brain and correlated with my spoken or written thoughts. But why should the system continue further in the direction of the centre? . . . It is . . . perfectly possible that certain psychological phenomena cannot be investigated physiologically, because physiologically nothing corresponds to them. (Wittgenstein [1953] 1967: §§ 608–9)

In this passage, Wittgenstein is suggesting that mental processes may not be imprints on the mind resulting from the impact of perception (as in naïve ontology, as per Sartre), but that they may be the aggregate result of the holism of the mental in its relation with an ever-evolving world. Thus, in attempting to plot out the limits of freedom of imagination, Needham was approaching the comparative task from a position that rejects a representationalist view of mind. The one notable predecessor in this approach is, as is so often the case, Bateson, who develops the concept of "stochasticism" to describe precisely the way in which such processes may occur. He claims that "thought and evolution are alike in a shared stochasticism" (1979: 162), which he defines in the following manner: "*Stochastic* (Greek, *stochazein*, to shoot with a bow at a target; that is, to scatter events in a partially random manner, some of which achieve a preferred outcome). If a sequence of events combines a random component with a selective process so that only certain outcomes of the random are allowed to endure, that sequence is said to be *stochastic*" (ibid.: 245). We conclude, therefore, that all beliefs (thoughts, images, concepts) that a person can entertain are propped on numberless other beliefs but that the processes of thought are stochastic, that is to say, they do not "continue further in the direction of the centre," as Wittgenstein would have it.

The stochastic approach means that we do not attempt to postulate the existence of universal forms of social imagination. Following Husserl's lead, we see the human condition as historically produced, "from our genes to the very neurological processes that provide for brain function, to all our ideas of the peopled world" (Toren 2012: 64). Thus, we aim to draw out to what extent human imagination shows evidence of being limited, that is to say, to what extent human societies are prone to recur and recidivate in the formulations they favor. For Bateson this was a feature in relation to which evolution and human mind operated in the same way. As he put it, "Random changes occur, in the brain or elsewhere, and . . . the results of such random change are selected for survival by processes of reinforcement and extinction" (1972: 255). Note that, immediately upon writing this, he goes on to argue that a specific meaning is here given to random, arguing that "the probability of a given change is determined by something different from probability" (ibid.). And, out of that, he then develops his idea of "an economics of adaptability" associated to habit formation (ibid.: 257). The argument is not about singular persons, but rather it is trying to address the same problem as Durkheim and Mauss in their *Primitive classification*: How is it that socially shared classifications impose themselves on people's imagination? Instead of assuming that such images "exist" in the mind as cognitive entities, rather this view sees them as the stochastic product of complex determination.

Durkheimian sociocentrism granted precedence to group processes of classification over personal processes of thought, but relied on the notion that collective representations and individual representations were isomorphic and that, indeed, they were both representations, entities of the mind (cf. Durkheim and Mauss [1903] 1963). Bateson's stochastic approach radically altered the terms in which collective and individual were conceived in twentieth-century social science.

THE PEG-ASPECT OF BELIEF

The turning point of Needham's thought on the matter is his long essay *Belief, language, and experience* (1972), where he asks: Why am I led to suppose that the verbal concept "belief" designates a set of experiences, propositions, or actions that denote the same human capacity or the same internal state everywhere around the world? Why is it that I suppose that the Penan concept *Peselong*, which I loosely identify with the English concept of God, is bound to activate in the Penan the same kind of response as would be activated in me if I were to say or to hear the sentence "I believe in God"?

This puzzle, which is the point of departure for his book, is not unlike a set of other such philosophical parables that marked deeply the questioning of the nature of human mind in the second half of the twentieth century. We are reminded of Quine's famous discussion of the meaning of *gavagai* ([1960] 2013: 23–72). Where Needham diverges from most philosophical authors is that he makes his question from the point of view of ethnographic theory. His is a radically empiricist approach, where theorization emerges not from first principles but from actual ethnographic comparison.

To return to his Penan parable, Needham sees that when he supposed that the Penan would know what it is to believe, he was taking belief, in all the multiplicity of its expressions and manifestations, as an invariant or natural capacity of humans. But even if one can translate the word *belief* into different languages, is that enough to suppose that such a word designates a clearly determinable mode of conscience of human experience (Needham 1972: 136)? Can one simply take for granted that particular belief statements constitute a plethora of occurrences that, from the deepest past to the furthest extreme of sublunar space, denote a capacity or faculty that determines all possible human thought and action?

In *Structure and sentiment* (1962), Needham had already started to produce concepts in which we see his distinctive mark, such as "primary factors of experience" or "proclivities of thought and imagination." There, he first engages the need to question the role of language in light of his study of the late work of Wittgenstein. He is progressively led to question critically the certitudes concerning the nature of human thinking that lay behind twentieth-century anthropological structuralism; certitudes about the relation between language and experience. He is eventually led to abandon the idea that the human mind is nothing but a set of (entity-like) categories whose processing depends on a determinable set of faculties. This means that the multiplicity of the expressions of belief is not reflected, nor is it regulated by either experience or language. In itself, this feature of the concept *belief* should immediately make us wary of the way it is recurrently used in ethnographic interpretation.

What characterizes concepts such as "belief" is that they operate in a very special manner. This is how Friedrich Waismann qualifies such words:

There is a group of words such as "fact", "event", "situation", "case", "circumstance", which display a queer sort of behaviour. One might say of such words
that they serve as pegs: it's marvellous what a lot of things you can put on them
("the fact that—"). So far they are very handy; but as soon as one focuses on them
and asks, e.g., "What *is* a fact?" they betray a tendency to melt away. The peg-
aspect is by far the most important of all. (1968: 59, original emphasis)

Because the concept of belief shares this peg-aspect, it produces the illusion
that there are certain specific manifestations that result from a fundamentally
immutable condition of belief. In social anthropology, this illusion generates the
assumption that different cultures, different societies—multiform and variable
as they may be—denote something that can be immediately translatable by
the psychological vocabularies with which we are familiar. The peg-aspect leads
us to believe that there are actions and expressions that refer back to the same
set of categories ordering collective ideas, in such a way that *to translate* would
imply to find something on the basis of which the actions, expressions, and even
thoughts would become stable aspects of human experience.

However, in light of the examination undertaken in *Belief, language, and
experience*, even a translation would always be a manifestation of a mutual understanding derived from a presence, an activity, or a substance that we do not
succeed in circumscribing either to experience or to language. Therefore, according to Needham, when psychology is at stake, "translation" has to be substi-
tuted by "interpretation" of the verbal concepts in question. These considerations
about "to believe" apply equally with *to act, to see, to mean, to think*, and so on.

Imagination, however, constitutes a sort of outlying example, for it prom-
ises to lead us to the matter of classification (Needham 1972: 134–35). For
Needham, classification constitutes one of the principal challenges that any ethnographer or comparativist can encounter—that of translating the peculiarities
of a classificatory ideology on the basis of one's own language (cf. ibid.: 133).
Now, since that is not really a very steady base, Needham is led to question
the certainties that anthropology assumes concerning what it is to classify. He
asks himself whether the multiple experiences, propositions, or actions that are
currently associated to imagination can be taken to suggest the existence of
something determinable, of some specific activity within the vast domain of
human experience.

Social anthropologists have inherited a set of *conceptual images* from their
disciplinary tradition (our toolkit of analytical concepts: e.g., clan, taboo, person,

filiation, descent, segmentation, structure, transformation, etc.). We must inquire as to the effective validity of their generality, that is, their analytical status. It would seem to be necessary to determine what such concepts actually denote; otherwise, owing to the infinite variability of connotations that apply in each particular ethnographic context, we run the risk of simply being ethnocentric. One of the principal contributions of Wittgenstein's thought to social anthropology would then be the call to undertake a critique of individual concepts. Such concepts are necessarily misleading since they "are taken to denote monothetic classes of social facts, whereas actually they are highly polythetic and cannot therefore have the uses that are normally ascribed to them" (Needham 1985: 150).

In a monothetic classification, groups are supposed to be formed by logical, rigid, and successive divisions, in such a way that the possession of a unique set of characteristics is simultaneously sufficient and necessary in order for a member to be included in the group thus defined. To the contrary, a polythetic classification associates entities that share a number of characteristics, but no singular characteristic is essential or sufficient in determining the inclusion of each individual member within the group. Needham defends that, from the point of view of anthropological comparativism, when what we want to compare are stochastic dispositions, the classificatory style must be necessarily polythetic. Owing to the nature of human communication, we will have to take recourse to a technique of comparison that contemplates the broadest possible number of variables.

Needham finds in Wittgenstein the inspiration for the answer to how we form the concepts that we use in anthropological analysis. He quotes the famous example:

> The tendency to look for something in common to all the entities which we commonly subsume under a general term.—We are inclined to think that there must be something in common to all games, say, and that this common property is the justification for applying the general term "game" to the various games; whereas games form a family the members of which have family likenesses. . . . The idea of a general concept being a common property of its particular instances connects up with other primitive, too simple, ideas of the structure of language. It is comparable to the idea that properties are ingredients of the things which have the properties. (Needham 1985: 17)

To sum up, the phenomena that we classify, for example, under the label *kinship* may be related to each other in any number of different ways. Kinship, therefore, is an *odd-job word*, an empirical generalization. An odd-job word is any phenomenon that shares a given set of distinctive characteristics, without it being necessary for all the members of the set to possess all of the distinctive characteristics. Such verbal concepts are formed by concatenation and sporadic similarity: they are formed by means of family resemblances. That is what Wittgenstein meant when he said: "[We elaborate our concepts] as in spinning a thread we twist fibre on fibre. And the strength of the thread does not reside in the fact that some one fibre runs through its whole length, but in the overlapping of many fibres" ([1958] 1967, § 67: 32). In other words, concepts cannot be defined absolutely: they chain up, they hook onto each other, they superimpose like the strands of fiber that make up the rope.

Needham concludes from this that we must reinvent a new kind of comparativism that is not foundationally theoretical, because our analytical concepts are not immune to the distinctive characteristics of any other verbal concept. This is essentially the proposed *change of aspect* that is enshrined in *Belief, language and experience*. To wit, the need for a comparative epistemology that is divorced from the idiom of certainty. This would,

> on the one hand, [bring] us more immediately, with systematically reduced prejudices, into relation with the distinctive features of those alien ideologies that we desire to understand. On the other hand, [it would] increase our knowledge of the most constant forms that cultural classifications may assume, and successively test their correspondence with our empirical appraisals of human nature, so we can elaborate a set of critical expectations that will prepare our perception of alien realities. In other words, comparative analysis can be pursued, by means of this dialectic of observation and self-observation, as a technique of apperception. (Needham 1972: 204)

PRIMARY FACTORS OF EXPERIENCE

Anthropological comparativism, therefore, would be a "technique of apperception" to the extent that it would be a way of situating new experience in relation to past experience. As much as it might distance itself eventually from our everyday experience of the world, the task of scientific or academic comparativism must be seen as originating in the same history of humanity as all other thought, not in a petition of first principles. But this means that we can only undertake the comparative task in the first place because there are recurrences in the way humans operate, that is, proclivities of thought and action, that allow us to recognize the humanity of what we observe, thus mobilizing our interpretive charity in specific ways.

Human experience manifests and is dependent upon these recurrent forms. They are very frequently encountered in the ethnographic record. But, more than that, they are a necessary condition for ethnographic verisimilitude: that is, in writing our ethnographies we take recourse to them (mostly implicitly) to help our readers and ourselves make sense of what is being said. The central argument here is that human beings within sociality are not simply free to exercise their imagination: they are constrained by predispositions that are inherited, not in any genetic or normative sense of the word, but in the sense of conditions for personal ontogeny; features of thought which are always anterior to any propositional thinking owing to the fact that sociality is a precondition.

The anthropologist is comparing forms of life that she wants to get to know on the basis of other forms of life that she already knows. But she cannot hope to achieve constant meanings concerning the human condition. Social life is highly unstable: one can observe rapid changes in the meanings of words and other symbolic elements; there are constant reformulations of social institutions; our intentions are innumerable and unpredictable (cf. Needham 1981: 17). In spite of this, however, experience does suggest that a high level of redundancy is present. Needham exemplifies this by reference to anthropological supervision:

> A particularly surprising realization is that often it is possible for an academic supervisor to guide and correct research into a society with which he has no direct or scholarly acquaintance. It is very perplexing, and against expectation, that this should be possible; for the more we think of men as directing their actions by free decision, and in the light of conflicting interests and purposes, the more striking it is that they should so regularly end up with very similar institutions. (1981: 20)

In short, we must avoid at all costs the all-or-nothing fallacy. While the *recognition* of a contextual correlation between the forms taken by institutions and thoughts does not allow us to entertain any expectation of prediction, we also have no certain reason to postulate absolute unpredictability. In fact, we observe a surprisingly high number of stochastic regularities and recurrences in the forms assumed both by social institutions and by classificatory ideologies. We

cannot say whether it is collective thought that is free of institutional conditionings or whether it is the structural dispositions of collective life that determine
the institutional variation; what we can say is that there are relational constants
that underpin both instances.

These universally distributed regularities and recurrences are what Needham
wants to capture with his idea of *primary factors of experience* (cf. 1972: 216–19).
By that he means the constants of human imagination that seem to be present
both in classificatory ideologies and in social action. We are not faced here with
the continuous development of a single form of classification, nor are we trying
to fit different forms into one mold by means of which other forms might be
compared; nor yet are we trying to establish two broad realms of comparison
that fit into each other.

Needham contrasts his idea of primary factors to the traditional idea of in-
nate ideas by means of five negative features:

1. They are of different types: perceptions, images, abstractions, logical constraints.
2. They are independent of the will; intrinsically they are neither created nor
   altered deliberately, but they originate unconsciously.
3. They are not a class connected into systems, but they can be variously combined.
4. They are primary but not elementary; each is analysable into a complex of
   grounds or possible determinants.
5. Characteristically though not exclusively, they are manifested in symbolic
   forms, not in cognitive or rational institutions. (1985: 70)

To start off with, when the anthropologist faces the symbolic elements that can
be encountered in the ethnographic record, these appear to diversify themselves
into a multiplicity of different human figurations of life. After a while, however,
it becomes apparent that there are constancies and regularities. It is as if there
were a repertory or a common ground of semantic units that human thought
and imagination have at their disposal: the right and the left, the color triad
(white, back, and red), the use of percussion, some recurrent geometric forms,
and so on, and so forth. Owing to their constancy, these allow one to have
a glimpse of what such a common repertory of symbolic components might
look like (Needham 1981: 34). It seems that what is required, therefore, rather
than trying to find a common code for the whole of humanity, as structuralism

attempted, is to try to identify and quantify semantic units or symbolic elements and whether there are specific recurrent (stochastic) relations among them.

This quantification constitutes a new mode (a poststructuralist one) of abstracting the qualities of the symbolic elements to which human thought and imagination take recourse. The systematic application of the method of polythetic classification will substitute the semantic study of symbolic elements, but it will do so in a different mode from that which is used in correlational analyses. If the symbolic elements are studied quantitatively, it is because the aim is to grasp the global incidence of particular elements and relational constants, not their coherence and/or their logical character within the general field of systems of classification. In *Primordial characters*, therefore, Needham insists that primary factors of experience "are heterogeneous: the contrast of textures pertains to touch, colours to vision, numbers are abstraction, percussion depends on hearing" (1978: 11) Then he goes on to argue that "they are vehicles for significance but they do not convey explicit universal meanings" (ibid.). Although they can be encountered widely around the world, "it does not follow that they will have further semantic properties in common" (ibid.).

It would seem, then, that, contrary to what is normally thought, in order to study human imagination we do not require a systematic approach to primary factors; to the contrary, we need a *factorial analysis*, which will reveal how these are condensed and concatenated owing to sporadic resemblances in such a way that they emerge as phenomena that can be grasped autonomously (cf. ibid.: 11, 17; 1980: 59–60). In factorial analysis we are not concerned with the classification systems; rather, we aim to grasp the syntheses that emerge from the general picture. Thus, Needham proposes a major methodological change: to invert the analytical strategy that characterized modernist structuralism. Rather than starting from first principles, the comparativist must start from our own capacity to recognize sporadic resemblances and work empirically at identifying where these emerge and how they are concatenated.

In turn, as his examination of the primary factors progressed, Needham concluded that there are two basic kinds of primary factors.[4] The first kind of primary factors he identifies are *abstract* ones. Of these, he only explores *binary opposition* (namely in his 1987 collection *Counterpoints*), but others might

---

4.   It should be noted that he does not close off the comparativist task. He is perfectly open to the possibility of anthropological comparativism eventually coming to discover a much larger number of such factors.

be suggested, as we will see below. The second family of primary factors is of a *perceptual* nature. They are human proclivities to react to recurrent changes in the world. They must be understood as stochastic events, not as automatic, mechanic, or in any way deterministically necessary. Rather, they are recurrent compound manifestations of very complex processes of human sociality in a world that is structured in similar ways: that is, similar answers to similar conditions. The most classical case Needham explored was the propensity to react to percussion as somehow triggering transcendence (cf. 1967), but others to do with basic colors (white, black, and red), texture, and so on, might be found. Again the list is purposely left open, as it is up to the comparativist enterprise to identify the existence of these and, offhand, we cannot predict where they will emerge.

SYNTHETIC IMAGES

In *Primordial characters* (1978) and *Reconnaissances* (1980), Needham moves to outline the synthetic character of some of the products of imagination, namely in terms of the concept of *synthetic image* and the correlated notions of archetype and paradigmatic scene. Distancing himself from the more commonly known use of the word by C. G. Jung, he defines an archetype as a primordial mental image, but not in the representational (ontologically naïve) sense of image, rather in the sense of a proclivity of the imagination, a recurrent and complex associative product. In fact, these archetypes are forms of collective mental behavior; they are cognitive institutions. They are synthetic images to the extent that they are dispositions to combine things in recurrent ways. Needham calls them "natural imaginative impulses," where natural is taken to mean unavoidable, recurrent, and inescapable.

In *Primordial characters*, he examines the synthetic image of the witch. He attempts to outline the most distinctive features of this synthetic image by taking recourse to factorial analysis. It is a synthetic image because, in a recurrent manner, images of witches involve opposition (of good and evil), inversion (a spatial metaphor), darkness, blackness, certain types of animals, flight, nocturnal travel, and so on. "I do not mean by this," he claims, "that the components of the image of the witch are always the same in number and character, from one tradition to another, but that there are characteristic features which combine polythetically (that is, by sporadic resemblances) to compose a recognizable imaginative definition of the witch" (1978: 33). Such a synthesis (because it is recurrent within a culture and across cultures) cannot be seen to depend either on specific individual cognitive operations, or on the collective manipulation of elements and relations, since the image is, on the whole, consistent with itself across a broad ethnographic spectrum.

The recurrence of the synthetic image of the witch (or of the half-man, which Needham explores in *Reconnaissances*, 1980) does not depend on the ideological or institutional arrangements of the particular ethnographic context from which it was gathered. Needham's hypothesis, which he is attempting to test with such cross-cultural comparisons, is that this is a series of elements, relations, and principles that constitute

> a common repository of factors to which men resort in the construction and the interpretation of social reality. The impression produced on the comparativist is that different traditions combine these factors, together of course with a great deal else that is contingently generated, by concatenation or by sporadic conjunction rather than by arrangement into discrete systems . . . and underlying many remarkable syntheses and extreme elaborations, certain factors have combined polythetically. (1981: 24–25)

These factors, and their condensation into synthetic images, can be recognized across the ethnographic register. They escape decidedly the sociocentric distinction (and isomorphism) between collective representations and individual representations that is so characteristic of twentieth-century anthropology. They are neither the product of a society that forcefully molds the intellect of an individual, nor the fruit of individual imagination or artifice (cf. 1978: 49–50). To that extent, they must be seen as a kind of collective unconscious; or, rather, they are recalcitrant to local definition (cf. 1981: 86–89; 1985: 66).

To conclude, Needham sustains that the notion of imagination can actually be taken to mean something truly intrinsic to the human experience (1978: 21), but the identification of imaginative syntheses requires the use of factorial analysis in order to show how the primary factors come together and link up stochastically on the basis of sporadic resemblances. These are fully polythetic conceptual processes that correspond to unconscious imaginative syntheses. There are no specific techniques that can help us identify them, since the method required—to take "social facts" as polythetic combinations—does not really tell us what we must look for, what characteristics are bound to be more distinctive or relevant (ibid.: 67). In order to unearth them, therefore, "a great deal depends . . . on an imaginative acuity such as is called for in the ultimate test of translation" (ibid.: 75).

This imaginative acuity consists in being able to identify the primary factors of experience at different levels of abstraction, since the condensation of symbolic elements or synthetic images is autonomously distributed, acquiring meanings that go way beyond particular local factors. This being said, it is necessary to stress that synthetic images are nothing but proclivities; they have no inherent or ultimate meaning. As such, they cannot be used to constitute a metaphysics (they will not bring together *one* human world).

Finally, if comparativists can succeed in sharpening their imagination in order to abstract the distinctive recurrences of human imagination, it is because they themselves are grafted onto world and onto sociality: "Fabricators, audiences, and analysts are bound together by common criteria of fantasy and common imaginative predispositions" (ibid.: 59–60).

METAPHORS

In the year Needham published *Reconnaissances* (1980), George Lakoff and Mark Johnson published a book called *Metaphors we live by* (1980), which was destined to have a major impact in philosophical and literary circles. Their basic starting point was that human conceptual systems are essentially structured by metaphorical thinking and, as thinking is part of the same "conceptual system" as communicating, language is par excellence the field where such metaphorical structuring of thought is seen to occur. They conceive their book, therefore, around the exploration of a set of linguistic commonplaces characteristic of West Coast everyday English, which they find to be structured by some major implicit (unstated) metaphors such as IDEAS ARE OBJECTS, or LINGUISTIC EXPRESSIONS ARE CONTAINERS, or TIME IS MONEY, and so on (note their use of capitals as diacritics, suggesting the uncertain epistemological status of these "metaphors"). They then proceed to explore a series of different instances where such "metaphors" can be postulated to occur. The book is full of very useful ethnographic insights concerning the worldview of the contemporary urban United States. Our argument here, however, is that the texts by Donald Davidson of the same period (e.g., 2001: 245–61), albeit less easy to read, bear a far more promising theory both of metaphor and of the veridical nature of belief.

The use of the concept of metaphor that Lakoff and Johnson propose is, to our mind, deeply problematic; let alone their attribution of determinate meaning to metaphors. As they define it, "Metaphor is principally a way of conceiving of one thing in terms of another and its primary function is understanding" (1980: 36). We do not have any real problem with the notion that understanding is associational; still we remain unconvinced that the authors really mean metaphor *stricto sensu* when they use the word throughout their book. Much like our colleague James Fernandez (1991), whose work on the subject was also very influential in its day, they use metaphor metonymically to mean analogical thought in general (thus both metaphor and metonymy, but also analogical mediation more broadly). Whilst they do have a short chapter on metonymy (1980: 35–40), the fact is they revert immediately after it to a use of the word *metaphor* that conjoins all forms of symbolic association and in particular those that take recourse to analogy.

The main problem with this is the lack of clarity concerning the epistemological status of the categories they use. This lack of clarity is not of a polythetic nature; rather it is the contrary, as they treat metaphors as if they were monothetic. For example, when they say, "The most fundamental values in a culture will be coherent with the metaphorical structure of the most fundamental concepts in that culture" (ibid.: 22), they are implicitly differentiating metaphors from concepts and treating value as a kind of adjectival adjunct to such concepts. They sustain that "the essence of metaphor is understanding and experiencing one kind of thing in terms of another" (ibid.: 5). But the problem is that, for human beings engaged in personal ontogeny, all ideas only exist because there are other ideas; the associational process by which each idea, image, concept, belief, exists is only possible because there are many more other such that support it.

The most problematic aspect of Lakoff and Johnson's proposal, however, is their treatment of metaphors as somehow existing as semiotic entities underneath cultural interaction: that is, their failure to understand the stochastic nature of mental processes and, in particular, of the constitution of meaning. Now, this reification of particular metaphors is of a piece with their proneness to condense analogical thinking into "metaphor," for if they had not done that, and had accepted that all human thinking is necessarily associational in analogic ways (with the inevitable indeterminacy associated to the holism of the mental), they would not be able then to go on to identify and give entity status (by placing them in capitals) to the metaphors they claim to unearth. They transform recurrent associations into images and then they postulate the existence of these as infrastructures of narrative proclivities. Rather than seeing human meaning proclivities as emerging stochastically from the immense complexity of associational forms of behavior that humans engage in when faced with a socially always preconfigured world, they are proposing that somewhere in the depths of each person's thought are inscribed these metaphors—some are universal (such as Good is up, Bad is down) but others are really West Coast-specific (such as Inflation is an entity, or Time is a machine). Moreover, these metaphors we are supposed to possess have a kind of collective existence; they are somehow the same in the mind of all the people who hold them (who have "learned" them), much like Durkheimian collective representations were meant to be.

Contrary to that, we propose that there is no such thing as collective thinking, properly speaking. Persons think, collectives do not. Propositional thinking is an activity that can only be entertained by singular persons who are engaged in personal ontogeny within human sociality. There is no such thing as collective thinking *and* indeterminacy and underdetermination cannot be pushed aside in terms of either intersubjective communication or subjective thought. Therefore, whatever recurrent features we may come to identify in the thoughts of a set of persons can only be of a stochastic nature. The kind of metaphorical recurrences that Lakoff and Johnson identify cannot be anything other than proclivities. In the end, their narrativist notion of metaphor amounts to a version of what Sartre called a naïve metaphysics of image. We agree, therefore, with Davidson when he insists that metaphors are to do with the use of language and that, for their occurrence, they depend as much on who produces them as on who receives them. Thus, metaphors are "brought off by the imaginative employment of words and sentences and [depend] entirely on the ordinary meanings of those words and hence on the ordinary meanings of the sentences they comprise" (Davidson 2001: xx).

There is one aspect, however, in Lakoff and Johnson's book that we find particularly useful.[5] In their exploration of what they term ontological metaphors, some really significant insights emerge concerning what Needham called the abstract primary factors of experience. The only one of these that Needham did explore in any significant way was binary opposition. In *Counterpoints*, he attempts to decipher the meaning of the human propensity for thinking in terms of oppositions and dyads. He concludes, however, that opposition "has no

5.   We are grateful to Giovanni da Col and Alex Ceccheti for having called our attention to this.

intrinsic logical form." It is "in practice an odd-job notion seductively masked by the immediacy of a spatial metaphor" (1987: 228). The principle behind the proclivity to think in terms of opposition is reversible direction; and that, in turn, is directly associated to our experience of our own body (ibid.: 71–72). It is, indeed, a spatial intuition (ibid.: 236).

Lakoff and Johnson propose that we should explore the idea that humans are prone to "impose artificial boundaries that make physical phenomena discrete just as we are: entities bounded by a surface" (1980: 25). The resulting broad dispositions may be treated as having the same status as Needham attributed to opposition: that of abstract primary factors of experience. There are two such features that emerge from Lakoff and Johnson's efforts: on the one hand, the proneness for *reification*—that is, the treatment of abstract entities as if they were material entities; on the other, *containment*—that is, "We are physical beings, bounded and set off from the rest of the world by the surface of our skins, and we experience the rest of the world as outside us. . . . We project our own in–out orientation onto other physical objects that are bounded by surfaces. Thus we also view them as containers with an inside and an outside" (ibid.: 29).

Both processes involve a manipulation of time and space: reification is a transformation of a recurrence into a spatial entity; containment is the transformation of a spatial proximity into a temporally recurrent entity.[6] It might be argued, as Lakoff and Johnson do, that these proclivities are metaphors, and it is undeniable that they are products of analogical thinking. But they are not metaphors in the narrativist sense that Lakoff and Johnson propose (e.g., TIME IS MONEY or LOVE IS TRAVEL), for they do not get learned as metaphors. Rather, they result from the recurrent (stochastic) way in which our embodied condition predisposes our cognition, loosely determining our thought dispositions.

We propose, therefore, that *reification* and *containment* should be treated as abstract limits of the imagination in the sense of proclivities of thought that can be detected in human modes of thinking fairly much everywhere in much the same way that Needham treats *opposition*. The very centrality of metaphor, metonymy, and analogy in human communication is dependent on these proclivities of thought. We have to stop seeing such rhetorical features as actual mechanisms of thought, and instead view them as the recurrent result of the stochastic operation of a myriad of processes.

---

6.   We are grateful to Joan Bestard Camps for calling our attention to this.

CONCLUSION

At this point, the reader may well be asking whether the sense of imagination that we have been exploring in this chapter has anything to do with the more common use that is given to the word: namely, to refer to the propensity humans have to design plans of action for the future and, in particular, ones that had not been previously entertained. Ontological naïvety encourages us to assume that we have ideas, concepts, or images in our minds and that these are transformed by imagination into new ones. This, however, as was argued above, is not how we should proceed if we want to avoid the dead end of representationalism.

Our argument in this chapter is that the two meanings of imagination are, in fact, deeply intertwined and that it is indeed only by reference to the transformational meaning of imagination that it makes any sense to call limits of imagination to the primary factors of experience. Once we give up on the Cartesian idea of images in the mind as imprints of perceptual experience, and thus we rid ourselves of the idea of there being such things as determinable metaphors in our minds, we then become free to see imagination as the associational process that situates thoughts within the holism of the mental. And, of course, therefore, there is a deeply ontogenetic side to imagination since it always sits on top of a history of personhood.

We are only free to imagine (new things, that is) because our thought is veridical—it engages the world of which it is a part. As in fuzzy logic, we are constantly correcting for error: "A creature that cannot entertain the idea that it might be wrong has no concepts, no thoughts" (Davidson 2004: 141). It is by questioning "what is" or "what is not" that we can entertain what might not yet be. Thus, there is a direct relationship between reminiscing and imagining as a destiny of openness; between pastness and futurity. We break with the naïve conception of mental images as somehow fixed. Time and space, as parameters of our human condition of embodied historicity in world, are always unfolding, thus giving rise to the dynamic process of *worlding* that we thematized in the previous chapter.

What we have discovered in the work of the Oxford poststructuralists is that humans are not just free to move anywhere they like. In order to imagine things, we are constrained by the fact that we live in a world with specific characteristics, that we are persons in ontogeny (i.e., in space-time), and that human sociality and its complex histories (forms of life) are the absolute condition for the very possibility of propositional thinking. The primary factors of experience limit our imagination to the extent that we are biological humans in sociality and that our personal ontogeny takes place in a common world. But so do synthetic images, paradigmatic scenes, and worldviews. The limits of imagination are constraints on our futurity—that is, on the way in which purpose (intentionality) is constantly part of our engagement with world and others. This does not mean that they have to be seen as a sign that there is no freedom in the human condition. Rather, it means that absolute freedom, like absolute truth, or absolute world, is an unthinkable goal. It is not only that they do not exist, but that they could not have existed. The ideas of absolute truth, of absolute freedom, or absolute world are contradictory in themselves; they are oxymoronic.

The sociocentric and representationalist dispositions that so deeply marked our discipline are correctly associated with the structuralist theoretical heritage inspired by the works of Durkheim or Simmel. It is legitimate to ask at this point whether a critique of sociocentrism and representationalism, such as proposed in this book, requires the wholesale abandonment of anthropology's structuralist heritage. We would be obliged to cast aside such precious jewels as, to pick a few examples, Lévi-Strauss' canonical formula of myth, Gluckman's "peace in the feud," Goffman's analysis of stigma, or Viveiros' demonic alliance. If, however, we take structuralism not as a theoretical starting point but as a methodological disposition, this need not be the case. While a new methodological structuralism will have to be analytically mitigated, there is no good reason to suppose that we cannot return to such tools as sources of inspiration, namely in our ethnographic analyses, for they remain brilliant windows into the human condition and its more recurrent proclivities.

CHAPTER FOUR

Person

> *We are so both and oneful*
> *night cannot be so sky*
> *sky cannot be so sunful*
> *i am through you so i*

> – e. e. cummings

At the beginning of this book, we observed that world is not only human but it is also personal. It is now time to take on the full implications of that and ask ourselves: If world is formed[1] by humans and if personhood is the characteristic condition of humanity, then how do persons come about in human sociality? This is a necessary step for querying how humans inhabit world.

The starting assumption is that, in the world around us, mind and body are one; therefore, it is not a question of matter, as there is no question of spirit.[2]

---

1. Note, we use the expression "formed" in its literal sense of "given form," not in the sense of "created."

2. This is one side of what Donald Davidson attempted to explain by means of his notion of "anomalous monism": "Mental states are as real as physical events, being identical with them, and attributions of states are as objective" (2001: 72). Contemporary efforts to reenliven panpsychism, and particularly attempts to grant substance to spirit (and notably in the shape of *Geist*—Gabriel 2015), are unwarranted, both empirically and ethically.

Life is a mode of in-forming the world that, once it accumulates, gives rise over time and in space to the consolidation of ontological scales of figuration. In turn, these can combine in complex ways, giving rise to the emergence of instances of dynamic stability: personhood is one such. As a process of life, personhood occurs in a human being who communicates with other humans, evolving progressively toward a person capable of reflexive thinking (we call that ontogeny). Thus, the mere existence of a live human being is only a necessary condition for personhood; it is not a sufficient one. We should not speak of the person aside from the process of her/his constitution in time: that is, we must reject the notion that there is any ahistorical essence or inevitability to personhood.

In the previous chapter, we saw that there are cross-cultural recurrences and similarities in the ways persons engage world and proposed that the notion of primary factors of experience could help us account for these. In particular, we concluded that personhood should not be approached as a neo-Kantian[3]-type entity (a category of the mind), but rather that it should be seen as a synthetic image, a stochastically recurrent set of features of thought and experience that operate by the combination of primary factors of experience within historically particular forms of life.

The occurrence of these synthetic images is directly related to the embodied condition of humans and the affordances that they encounter in world, but not as logical impositions or preconfigured molds. To the contrary, synthetic images emerge in a complex stochastic manner out of the myriad forms that communication within human sociality assumes in history. Now, if this applies to the more abstract proclivities (containment, binary opposition, reification), it must also apply to personhood, where, as Mauss highlighted from the beginning of the discussion, the variability in modes is immense within the ethnographic record. This variability, however, is not complete; there are limits to it. That is, there are recurrences and proclivities that can be observed to operate in all contexts of human sociality.

We start, therefore, from the idea that there are limits to the ways humans imagine their social condition and that one of these is the proclivity to assume entities of a kind that anthropologists have chosen to call "person." Departing

---

3. Note, however, how Godlove argues convincingly that Durkheim's French neo-Kantianism was inspired by Charles Renouvier and, in these matters, actually dependent on an incorrect interpretation of Kant (e.g., Godlove 1996: ix; see also Keck 2008).

from personhood as a factor of experience, this chapter dialogues with a number of attempts to reformulate the theoretical bases of the comparative study of kinship. It aims to emphasize the central relevance of personal ontogeny to human sociality. It is an effort to bring a series of critical insights to bear upon the age-old anthropological questions concerning kinship in terms of filiation and alliance.

PERSONHOOD

Humans act collectively but always through the agency of the person. All that is human arises from the person, each and every one of us inescapably personal. It is to persons that we can trace back the path of all the amazing marks humans have left in the world throughout the history of their species. Note, this is not a declaration of individualism or even of personalism; it is nothing but the empirical recognition that human sociality (emerging from the evolution of our species) inheres in the person and can never exist beyond it. Human sociality as we have known it since the development of language and the inception of *Homo sapiens sapiens* is rooted in the action of persons endowed with reflexive thinking. Persons are emergent entities that arise within human sociality (cf. Hattiangadi 2005).

While we disagree with Durkheim's sociocentrism, we validate Mauss' original observation that all known human forms of life have depended on some shared agreement about what it is to be a person. In spite of interpersonal indeterminacy, there is no doubt that, when you become a person, you do so within a narrative context where what it is to be a person is already a largely determined field. Furthermore, the expectations associated to personhood are echoed in all sorts of other facets of a form of life, which present themselves to the person as affordances (see Chemero 2003), such as modes of dwelling, forms of care, gender relations, relations of kinship, and so on. The boundaries of personhood may be questioned (as in slave-holding societies), the nature of what makes persons operative may vary (as in different forms of conceiving of spiritual essence), even personal embodiment can assume diverse aspects (as when Ingold argues that we do not all see in the same way—2010). The ethnographic record, however, leaves us in no doubt: the existence of globally recurrent values and associations concerning *personhood* is a central element of all forms of human life. More than that, across different sociocultural contexts, it has been systematically observed

that these values and formulations of personhood are of foundational importance for human forms of life.

In chapter 2, we observed that the world offers itself to persons in ontogeny
as a form of extension (space and time) where things are founded and order can
be built—that is, worlding is a central part of human existence. This process of
worlding is the result of a disposition that humans share with all animal life to
relate intentionally with world. I was inspired here by the account of intentionality and *purpose* as the bases of all meaning that T. L. Short (2007) derived from
a historical reading of Peirce's late "semeiotic."[4] Short defines intentionality as
the act of being attentive to an object. Any act of attention interprets a facet of
world, but it need not be a component of a thought in the propositional sense.
As intentionality is an active engagement with world, it implies a constant assessment of the impact that features of world have on the agent. In intentionality, the act of attention presupposes purpose. This means that error assessment
is necessarily the ground upon which thinking is based, that is, intentionality is
veridical. Furthermore, inasmuch as "meaning is not contained in a moment but
is future-directed" (ibid.: 44), space-time is part of all thinking, and worlding
ensues.

Such a view of intentionality can be very useful for the anthropological project, since it opens up the way for *a theory of meaning that is naturalistic and yet is
not limited to mechanistic notions of causality*. All animal life is based on sociality
(the achievement of collective action), and this depends on information sharing
(communication). In turn, communication is not primarily a dyadic relation
between two agents. Rather, as Davidson has taught us, it is a triangulation
with world; it requires world (2001: 128). Intentionality is what makes possible
communication among the members of a species, for it is what opens up world.
Sociality and intentionality, therefore, are codependent.

This is the reason why there are serious problems with proposals that aim
to extend the first-person plural of scientific analysis (the so-called "ecumenical

---

4.   According to Short, the principal problem with Peircean "semeiotic" is that "it has
      gotten amongst the wrong crowd" (ibid.: ix), that is, it has been made implicitly to
      converge with the kind of Saussurian semiotics that constitutes the epistemological
      bread and butter of most anthropological undergraduate degrees. Furthermore,
      Short's more abstract version of intentionality seems better suited to our project
      than that proposed by Alessandro Duranti in his recent book on "intentions"
      (2015), where the concept is treated primarily to refer to dispositions of human
      consciousness of a representational kind.

we"—see Praet 2015) to include, for example, whole planets, way beyond what has been considered life. The issue is not if planets, as the example goes, are "like us," since all things are "like" all other things in some way; but whether a planet is capable of "we"—in other words, whether it possesses the capacity to address and respond to the affordances provided by world through a system of communication among members of a species and beyond it. If it does, it is capable of "we" (as Lévi-Strauss argued for amoebas—2000); if it does not, then to classify it as "we" or "us" is to engage in metaphorical, poetic thinking. In short, the social teleology of intentionality—Peirce's "purpose"—is a condition for the very occurrence of a "we"; beyond teleology there is no sense in talking of "we/us," for this is not simply a definitional matter.

In contrast, one must be equally weary of the anthropocentric proneness to identify intentionality with "the mental" or with consciousness. In humans, intentionality is a central feature of everyday life that continues to operate throughout a person's life as a basic disposition. Processes of sociality occur among other species; other species also have complex forms of information sharing; what there is not in other species is thinking reflexive subjects endowed with *presence*, such as fully formed persons. While intentionality is a characteristic of all animal life, reflexive propositional thinking is exclusive to persons.

The entry into personhood, however, is a staged process that requires us to be in sociality with other humans who have already been called into personhood. The material person is born as a member of the human species but it is only in *personal ontogeny* that it enters fully into human life by postulating its own presence. The intersubjectivity of others provokes the intersubjectivity we share with them. This is the marvelous result of the evolution of our species (see Schaeffer 2007). Human sociality has much in common with all other forms of sociality, but it is distinctive in that way: children in human sociality are prone to develop propositional thinking out of a joint engagement with world.

We are born wired in such a way that we have a propensity for entering human communication (Edelman 1992) and remain within it through memory (Kandel 2006). For that, however, we have to be called into personhood by other humans who had already been called by others before them, in a long chain of mutuality. If the proverbial catastrophe were to occur and only newborn babies were to survive—however many of them might survive, however many books and computers survive with them—that would be the end of humanity, for it would be the end to an uninterrupted history of transgenerational personal mutuality.

By human sociality, therefore, we mean the ongoing contexts of information sharing as instituted in the history of our species (cf. Ingold 1996). It is very important to understand that this is not limited to matters of propositional (symbolic) thought.[5] Rather, communication involves the possibility of achieving joint action, and that is a feature of most life forms. Sociality, as the passing of information between the members of a species in order to achieve collective action, is the root of intentionality. And, as we saw above, intentionality assumes space and time, it involves pastness and futurity—that is, the variation in mode that results from the causal trace of both effective and possible intentional engagements.

Contrary to intentionality, propositional thinking as it evolves in human infants from about one year of age is something that only persons can do: not parts of persons, not groups of persons, not books, not computers (see Hutto 2008). Persons and only persons. And, in order to be a person, we have to be called into personhood by other persons; not only one other but various others. This is why Levinas (1996) claims that being called into personhood by other persons constitutes an *anterior alterity*: "anterior" in the sense that it is not symmetrical with identity, for it is, rather, constitutive of identity. The point is that I can only become aware of myself as a counterdistinction. Intelligibility always precedes me; I am not the ultimate source of my own thinking, because it is from within narrative that I emerge—this is how we propose to read today Anselm's insight concerning belief and reason.

To recapitulate: intentionality (*basic mind*) is a precondition for propositionality (*scaffolded mind*). As humans, when we are born, we possess capabilities that distinguish us from other species. Human babies have a disposition to sense what others are experiencing—developmental psychologists call this *alteroception* (Bråten [1998] 2006). This disposition means that humans are prone to respond together with others in the world, engaging the world jointly. This *shared intentionality* is an embodied disposition that evolved phylogenetically, not some sort of mental or spiritual disposition, as we were told of old (see Tomasello 2008). Through it, we integrate our own perspective with that of those with whom we are experiencing alteroception. There is nothing conscious about it—at least before we become fully persons. Shared intentionality is what allows humans to come together in the world, to find each other's rhythm

---

5.   I specifically avoid here a semiotic account of human sociality—much like, in fact, the older Peirce also did (see Short 2007).

without even trying to do so, to sense each other's needs; whether one is cooperating for action or whether one is fighting each other to death. It is as important in love making as in karate.

Humans have been endowed by evolution with a proclivity to respond to world in joint perspective with our close partners in that world (Chemero 2009). This process is what makes us prone to learn how to communicate *as humans*: that which has been called intersubjectivity.[6] Child psychologists have demonstrated that intersubjectivity is the door through which human babies enter the process of communicating by means of gestures and, eventually, through language (Trevarthen 1980). As we have learned of old with the instances of feral children (*enfants sauvages*—Newton 2002), if one is not called into this form of primary intersubjectivity with humans, one will never develop human thought processes fully.

This process of entering into communication by engaging in intersubjectivity with others in a dwelling environment occurs in steps, and it is what makes us become persons and, eventually, fully thinking persons with a reflexive knowledge of our own existence in world. Intersubjectivity, however, is operative in each of us even before we develop any notion of our own separate existence as persons; before each one of us has constituted his or her own singular arena of presence and action before world (Bråten [1998] 2006). This is why "being-in-the-world" is inevitably a "being-with-others," to use Heidegger's dictum.

In order to understand this, we must grasp that the emergence of the person (personal ontogeny) is a layered process. The distinction between primary and secondary intersubjectivities can help us grasp this layered coming into being of the person. Shaun Gallagher proposes that, being based on intentionality, *primary intersubjectivity* is already present in the newborn and never stops throughout life. It is a nonmentalistic, perceptually based engagement with the intentions and attitudes of others. Eventually, for a child who is cared for by humans, this is superposed by a *secondary intersubjectivity* that evolves from around one year of age and that already assumes the scaffolding of world to the extent that it involves engaging persons and their intentions in light of their contexts of action (see Gallagher and Jacobson 2012).

---

6.   Contrary to Alessandro Duranti (2015: 7), I do not believe that the word should be synonymous with shared intentionality. The two notions refer to processes that overlap significantly but have very diverse implications, as Shaun Gallagher's distinction between primary and secondary intersubjectivities highlights (Gallagher and Jacobson 2012).

This secondary intersubjectivity, in turn, involves two layered modes: firstly, the child moves from understanding others to making sense of the world—through shared intentionality, the child becomes aware of the way others grasp pragmatically the affordances in the surrounding environment; secondly, the child moves from understanding the world to making sense of others—it comes to grasp the roles that others play out in the world by engaging in the everyday pragmatic routines of the dwelling environment (the "jobs" that the child so wishes to accomplish, according to Trevarthen[7]). In short, there never is an original moment in which the child is itself alone facing others; being-in-the-world is being-with-others from before the child constitutes its own presence. And then, throughout life, as we engage new situations, the layered process of personal ontogeny never stops, so that anterior alterity is a feature of personhood that is constant, not only at the beginning of life.

THE EMERGENCE OF SINGULARITY

In light of that, plurally cohabiting the world—*company*—is the inescapable condition of personhood. The arousal of subjectivity in the person—that is, the oncoming of propositional thinking—happens through an engagement with a plurality of human beings, as the result of triangulation.[8] Singularity and partibility coexist in the human condition, mutually creating and destroying each other (Strathern 1988: 11–14). Meyer Fortes ([1973] 1987) has famously demonstrated that, for the Tallensi, it is only after death that a man can fully achieve the status of full personhood. As it happens, there is a profound universalism in that particular aporia, since it highlights that personhood is a variable, even in contexts where it is not presented as such. As a matter of fact, in the course of personal ontogeny, each one of us will never be more than an almost-one, that is, singular but only almost so, because indeterminacy and underdetermination are inescapable conditions of propositional thinking. We can only think to the

---

7. Extract of oral communication in
    http://www.educationscotland.gov.uk/earlyyears/prebirthtothree/
    nationalguidance/conversations/colwyntrevarthen.asp (accessed 30 November
    2014—no longer available).
8. For the backing to this account in studies of cognition and developmental
    psychology, see Hutto (2008), and Trevarthen (1993, 1998), respectively.

extent that we are within sociality, and that is a communicational condition that has to happen in a historically specific location, in a world of becoming. In his foundational lecture on the category of the person, Marcel Mauss noted that there never has been

> a tribe, a language, in which the word "I", "me" (*je*, *moi*) . . . has never existed, or that it has not expressed something clearly represented. . . . As well as possessing the pronoun, a very large number of languages are conspicuous for their use of many "positional" suffixes, which deal for the most part with the relationships existing in time and space between the speaker (the subject) and the object about which he is speaking.. ([1938] 1985: 2–3)

While this is true, it must also not be forgotten that pronouns do not all function in the same way. Long ago, Émile Benveniste demonstrated that the first-person and the second-person pronouns operate differently from the third-person pronoun (he/she) in that they are "empty," as he put it: "Their role is to provide the instrument for a conversion . . . of language into speech" (1966: 254). In short, he argues that while *I* and *you* are positional indicators, *he/she* are substitutes for objects of speech (as in, "Peter ate the apple. *He* loved it"). *I* and *you* are positional, they do not demand a reference external to the speech act; to the contrary, *he/she* stands for something that is external to it.

There is, indeed, a profound truth to this observation, for it has implications in the matter of early personal ontogeny. We must not assume that there is any anteriority to the first or second persons, for if we did we would be falling into the trap of separating language use (speech) from the historical process of the constitution of the speaking person, both in ontogeny and in phylogeny. We have to understand that the "substitution" that the third person operates, to use Benveniste's terms, is the original process that allows for the constitution of the other two: as we have come to know, primary intersubjectivity antedates subjectivity, not the other way around (see Trevarthen 1980).

Dividuality results directly from the process of being called into personhood by one's early carers, which is not something that is planned or consciously enacted each time. Adults call children into personhood because they too experience alteroception, that is, they too are prone to include babies in their lived worlds through the effects of shared intentionality. Intersubjectivity is not a choice; it happens. It is all rather inevitable once a baby is among humans and is being cared for during the long period of maturation that the human species demands. The oncoming of reflexive thought is what allows for the arousal of subjectivity in the person. The child experiences shared intentionality with those carers who are physically closest to it. It experiences that as participation (à la Lévy-Bruhl), to the extent that it sees itself and the carer *as being intrinsically the same* before the word. The child is encouraged in that by the fact that the carers themselves are also prone to this same process of participation.

Now, as Donald Winnicott (1971) came to understand when studying children, there never is only one *other*. It is when further carers—third parties in the theater of personal ontogeny—come into contact with the child and with its initial closest carer that it experiences for the first time that terrible sense of betrayal, of aloneness, which Levinas (1996) theorised. This is what William James called "the law of dissociation": "What is associated now with one thing and now with another, tends to become dissociated from either, and to grow into an object of abstract contemplation by the mind" (1918: 506). In sum, memory of crossed identifications is what produces personhood: the emergence of *presence* is a function of the aloneness of being singularly identified in the world.

This is a process that depends on the spontaneous operation of the abstract primary factors that we listed in the previous chapter: opposition, reification, and containment. These three modes of operation come together in a process of triangulation that is never completed: ontogenic triangulation goes on happening for as long as the person remains alive; and, in turn, participation reimposes itself after separation. The person will face an *other* (person or, for that matter, animal) and experience again alteroception leading to shared intentionality— and intersubjectivity starts once more!

What this means is that there is a permanent evanescence to identity. James' law of dissociation is a continuous dynamic of human creation. Alterity—the fact of having been called into being from the outside—will never fully resolve itself into identity; it will always remain anterior. Therefore, there is no stability in identity, as Levinas (1961) has demonstrated. The asymmetry of alterity imposes itself at every new encounter and humans will have no rest as humans. Persons as reflexive agents will ever be the unsteady products of sociality.

There is, in short, a fundamental ambiguity in personhood that never resolves itself throughout ontogeny, for if I were to become "one," I would betray the other in me and, in that way, I would lose the possibility of being myself. Personhood, as an emergent property, is never unitary; it is always an almost-one. In the theatre of personal ontogeny, I am close to another (contiguity, neighborhood) but I am also another (substitution, surrogation—see Pina-Cabral 2013b). In that sense, participation (à la Lévy-Bruhl—see [1949] 1998) involves both proximity and substitution (as Levinas identifies—see 1996).

In fact, I can only come to communicate propositionally with other humans because primary intersubjectivity disposes me congenitally to assume that others around me may make sense because they are with me. Mutuality is foundational of the person: at the root of propositional communication there is the ethical posture of Quine's interpretive charity. Ethics, therefore, is not a contract that the person enters into, nor is it a set of rules that the person has accepted to follow in order to be a member of the social.[9] At root, corresponsibility is there as a condition for me to become a person. Therefore, it is *an imposition*.

Much like with meaning, where we discovered that indeterminacy and underdetermination were conditions of, not impediments to, thought, so here, in personhood, the ineradicable presence of the third party in the theater of ontogeny, leading to the challenge posed by anterior alterity, must be seen not as a source of invalidation of the human, but as its very condition of possibility. The compositeness and ambiguity of the person are the source of ethics and politics.

The person discovers him- or herself as other, and as other of another. In propositionality, the presence from the start of the third party, questioning the identification of the intentional engagement with world, is the mechanism that launches reflexivity, making possible the scaffolding of thinking. Thus, the emergence of personhood as singular is experienced as a disturbance, an uncertainty, a contradictoriness—*the emergence of personhood is traumatic*.

This kind of language may discomfit anthropological readers, who are bound to find it too abstract, bordering on meaningless. But it is an unavoidable moment of anthropological thinking, for part of the problem we have identified with our disciplinary tradition and its incapacity to register some of the more provocative findings of poststructuralism is precisely its proneness to reify excessively and to avoid the conclusion that transcendence in personhood is a part of becoming a person, not a "culturally" imposed mode.

---

9.   Philippa Foot's disquisitions about goodness can be read as implications of this
      feature of personhood (2001).

STEPS OF ONTOGENY AND WORLD

Our motto in the following section is Heidegger's assertion that, by relation to stones, persons are world forming;[10] and by relation to animals, they do so in a richer fashion ([1929/30] 1995). We will transform that observation into contemporary anthropological terms by demonstrating that configuring world occurs in full isomorphism with configuring personhood; *the two processes are codependent* and they occur through a series of four steps that we will now identify. For obvious explanatory reasons, we do so from the perspective of early ontogeny; but the reader must keep in mind that the process that launches ontogeny and gives form to world goes on happening for so long as the person remains alive. Owing to the unfolding of personal ontogeny, the person is a constant engine of world building; thus, the steps we abstract below are happening all of the time. That is, they are not chronological steps in any strict sense, but a process of constant implication. The chronological sequence we propose below, therefore, is essentially expository.

The gateway to personhood—the *first step of ontogeny and world*—is the motivated perception of others that is based on an immediate response to the other's body movements (Trevarthen calls it alteroception—see 1980 and Bråten [1998] 2006). By means of it, the newborn child is drawn into identification with its proximate others. This occurs primarily with its first carer (often the breastfeeding mother), and subsequently with more and more persons in its immediate dwelling environment. These relations of participation (specifically of surrogation—see Pina-Cabral 2013b) are driven by shared intentionality and give rise to primary intersubjectivity. Clear boundaries are not demarcated and worlding occurs in a diffuse manner as a process of extension outward in time and space. The world is lit, as it were; it embraces the emerging person as an awareness of an area of possible movement: world arises as *source* (as aspect [i] of world, as elicited in chapter 1 above).

The *second step* is when the child is confronted with its carers interacting with each other and performing "tasks" in its immediate dwelling environment.

---

10. "Forming in the multiple sense that it lets world occur, and through the world gives itself an original view (form [*Bild*]) that is not explicitly grasped, yet functions precisely as a paradigmatic form for all manifest beings, among which each respective Dasein itself belongs" (Heidegger 1998: 123). Once again, we meet here with the principle of non-wellfoundedness—i.e., a part that relates to a whole of which it is a part—as the mode of emergence.

As the carers interact with each other, manipulating separately the diverse features of the dwelling environment, the child is treated as a third person. It too engages actively with surrounding affordances, thus discovering its own agency.[11] In this process, the child's original participations with its immediate carers are challenged owing to triangulation. Thus, the child confronts its absence from its primordial participations.

This is the moment when duality emerges, for the child is split from itself (itself as one with each of the immediate carers). It is the ethical moment of betrayal when the emerging person is confronted by the possibility of its own absence. It is a breach of continuity, like dividing the left side of the body from the right side of the body. It is at this point that perspective on world arises. By relation to a world that no longer includes it, the person becomes a perspective on world, which is now an encompassing world that is placed not in mere continuity with the person, but by contrast with him or her—that is, as *domain*, as aspect (ii) of world.

The *third step* is when the child discovers him- or herself as other. This is the moment of emergence of the arena of presence and action (see Johnston 2010). The process is one of both reification and containment. Through memory, an internality takes shape that relates spatiotemporally with world. That is, I look at myself like yet another thing in the world—a world which contains diverse things; a world divided by boundaries. The now reified person can engage the world reflexively from the point of view of his or her internal arena of presence and action, his or her self. The scaffolding of mind—in Peircian terms, the achievement of symbolic thinking—occurs concomitantly with the emergence of the arena of presence and action. Language acquisition is part of this process of scaffolding, which is a process of acceptance of *limits* upon world. Limits that, much as they are formative of the person in secondary intersubjectivity, appear as external to the person's actions—it is the arising of aspect (iii) of world.

The *fourth step* is when the person discovers him- or herself as internally complex by crossing his or her reified existence with the identification he/she has with those with whom he/she shares the world. The plural emerges as an extrapolation of self-identity, a symmetry between levels. Persons form non-wellfounded sets (cf. Moss 2014) to the extent that they create wholes together

---

11. By taking recourse to the neutral pronoun here we seek to achieve two things: (a) to postpone the attribution of personhood at a point when it is being constituted and (b) to postpone the attribution of gender at a point when it is being negotiated

with wholes of which they are a part (Hattiangadi 2005: 89). The person's own disposition for dividuality comes to mirror the collectivity's internal plurality. Sociality is no longer just a disposition to collaborate for self-interest (as in intentionality) but becomes a relation between hypostatized dividual entities.

The singular and the plural, therefore, are copresent. It is the interaction between duality and singularity/plurality that leads, through broken symmetry, to the process of transformation that Thompson (2007) calls morphodynamics.[12] Opposition shatters continuity as alterity shatters participation; it creates relation (which occurs within propositional, symbolic thought). But, as there is a constant reengagement, owing to the constant operation of intentionality and alteroception, the whole process always starts again. For this reason, the relations between internally plural hypostatized entities resulting from the fourth step are ever incomplete.

Lévi-Strauss warned us famously against putting the focus on entities and not on relations, but then he went on to enshrine absolute duality as the primary relation. Marilyn Strathern, on the other hand, pointed out that, in human sociality, the founding opposition is not between the "one" and "others," but between the "one/many" and the "dual":

> In one sense, the plural and the singular are "the same". They are homologues of one another. That is, the bringing together of many persons is just like the bringing together of one. The unity of a number of persons conceptualized as a group or a set is achieved through eliminating what differentiates them, and this is exactly what happens when a person is also individualized. . . . In other words, a plurality of individuals as individuals ("many") is equal to their unity ("one"). (1988: 13–14)

There is, therefore, a dynamic process that is operated by opposition and reification. Strathern again: "To be individuated, plural relations are first reconceptualized as dual and then the dually conceived entity, able to detach a part of itself, is divided. The eliciting cause is the presence of a different other" (ibid.: 15). This

---

12. In this, Thompson is inspired by Merleau-Ponty, but opts for a definition that uses the language of physics: "Structures are essentially dependent on *critical phenomena*, i.e., on phenomena of symmetry breaking which induce qualitative discontinuities (heterogeneities) in the substrates. . . . Discrete structures emerge via qualitative discontinuities . . . a system of qualitative discontinuities in a substrate is called a *morphology* and dynamic theories of morphologies belong to what is called *morphodynamics*. There is therefore a close link between the concept of 'structure' and morphodynamics" (Petitot quoted in ibid.: 71, original emphasis).

dynamic of partition is a dynamic of mutuality, as explained above; it operates continuously and is at the root of sociality to the extent that there is no point in which a number of separate entities get together to form a collectivity. Groupness and personhood (collective and singular) arise out of each other. This is why groupness is not the same as sociality, for the latter is constitutive of the very persons who form groups—something that twentieth-century sociocentrism failed to grasp. The neighbor is always already there, to revert again to the more poetic language of Levinas.

Notice that, in describing the steps of ontogeny and world, we hesitated on the attribution of gender (it, he, she). This is a matter of enormous relevance, as we will see in the remainder of this chapter. It is indeed in the dynamics of triangulation through which the person emerges that gender identity starts to consolidate. In fact, there are no ungendered persons, although there may be all kinds of gender complexities, as we have come to know. Gender presents itself from the start as a factor in the theater of ontogeny and never leaves it again. It is a central facet of the process through which the self emerges in alterity and all persons are gendered persons, since the immediate environment of caring where the child experiences its original moments of ontogeny is already divided in that way.

Step 1. (xB) (xC)

There is an identification of the emerging person (x) with proximate others: the first carer (B) and, progressively, other close carers (C) in the theater of ontogeny. *Alteroception is the gateway to personhood—world (i) as* **source**.

Step 2. (BC) ¬ x

In witnessing B and C participate in each other and the surrounding environment, x is excluded from its earlier participations (¬ x), it is treated as a third person. *Triangulation gives rise to dividuality—world (ii) as* **domain**.

Step 3. x ⇒ A

The emerging person (x) discovers him- or herself as an other (A). *The emergence of presence—world (iii) as* **limit**.

Step 4. (A + B + C) ⇒ A'

Dividuality emerges at the same time as plurality. It is the child's own participation that challenges its arena of presence and action and allows for a constitution of identity at a superpersonal level. *Relations arise.*

ASPECTS OF PERSONHOOD[13]

As outlined above, an awareness of one's own separate *presence*—one's singularity as an arena of presence and action—is a central feature of personhood. Contrary to what we normally assume, this process of discovery of one's own singularity in the world as person is not merely "mental," as it is both narrative and organic (it is inscribed in the world—presence implies action and vice versa). It can only happen to embodied humans, and it happens in all historical human social contexts known to us, albeit in a diversity of ways. We must keep in mind the findings of embodied cognition, which tell us that "Mind . . . is congenitally predisposed to seep out into the world" (Clark 2010: 8; see Clark and Chalmers 1998). In short, propositionality is not merely an "internal" matter; as cognition occurs in world, propositional mind inheres in the socialized world where human persons constantly pursue their ontogeny (cf. Hutto 2008; Anderson, Richardson, and Chemero 2012). The person's mental life has to be seen as a form of communication in sociality.

We know of the examples of cultural contexts where personhood has been attributed to beings that are not embodied, to material features of the environment, or even to animals (e.g., the famous case of the Tallensi sacred crocodiles—see Fortes [1973] 1987). Furthermore, we know of many ethnographic cases of persons who are not treated as being persons, or to whom some part of personhood is denied, or who are undergoing liminal processes during which the normal attributions of personhood are not held to apply to them. All of these are familiar instances in the ethnographic record. Moreover, we are not claiming that all such attributions or denials of personhood are metaphorical in the sense of staged or artificial; all we observe is that the *focal meaning* of personhood is associated to human persons and that other uses are extensions of this focal usage that are dependent on it. It is only to the extent that we (i.e., ethnographers, anthropologists, comparativists) are persons that we can achieve a notion of what it is to be a person (both in "our" and in "other" cultures).

It is not because they know that the crocodiles are persons that the Tallensi attribute personhood to human persons, but the other way around. The culturalist suggestion that, for the Tallensi, crocodiles are as personal as human persons does not actually stand up to the ethnographic evidence as Fortes presents it.

---

13. In parts of this section we rely on arguments already developed with other intentions in Pina-Cabral (2016).

Similarly, whether the tiger is a person to a person and the person is a tiger to
him or her, or whether the person is a person to him- or herself and a tiger to
him or her, might be held to depend on a kind of free signifier: personhood.
But does this interpretation withstand scrutiny? Would we (i.e., I and my readers) be able to understand the essential anthropomorphization of animality that
Amerindians undertake if we started from tigers instead of persons? In short,
how would we query a tiger about what it is to be a tiger when faced with a human? We only know that tigers think they are persons because we know what
it is to be a person when faced with a tiger, and this we know because we share
our condition of being a person with the Amerindians and we can communicate
propositionally with them and learn from them what it is to be a person when
faced with a tiger.

It is not a question of defending some kind of ahistorical or objective
knowledge of personhood; no, indeterminacy rules. And yet we know that we
can achieve quite large measures of mutual understanding across the cultural
(and historical) divide.[14] Furthermore, there are no persons in general but only
specific persons made different by their specific personal history, their ontogeny (cf. Bloch 2012: 33). In short, since there is a foundational alterity in personhood, it makes no sense to assume that it has a clean beginning. Not only
do persons emerge from the embrace of earlier persons in child-rearing, but
they also see themselves as causally linked to earlier persons (that which anthropologists usually refer to as "filiation"). Such a process is not a generalized
condition; rather, it is grounded on specific human relations whose history is
unique in the case of each one of us: our personal history of ontogeny. Whilst
the history of each one's existence as a determinable person is immersed in the
long history of sociality, none of us can be reduced to a simple manifestation
of an overarching totality—our carers are particular others, not a generic other
(see Pina-Cabral 2013b).

In his book about the challenge that developments concerning human cognition represent to anthropology, Maurice Bloch (2012) aims at providing a
formulation of what constitutes a human person. As is necessarily the case in
a field with a history as long as ours, he is immediately confronted by terminological problems. Words, as they have a history, carry with them a bagful of

---

14. Not ever completely, of course, but then again the notion of complete understanding,
where human communication is at stake, is itself absurd, owing to the exigencies of
the very nature of communication, that is, the inevitability of indeterminacy.

implications. What word should one use to describe a phenomenon the nature of which one is precisely trying to extricate from previous formulations? This is a challenge that anyone who attempts analytical deconstruction characteristically meets. In the past, a number of rhetorical strategies have been devised to deal with it. In this case, Bloch wants to examine "what kind of phenomenon human beings are." He immediately meets with a large list of concepts, such as "self, the I, agent, subject, person, individual, dividuals, identity, etc." (ibid.: 120). Instead of picking one of these old words and reformulating it, he decides to bracket the issue, to sidetrack the categorical problem by using the empty word "blob."

I contend that this stratagem failed him in this instance. In English, blob is primarily "a drop of a thick liquid or viscous substance" from which derive two secondary meanings: "a spot of colour"; and "an indeterminate roundish mass or shape" (OED). Immediately we realize that the word implies unicity, identifiability, and palpable materiality. A blob is no longer when it gets divided into two blobs. Bloch, thus, short-circuits from the start the very purpose of his exercise by attributing easily identifiable, material unicity to the understanding of singular humans.[15]

To the contrary, in line with a poststructuralist procedure, I suggest that we should go about this otherwise: instead of characterizing from the start the unicity of what we are about to discuss, we must group the whole range of phenomena we want to discuss adjectivally. For example, instead of speaking of societies or cultures, words that were becoming so problematic for anthropological theory in the 1990s, Strathern chose to speak of socialities, and, as we have seen, sociality is not to be confused with groupness. It seems reasonable to follow this lead: instead of speaking of selves, individuals, agents, or subjects . . . blobs, as our subject matter, let us advance laterally by debating conditions of personhood.

If, then, we do not take for granted the blob's unicity, we come up with an interesting observation: it is not the object itself which fades away, but rather our epistemological disposition toward it that gets profoundly altered. As with Strathern's socialities, societies and cultures remain roughly identifiable processes in history and their existence is not put into question. Rather, it is our

---

15. After all, it would seem, the repeated recourse to the word "individual" throughout the book carries greater implications than the mere practical strategy of using a word that we all can be expected to understand (Bloch 2012).

epistemological relationship toward them that alters. Similarly, we discover that much of what was observed for "selves, persons, individuals, agents, blobs, etc." continues to be valid, but we discover that within the general field of person-hood that those concepts elicit, there are phenomena of different epistemological statuses that call for analytical differentiation.[16] Moreover, in this regard, the word *person* has clear benefits over alternative words, for reasons that have to do with the history of the discipline (back to Leenhardt, Fortes, and Mauss, but further back still to Kant and even Spinoza); but also because this was the word that allowed us to start criticizing the individualist ideology that was at the root of the individual versus society/culture polarity, which structured all sociocentric thinking throughout the twentieth century.

As an emergent entity that arises within sociality, then, personhood presents *three different aspects* of interaction with world (see diagram 2). These three aspects[17] are all coterminous and interdependent to the extent that they are different perspectives on historically singular processes:

(α)   the organic human person in ontogeny—broadly speaking, an individual phenomenon;

(β)   the "arena of presence and action"—a dividual and partible phenomenon;

(γ)   the historically constructed frameworks of personhood that pervade the environment within which personal ontogeny occurs—here individuality and dividuality are combined in very many different ways, depending on the variation between what anthropologists normally call culture.

The three aspects, it must be stressed, are aspects of each and every person, they do not exist per se; even the frameworks of personhood produced by human sociality (γ) are only present to the extent that they are present in actual persons. Aspects α and γ are in constant interaction with world, and they are subject to the dynamics of worlding. This means that the forms of life produced by human sociality (γ) come to be hypostatized in the world as *habitus* and, in that way, they present themselves as affordances to the organic person (α).

---

16. For example, we can now see that Bloch's blob remains essentially throughout his book a "cognitive" phenomenon, which is a rather unfortunate aspect, for it reproduces the individualist, cognitivist, mind-versus-world polarity that we all agree needs to be overcome.

17. I am using here the word "aspect" in the sense that Wittgenstein gave to it when he proposed the famous example of Jastrow's duckrabbit ([1953] 1967: II xi, 193–229) and that Needham further developed in *Against the tranquility of axioms* (1983).

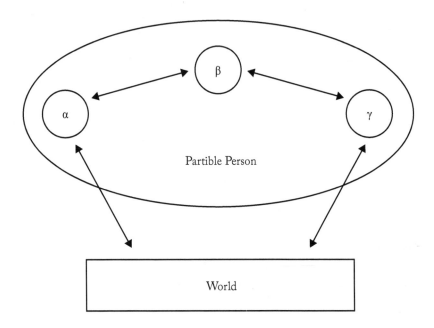

Diagram 2. The partible person.

Persons are constitutively "amidst," as Heidegger liked to stress, and that is one of the reasons why pastness in humans is inescapable. This is also the reason why simply separating between individual and individualism, as Nigel Rapport (2001) proposes, is not enough to solve the matter of personhood, since even our formulation of personhood γ could raise problems, for it might be interpreted as implying that people have concepts in their heads that their culture gave them as concepts and that they share with the other members of their culture as concepts, having learned them as concepts. And yet such a representationalist approach is false, as we have seen: the cognitive processes of each one of us are indeterminate and cannot be repeated. The integration of meaning within language (the scaffolding of mind) is fully personal. Contemporary philosophy, inspired by phenomenology, has been calling our attention to the need to overcome this limitation and to assume a "radically embodied" notion of personhood where meaning is seen as relational (e.g., Clark and Chalmers 1998; Chemero 2009; Hutto and Myin 2013).

Thus, the "Nuer notion of the person" is nothing but the identification by the ethnographer of a statistical recurrence among the Nuer in the ways they cope with personhood: it is the fact that, in order to circulate in a Nuer world, one must assume a determinable but open-ended set of associations and recurrences that amount to broad parameters of what persons are in that particular human historical setting. We have been alerted to this for a very long time—it was, after all, the central quandary that engaged Robert Feleppa (1988) in his important book on the philosophical problems that face the comparative study of culture—but most of us took a while to come round to admit that we needed to face the problem of representation head on. We have been too slow to take the conclusions required by the shedding off of what Sartre, as noted above, called a "naïve metaphysics of the image" (1936: 3).[18]

It is important not to jump to the conclusion that the organic person (α) is universal; the arena of presence and action (β) is individual; and the historically constructed frameworks of personhood (γ) are culturally unique. This would be to assume both a mind–body polarity and a representationalist model of mind—analytical dispositions that we reject. We should be clear, therefore, that the material person in ontogeny, the reflexive person, and the culturally shared frameworks of personhood are all both universal and historically specific. The notion that human inherence in history is divided into neatly separable cultural worlds ("ontologies") is a primitivist mirage that has produced much misunderstanding and hindered our anthropological theorizing very seriously over the years. But so is the notion that one might be able to have any grasp of a culturally shared framework of personhood (e.g., the Nuer notion of person) aside from its instantiation in actual singular human persons ($\alpha + \beta + \gamma$). It would be like suggesting that there are cultures whose identity lies outside of history, the complex history of human interaction. Only organic, reflexive, and interactive persons can come together in culturally identifiable modes of being a person. In short, there are no generic Nuers.

The person, therefore, is an ontological hybrid, an emergent entity that is consolidated over time—personal death is the collapse of that effect. What makes the person specific among other forms of life is that it is a combination of phenomena occurring at three different scales of figuration: the person is a hybrid between an organism (α), a complex of cognitive attitudes (β), and a combination of hypostatizations of cognitive attitudes (γ). Ontologically, all the three are similar, for they are space-time phenomena, to the extent that they are

---

18. For a more contemporary take on the issue, see Hutto, Kirchhoff, and Myin (2014).

stochastically emerging recurrences. This is as much the case for the organismic life as it is for the mental actions and the hypostatizations—in a sense, the latter are the more "material" of the three kinds of processes.

The organismic (α) and the cognitive (β) are combined with the historically preexistent modes of species-specific response to environment (γ) in all forms of intentional life; but in the human person in ontogeny there is a further complexification of the processes of sociality owing to symbolical scaffolding—that is, the hypostatizations resulting from *habitus* that accumulate over time as the result of human forms of linguistically configured communication. Presence is a combination of the three factors and it is what allows the person to *transcend* his or her immediate conditions of life and participate in forms of sociality that overreach time and space. Note, personhood never escapes time and space, but persons can operate beyond them in an indeterminate manner. There is a freedom to all forms of life, as Spinoza discovered and the enactivists stressed; but, because personhood transcends, human communication achieves a yet greater freedom. As we have seen, this is never absolute freedom; there are no absolutes in the world of live beings to the extent that time and space (death, to put it succinctly) will always reaffirm themselves.

Many contemporary psychologists (e.g., D. Siegel 2016) have chosen to refer to the relevant level of emergence as "mind." This raises two problems when we consider personal ontogeny as a process rooted in space and time— that is, in worlding as it occurs with all live beings. On the one hand, it fails to differentiate between what we have been calling basic mind (the modes of intentionality) and scaffolded mind (those of propositionality), whilst we have seen that the former supervenes on the latter. Moreover, these psychologists' association of mind with consciousness is deeply anthropocentric and, therefore, poses problems to an anthropological analysis. On the other hand, as far as personal ontogeny is concerned, it concentrates our attention on β (the arena of presence and action), dissociating it from α (the organismic aspect) and γ (the effects of the *habitus*). Although these authors make a whole lot of the embodiment of mind, they fail to understand that β is a property that only emerges in α in the presence of γ and cannot ever be dissociated from them, for there are no persons outside sociality. Anterior alterity—the non-wellfounded nature of personhood—is the very mechanism of personal ontogeny and there is no such thing as mind outside of it.

FAMILY AND MUTUALITY

Since the person is constituted in the way described above, the original experience of being a person is marked by links that the person will carry throughout
his or her whole life. No one, therefore, can cast away the constitutive implications of the initial processes of self-constitution, one's personal *primary solidarities* (see Pina-Cabral 2002b): that is, personhood is of necessity familial. These
identifications connect the person not only with one carer, but also with a multiplicity of carers. The plurality of the family is part of the theater of ontogeny; it
is implicit in the role of the third person that elicits the founding triangulation.
As Fortes (1969) argued long ago with his notion of *amity*, at the root of all
family behavior (what anthropologists have called "kinship") there is a disposition to feel that the other is part of me: that is, my condition and that of the
proximate other overlap constitutively; mutuality occurs.

Cohabiting, therefore, cannot be dissociated from kinship, for kinship is
something that only occurs to persons, and personhood is constituted in intersubjectivity: place and company interact; being-in-the-world is being-with-
others. One of the principal sources of analytical confusion in the history of
kinship studies is the propensity to polarize kinship and residence, dealing with
them as phenomena of radically different natures (cf. what I called "the heritage of Maine" in Pina-Cabral 1989). I propose to overturn that by focusing on
the evidence that personhood is never a self-enclosed, neatly bounded, unitary
phenomenon. Plurality and singularity are constantly reinstituting themselves
through living together in close cohabitation. Owing to James' law of dissociation, *personhood is intrinsically approximate*, almost-one—not only personhood β
(the reflexive, interactive person), but also personhood α (the organic person in
ontogeny), since the difference between α and β is one of aspect to the observer.
It is an analytical distinction; a matter of essence, not of existence, so to speak.

In ontogeny, therefore, at one moment, I am one with Mary, then one with
John, then I emerge before myself as Rita. But, just at the same time, I realize
that Mary, John, and Rita all feel they are, in some sense, together. Then *relation*
emerges, that is, mutuality institutes family as collectivity: $(A + B + C) \Rightarrow A'$. Being together in a dialectic of mutuality is continuously reenacted and reenforced
by living together in an ever-complexifying chain of relations that, as they are
invested in the dwelling environment, become increasingly independent of the
actual persons involved. Singularity emerges from plurality; the thinking person
emerges from an experience of mutuality of being (see Sahlins 2011a) just as

much as plural entities (familial entities) arise from singular persons. The process is one of being together whilst being different; of having the same perspective upon the world and yet inhabiting different places.

Now, as Rodney Needham has demonstrated in *Counterpoints* (1987), duality is always indeterminate and binary opposition is always incomplete. Whilst thinking indeed operates through the creation of caesuras (breaches that create meaning in the world by separating sides—Thompson's "morphodynamics"), these are ever evanescent for the reason that anterior alterity (i.e., the ground upon which all human thinking is constructed) ever reimposes itself (Pina-Cabral 2010a). Thus, the essential condition of all dyads is their ultimate indeterminacy (Needham 1987: 236). All singularity returns to plurality and all plurality is incomplete, in-becoming.

For persons, to be is to start being, and identity only exists as a relational inscription. This, in any case, seems to be what modern mathematics has come to discover after Gödel. Totality is what there is, and it is incomplete in its indeterminate multiplicity. When Marilyn Strathern declares that "the eliciting cause is the presence of a different other" (1988: 15), she is right, of course, but not in any sense of closure. That is, ontogeny never stops; the eliciting cause remains a cause both historically as a memory, and prospectively as part of daily interaction. Otherness is anterior but it also constantly reaffirms itself. The clear-cut opposition of the duo and the closure of the duo's integration into a higher-order unity are mirages if seen in the course of time—and time cannot be stopped, not even in the make-believe world of synchronic structuration. Space-time is all there ever is for humans; indeterminacy and irreversibility ultimately rule. Thus, all duos eventually dissolve into pluralities and all singularity is relational—a figure upon an indeterminate ground.

As we have seen, personal existence starts within triangulation in a process characterized by friction and ambivalence (as with the example of Mary, John, and Rita). This is an emotionally charged process that can be understood as a type of betrayal, in the terms proposed by Levinas. This menaced ambivalence remains ever part of personhood and institutes a complex dynamic to the interaction between the three different aspects of personhood: the organic (α), the cognitive (β), and the social (γ).

Although humans have a propensity for thinking in opposites, the fact is that "the relationship between [two terms] has no intrinsic simplicity" (Needham 1987: 224). This means that opposition as a factor of experience is grounded in the human body and on the way in which causal relations are present in

perception (see also S. Siegel 2010: 117ff.). "The principle of opposition is reversible direction; and (directional) opposites are based on the spatial experience
of the human body" (Needham 1987: 71–72). As we saw, a similar argument can
be built for reification and containment, the other two abstract primary factors
of experience identified above.

As such, human categories are guided by practical reason and are, therefore,
ever prone to being polythetic categories (Needham 1975); propositional thinking is a form of acting within sociality, in the sense of engaging in language
games. This should be seen not as a human shortcoming, but as humanity's great-
est strength, as its ultimate capacity for creativity and imagination. As we have
seen above, humans think approximately, through assessment of relative error, in
the sense that *fuzzy logic* has tried to emulate (cf. Zadeh 1987; Kaehler 2015).

What I have been describing for the person's coming into being applies
indeed to all forms of *institution*: that is, all processes through which sociality
grants entity status to certain features of the world (cf. Pina-Cabral 2011). To
institute is to prop up, to hypostatize by situating contextually certain portions
of the world. It is an exercise in prospective memory, as it involves recogniz-
ing that a set of patterns will thenceforth concur. Instituting, thus, is a future-
oriented gesture that invests a set of patterns with conditions of continuity: it is
a project in singularity.

Furthermore, humans are in the world socially owing to the nature of intentionality; thus, the project-nature of instituting (its purposefulness) is necessarily coextensive with sociality.[19] The world's diffuse multiplicity is the basic and
ever-recurring condition; singularity and its partibilities are what human life
produces. Instituting is a process carried out by persons who, being mutually
constituted, are always in the process of becoming singular persons in "presence." What gives rise to the expectation of singularity is what James called
the law of dissociation: the overlap by triangulation of memories between the
persons involved (Mary, John, and Rita, as above).

As such, the condition of instituting is mutuality, not some kind of negotiation between dyadically related partners. This is why a vision of collective

---

19. Cf. Peirce's notion of purpose: "If an interpretation can be grounded, then it must
     have a purpose; for a ground is something that justifies with respect to a purpose. It
     follows that interpretation is purposeful and, hence, that significance exists relatively
     to a possible purpose. But sign interpretation is not limited to human consciousness
     in Peirce's mature semeiotic. Thus, there must be at least the possibility of purposeful
     action without consciousness of purpose" (Short 2007: 54).

rationality as proposed by Jon Elster, for example, will never satisfy anthropologists, as it naturalizes modern Anglo-American individualism and fails to see that sociality is immanent to the person (1983, I.5: 33–42). The mutual engagement between the persons involved is rooted in early ontogeny, a form of primary intersubjectivity anterior to any conscious, linguistically shaped decision making: it has less to do with thinking than with *being in company*. In this sense, the environment of cohabitation where personal ontogeny is launched (the *casa*, *maison*, the primary social unit—see Pina-Cabral 1989) is the original ground for institutional construction.

It is the intentionality of basic mind (i.e., the proneness to address the world by forming purposes) that allows the child to engage with the affordances that the dwelling environment and the adults within it provide it with, turning them into invitations for action (cf. Gibson 1979 and Ingold 2000). But, in turn, for those who surround the child, the potential of fertility in sexual reproduction and eventually the actual newborn child constitute affordances that adults can choose to engage with in the process of family building. Children, thus, as they become persons, do so through a process in which they afford familial relatedness to adults. Therefore, persons are existentially familial, since they are centrally involved in the modes of participation, collaboration, and authority that familial life presumes.

This is a matter that Robert Parkin (2013) addresses in a paper in which he attempts to extricate anthropology from the old dichotomy between "culturally held notions of reproduction" and "biological reproduction" that so engaged culturalist relativists in the second half of the twentieth century. Indeed, we agree with Parkin that this polarity is false (as it sits on the emic/etic distinction) and that it is not necessary to engage it if we realize that transcendence is an inherent part of kinship. Parkin notes that relations of kinship always involve spiritual, ritual, or cosmological formulations that, on the one hand, interact creatively with local understandings of organic reproduction and, on the other hand, operate as modes of association/dissociation of particular persons from relevant contexts of action. For him, kinship transcendence opens up the possibility of "the overcoming of potentially but not necessarily divisive dichotomies to ensure the production of harmony and unity in any collectivity" (ibid.: 10).

This stress on transcendence is much to the point, but personal transcendence as an embracing disposition of persons should not be limited to spirituality or religion: what gives rise to transcendence is the person as it emerges in personal ontogeny (as Heidegger insisted—1988: 299). Transcendence is central to kinship in that a person's capacity to be reflexively aware of his or her own existence (the dissociation that institutes "presence") is a condition for the process of scale-change that institutes collective existence: $(A + B + C) \Rightarrow A'$.[20]

In one sense, of course, collectivity preexists the person in ontogeny, but at the same time it is conditional upon personal transcendence: that is, what mobilizes the institution of collective identity is presence, the capacity of the person in propositional (symbolic) thought to rise out of his or her own world-immersion and reflexively hypostatize his or her own existence. As a function of the process of personal ontogeny, transcendence opens up the way to collective inherence and, therefore, enhances considerably the potential for collective action that distinguishes human sociality from other forms of animal sociality. Kinship, as Parkin intuits, is the essential mode through which separate personal presences come to cohere into collective presences by means of transcendence.

FILIATION AS CAUSALITY

Persons are placed before human reproduction in one of two ways: males and females. That is, in terms of the conception of new humans, males and females are marked by distinct roles, corresponding to distinct bodily features. There are, of course, a number of humans whose bodies are ambiguous, but these are sufficiently exceptional for the binarism of sex to impose itself overwhelmingly: sex is an overriding affordance. This, however, is no exception to other dualities: as it becomes a part of the process of ontogeny, *sex* becomes *gender*. The reason anthropologists emphasize this difference is not due to some sort of vacuous political correctness, but because the ethnographic evidence collected by professional ethnographers throughout the twentieth century strongly suggests that, at the onset of personal ontogeny, the original binarism of body shape and function is turned into a polythetic classification open to redoubling, to complex resignification, to ambivalence, to manipulation.

In short, as with everything else in personal ontogeny, the organic dualism of sex dissolves into the complex mutuality of gender once propositionality establishes itself and presence arises. In particular, the constitutive role of intersubjectivity means that persons are copresent: that is, their sense of personhood is

---

20. We are reminded here of Strathern's notion of holography as explained by Alberto Corsín (2004).

porous and mutually engaged. Since we are all partible, and since we are formed in bigendered environments, no gender identity can be exclusive, unitary or clear-cut.[21] All gendered differentiations will be incomplete, temporary, and approximate in spite of the foundational role they play in sociality.

The second major differentiating feature of early human ontogeny is the fact that humans are not all born at the same time and that some are born as a result of gestures undertaken by others who, in the largest majority of cases, are conscious of the fact that the acts of mating they undertake may redound in the possible affordance of the emergence of a future person. The actual circumstances of conception and gestation may turn out to have important implications later on in the person's life; however, on the whole, in matters of personal ontogeny, these are secondary aspects. Rather, it is the early acts of nursing and caring for the child within a context of cohabitation that institute the major marks of generational differentiation which shape the child's first social associations: that which anthropologists have called "filiation" (see Porqueres 2009). Filiation, therefore, is a form of futurity; yet, seen from the angle of pastness, it is a kind of causal attribution. Mary and John recognized an affordance in their reproductive potential and caused Rita to become a person. In time, the relations of filiation come to be instituted in the dwelling environment, and in this way become increasingly independent of the actual persons involved. They are a personally constitutive attribution of causality.

In different cultures and at different times the formulations of filiation differ considerably, as persons are products of profoundly diversified sociocultural histories. And yet no one denies that a "family resemblance" can be observed among all forms of human filiation. Part of this resemblance certainly results from the fact that sexual reproduction constitutes an "affordance," in that it is both a ready potential for the creation of new persons and a limitation upon social imagination. In fact, primatologists argue that this family resemblance connects us directly with our evolutionary history, for it is due to the specific nature of primate sexuality (e.g., Gettler 2010).

Definitionally, filiation (the parent/child link) embraces maternity, paternity, and filiality. But while the former two are endlessly discussed in the literature, the integration of the three into a field mobilized by the occurrence of *filiality* is seldom analytically considered. Most social and biological anthropologists simply assume that we all agree concerning the meaning of the word *filiation*.

---

21. For an ethnographically based demonstration of this point, see Pina-Cabral (1993).

Yet, anyone who has been attentive to the history of kinship studies in twentieth-century anthropology will agree that the concept has been "a fountain of aporias" (Bonte, Porqueres, and Wilgaux 2011: 16). When we attend to details, we find that there is no agreement at all concerning its meaning or implications. The matter is especially polemical in relation to so-called "biological" and "social" understandings of filiation, namely in the interdisciplinary clash between sociocultural anthropology and evolutionary psychology (Shapiro 2008).

Filiation links people with each other in such a way as to constitute histories of causal linkage: Rita, daughter of Mary, daughter of Herbert, and so on. As Donald Davidson has put it, "A male is a grandfather if he has helped cause a child come into existence who has helped cause another child into existence" (2005: 287). Collective belonging is marked by the generational inscription of the person within a familial history of personal causation. The number of persons who are responsible for bringing the child into the family and for nursing it can be anything from two to many. Filiation, therefore, is not *a* relation between persons, as it used to be presented by the European legal tradition; rather, it is an abstract term that refers to a network of causal relations between persons across time.[22] In the ethnographic record, filiation is often typified as maternal or paternal, but it can be both or neither (see chapter 5): it is a diversified field of relations that place the person vertically in time in terms of a *causal history of personhood*. The important thing to note is that all historically evolved forms of sociality that have come to the attention of anthropologists and historians present strong typifications of a field of relations of this nature. This conforms to the kind of factor of experience that Needham called a paradigmatic scene (1985: 67–69). The modes of relating that such traditions of filiation trigger off carry a long and lasting impact on the person and on the way people come together in collectivities. In turn, in their plurality, such collectivities come to acquire aspects of singularity (*A'*—even what anthropologists have called corporateness; see Fortes 1969: 308).

Recently, the study of the complexities brought about by assisted reproduction has highlighted how the participations out of which the child emerges as a person cannot be typified in the simple triangular terms of what used to

---

22. This is an issue about which we can no longer agree with Rodney Needham. Surprisingly, he seems to have held on to his high structuralist convictions concerning "descent" even in the face of his own later findings concerning human thinking (e.g., 1985: 65).

be called "the nuclear family" (e.g., Edwards and Salazar 2009; contra Shapiro 2008). Rather than focusing on maternity and paternity, as was characteristic in the twentieth century, we must be especially attentive to the conditions of filiality. The infant becomes a person out of a complex process that involves a number of people engaging in practical activities and interacting with each other in the caring environment. This even goes beyond the immediate dwelling group: the permanent presence of more than one family (typified in anthropological history by the figure of the mother's brother) must be taken into consideration. The person is familial both because he/she is brought to personhood within a familial environment and because he/she perceives him/herself as the causal product of participation: from the beginning the child both stands with and stands for other persons (contiguity and surrogation, respectively). The person is a familial person because his or her own sense of who they are, what responsibilities they have, and whom they can closely depend upon is shaped by those who brought them into the family—by the causal history of personhood enshrined in filiation narratives. Different cultural traditions have widely diversified modes of shaping such processes. European tradition, for example, is prone to treating relations of cohabitation as being of a radically separate nature from those of filiation (falsely, as it turns out, even for itself—see Pina-Cabral 1989). To the contrary, the constitution of contexts of cohabitation into collective singularities (*maisons*, households, and suchlike) is the very essence of processes of constitution of the familial person.[23]

Whilst gender belonging appears to be unitary and then turns out to be a central field for partibility, filiation appears to be a multiple, diffuse process and then turns out to be one of the principal processes of producing collective singularity, that is, of producing suprapersonal social entities (*A'*). To that extent, the two major axes of personal differentiation (*gender* and *generation*) are to be seen as synthetic images. They cross each other in one of the most constitutive processes that the ethnographic register has encountered: what we have learned to call, after Lévi-Strauss (1973), *alliance*.

---

23. This is how Emmanuel Levinas puts this idea in his characteristic language: "The 'moments' of that identification [of oneself]—the body, the house, work, the economy—must not be conceived as contingent and empirically given, as if they were stamped on the formal scaffold of the Same. They are the articulations of that structure" (1961: 27).

ALLIANCE AND THE DIVIDUAL

Human sociality is characterized by a horror of the individual, that is, of entities that are not partible. The confrontation between two such entities would be a dead-end; it would yield no fruit. This *horror vacui* is not a charter of some sort, inscribed by a structuralist demiurge upon the heads of humans. Rather, it is the necessary outcome of the need for intersubjectivity in order to produce reflexive persons and to reproduce the species. As a body, a human being is not very dividual, to the extent that one cannot cut it into parts and keep these parts alive. All parts that one slices off a human body are dead waste, and if that partition is sufficiently radical, the whole body even ceases to function. A person ($\alpha + \beta + \gamma$), however, is far more dividual, since slicing the person, reconnecting the person, mixing the person, superimposing the person, and so on—that is, the acts of partibility—are the very constitutive processes of personhood. Persons are *dividuals*, therefore, to the extent that they cannot ever survive as persons whilst remaining closed onto themselves (Mariott 1976; Strathern 1988). This being said, the singularity of personal presence does have to be protected. Although it is permanently challenged through the acts of partibility, personal singularity cannot be simply abolished without serious consequences for the person's social interaction (see de Martino [1959] 2001). This does not apply only to Melanesia or to the depths of Africa; rather, it is a universal condition that applies to every person everywhere—even those who, being enthralled by the utopia of modernity, fancy themselves as fully independent individuals.

Long ago, Lévi-Strauss called our attention to an interesting facet of the ethnographic register. Whilst, biologically speaking, persons are like individual flowers, like specimens of a variety, the fact is that the way societies deal with persons is more akin to the way they deal with species than with individual specimens: "Social life," he argues, "effects a strange transformation in this system, for it encourages each biological individual to develop a personality; and this is a notion no longer recalling specimens within a variety but rather types of varieties or of species" (1966: 214). In the two memorable chapters of *The savage mind* that he dedicates to personal naming, he observes a set of regularities that are confirmed by my own material concerning the comparative study of personal naming in Portuguese-speaking contexts:[24] social practices relating

---

24. Cf. Essays on naming in Portuguese-speaking contexts (Pina-Cabral 2010c, 2010d, 2012a, 2013b, 2016).

to the naming of persons (and domesticated animals) are ambivalently placed before singleness and plurality. Proper naming works actively at constructing dividuality, affirming the intrinsic plurality of what is identified as single.

What this means is that the history of our species, as a history of sociality, has come up with modes of producing persons that ensure the intrinsic plurality of the person. This is primarily done through filiation, as defined above. If contexts of cohabitation leading to human reproduction were closed onto themselves (i.e., if "houses" were individual entities), they would be closed to the ever-pulsating dynamic of history: a history of sociality; a history of relating; a history of humans causing other humans to exist. I suppose that was the principal lesson that Radcliffe-Brown and Lévi-Strauss had to deliver to us concerning kinship and the role of the mother's brother (Racliffe-Brown [1940] 1952; Lévi-Strauss 1973). Two objects that are closed within themselves may confront each other but they cannot connect. The human species would not have survived, considering the enormous dependence that it has on sociality (and communication) for survival, if its constitutive elements, persons, were individual units.

As such, throughout history, we observe that new persons are never produced by fissiparous processes out of singular persons. Similarly, at a suprapersonal level (A'), the entities of cohabitation where early ontogeny unfolds (the primary social units—the house, *maison*, the kraal; see Pina-Cabral 1989) are also necessarily plural. As Radcliffe-Brown commented long ago, all social contexts known to anthropologists and historians have instituted modes of filiation which ensure that each person is connected to at least two different histories of sociality (Radcliffe-Brown and Forde 1950: 4). One may lack a father or a mother (to simplify the description), but one is better off if (having both) these come from different historical chains of filiation.[25]

What seems relevant to retain here is that, whilst scholars have normally described this feature of human history as a prohibition (the *incest prohibition*), it seems more adequate not to see it as a prohibition but as an *affordance*: the increased benefits to human communication derived from persons being founded on essential partibility, on a diversity of the histories of personhood (filiation).

---

25. Nevertheless, it is probably necessary to insist that we are *not* here keeping to Lévi-Strauss' original definition of alliance as the exchange of women among groups of men. We have come a long way since then. A much closer source of inspiration is Viveiros de Castro's discussion of "cannibal alliance" (2007; for an ethnographic instancing of the argument, see Pina-Cabral and Silva 2013: 123–43).

Alliance, therefore, as a constitutive process of human sociality, is rooted in personal ontogeny and *not* in "marriage."[26] This position is a radical break with the basic assumptions that dominated anthropological kinship theory throughout the twentieth century. Whether a society has or fails to have an institution akin to the institution of marriage that evolved in Europe from the late Middle Ages is beside the point (cf. Rivière [1971] 2004). The central feature is that a person's integration in sociality is maximized by their being constitutively plural. Children's dual life connections (double affiliation) must be seen *not* as an instance of ambivalence (as Sahlins suggests—2011b: 236) but, to the contrary, as the very ground on which sociality is stochastically constituted and collectivity instituted—that is the upshot of Lévy-Bruhl's and Strathern's prophetic lessons.

The latter formulated this dialectic of mutuality in the following terms: "Single, composite persons do not reproduce. Although it is only in a unitary state that one can, in fact, join with another to form a pair, it is dyadically conceived relationships that are the source and outcome of action. The products of relations—including the persons they create—inevitably have dual origins and are thus internally differentiated" (Strathern 1988: 14). This internal differentiation is the dynamic principle (the spring, *fons*) that ensures the continuity of human sociality in history; and whilst that was already the case in all forms of sexed reproduction in the animal kingdom, in the case of humans it is a condition for the emergence of the more complex (richer) forms of human communication and, in particular, language.

CONCLUSION

The dividuality of the person means that those who, as a result of the operation of filiation, are brought up together in a context of cohabitation are again deeply divided by *gender*, as the earlier *generation* also was. The sibling group emerges out of the crossing of filiation with generation and constitutes the founding nucleus of larger superdomestic kin groupings (kindred, lineage, clan, etc.).

When I speak of sibling group, I mean to define it, of course, not as the children of a common mother and father, but rather as the group of contemporaries who have been brought up together by the same persons in close proximity of cohabitation and care. Each cultural tradition has different forms of

---

26. For an ethnographic instancing, see Pina-Cabral (2010d).

defining these modes of association, but their being rooted in the sibling group must be seen as broadly general to the human condition, as a primary factor of experience—much as indeed Radcliffe-Brown ([1940] 1952) found out when he argued for the unity of siblings. Such siblings cohere into a kind of unity, but they are constitutionally plural, since they bring together in themselves the separate familial histories of their parents—they are bearers of more than one *continued identity*. Gender, however, comes again between them, for their own children, much like them, have to have different historical sources (owing to the advantages of alliance), so the sibling group has to split in some way or another (often along gender lines).

And, whilst the plurality of siblingship is reinstated upon adulthood, its essential singularity also reimposes itself; siblings remain company to each other in some sort of constitutionally deep form to the end of their lives—their primary solidarities do not simply vanish into thin air with the onset of adulthood. Furthermore, as classificatory fathers or mothers, or as mother's brothers or father's sisters (these are used here as conventional anthropological labels to describe vast areas of similarity in the ethnographic register), they reproduce their condition of company (their histories of personhood) to the following generation.

In this way, families over time are structured by a criss-crossing of *continued identities*: a set of markers in the world that frame people's constitutive actions of personhood in terms of the constitutive actions of those who preceded them in the causal chain of personhood: as the Lovedu of northern South Africa used to say, the bride follows the cattle's footprints upon the sand—she follows the traces of her own mother's marriage payment (Krige and Krige 1965). Upon such simple props are constructed the gigantic edifices of kinship systems that continue to puzzle anthropologists today quite as much as they did in the past. Much of our puzzlement, however, continues to be driven by our distaste for fuzziness, polythetic classification, partibility, dividuality, non-wellfounded sets, incompleteness, and indeterminacy. We are prone to search for structuration, equilibrium, and unitariness, and, as we do that, we turn what is complex and ultimately indeterminate into a paradox to be struggled against.

And so, at the end of this summary statement, we come back to Donald Davidson's notion of *company*—as when he claims that "the possibility of thought comes with company" (2001: 88). But while company—cohabiting the world—is the indispensable condition for personhood, personal transcendence is what institutes collectivity. In this chapter, we have dealt with personhood from a comparative perspective. In tracing the steps of ontogeny, we saw how they were also steps of world constitution. The aim, at every point, was not to sever from each other the three aspects of personal ontology ($\alpha + \beta + \gamma$). In order to do that, we relied on the lessons concerning embodied cognition accumulated from previous chapters. In the chapter to come, we will focus on world again and how human social life is necessarily based on collectively shared configurations of world. These, in turn, assume specific modes of personhood.

CHAPTER FIVE

Worldview

The ideal is to return home, for
"The only place one never returns to is the womb."

– Eileen and Jacob Krige (1965: 323)

In his introduction to Kant's *Anthropology*, Foucault stresses how the aging master's lectures about world were structured by three concerns that were transformations of the three original questions that had guided his youthful *Critiques*:

> The corollary of the possibility of conceiving of other worlds—this one being,
> *de facto*, only a domain—is the impossibility of moving beyond the world we
> inhabit and the imperious necessity of accepting its *frontiers as limits*. Thus the
> world, once again taken to mean the *"Inbegriff des Daseins,"* appears on the basis
> of the three-part structure . . . of *source, domain*, and *limit*. (Foucault [1961] 2008:
> 82, original emphasis)

Thus transformed, Kant's critical questions become the guiding concerns for
the establishment of his Anthropology, that is, an undertaking for which, by
its very nature, human being "is neither a *homo natura* nor a purely free subject;
[rather] he is caught by the syntheses already operated by his relationship to
the world" (ibid.: 54–55). Foucault explains that anthropology works with the

broken symmetry[1] resulting from the unsteady conjugation in presence (β) of the synthesis produced by the organism (α) and the limits imposed by human interaction (γ).

As it happens, this classification echoes closely Heidegger's three moments of occurrence of the Dasein: "(1) holding the binding character of things towards us; (2) completion; (3) unveiling the being of beings" ([1929/30] 1995: 348). However, Heidegger's formulation turns out to be less convenient than the one proposed by Foucault/Kant (cf. Godlove 1996), since our contemporary discovery that intentionality refers to phenomenal experience that does not involve mental content—that is, representation—will necessarily alter significantly Heidegger's understandings of being-in-the-world (Hutto and Myin 2013). In fact, contemporary biologists have been demonstrating how surprisingly complex forms of collective behavior depend not on preconceived patterns or on central control, but on the chain reactions of local responses among the different participants in a set environment. Ants, birds, and fish (and, of course, humans in crowd behavior) move not according to previously conceived (collective) designs but by assessing each one's convenience in the surrounding world.[2]

Our personhood is indissolubly linked with the world we live in and its history. People's world worlds in a social way; it is held by persons whose ontogenies are perspectivally focused on dwelling environments and histories of personhood that preexist the person. As Davidson put it, "The correct interpretation of what a speaker means is not determined solely by what is in his head: it depends on the natural history of what is in his head" (2001: 44). *Pastness* is the feature of world that allows the person to carry out his or her path of ontogeny within the complex jungle of broken symmetries that we are bodily endowed to attune to (Lederman and Hill 2004; Thompson 2007: 71).

In the above chapters, as we examined the conditions of possibility of personhood, we came to the conclusion that there were three aspects to personhood and that these correspond closely to aspects of world. In short, the world of persons worlds in three principal modes that correspond to the three aspects of personhood (see diagram 3):

---

1. He calls it "dissymmetrical symmetry."
2. See Iain Couzin: https://www.youtube.com/watch?v=_2WqH_HUxz8; or Deborah Gordon: http://www.ted.com/talks/deborah_gordon_what_ants_teach_us_about_the_brain_cancer_and_the_internet#t-59396 (accessed January 11, 2017).

(i/α)   world offers itself as a space-time of existence (it embraces as *source*);

(ii/*b*)   world places the person perspectivally (it encompasses as *domain*);

(iii/γ)   world establishes modes of containment (allowing for *limits* to emerge stochastically over time).

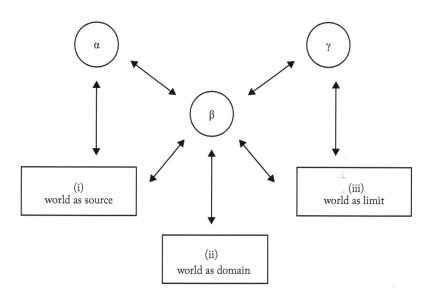

Diagram 3. The aspects of person and world.

The arena of presence and action (β) constitutes the mediating process—the root of propositionality—that allows for the other two aspects (α and γ) to co-here. But personal presence is also what allows for world to encompass person as a *domain* of action (ii) and thus to mediate between the world that worlds (i, world as *source)*, and the bounded world of shared human imagination (iii, the *limited* world), that is to say, for essence to emerge out of existence. Thus, as the world of persons is ontologically dependent on personal presence, which is a form of transcendence,[3] it is ever moved by the unstable dynamics of personal partibility. Therefore, as we will see in this chapter, it is a matter not of there being many worlds rather than one, but of world being metaphysically plural.

---

3.   As Heidegger put it, "If it is indeed in transcendence alone that beings come to light as beings, transcendence comprises an *exceptional domain* for the elaboration of all questions that concern beings as such, i.e., in their being" (1998: 123, original emphasis).

Where our contemporary understanding parts ways with the long and pres-
tigious tradition of querying world that Kant, Heidegger, Foucault, or Derrida
represents is in the matter of consciousness (cf. Gaston 2013). In the wake of
Francisco Varela, many of us have come to question the anthropocentric tendency to see reflexive consciousness as the defining instance of thought and
thus to distance ourselves from the founding assumptions of the European
philosophical tradition. António Damásio, for example, makes a clear distinction between core consciousness, that is, the reflexive awareness of thought in
human adults, and extended consciousness, the diffuse sense of self-interest that
is associated to intentionality (1999: 15–19). In this book, we have avoided the
word *consciousness* precisely because of the way it creates the conditions for us to
fall back on anthropocentric assumptions concerning mind, which unwittingly
naturalize Augustinian notions of "soul" (cf. Givens 2009).

This chapter will move from the personal to the collective, attempting to
show how the two scales are mutually dependent. An examination of what constitutes sociality will open the way to the formulation of a methodologically
richer notion of worldview. The chapter concludes with an examination of relatedness as the central formal tool of social analysis.

SOCIALITY

To be alive is often defined as "accurately transmitting a genetic blueprint"
(Kirschner, Gerhart, and Mitchison 2000: 79); that is, living beings are self-
organizing to the extent that they operate a continuity of form in the face of a
constant change of composition. Organisms operate a boundary system: "A cell
. . . is a self-sustaining unity, a unity that dynamically produces and maintains
its own identity in the face of what is other" (Thompson 2007: 147). This means,
as Kant had already noted, that organisms are endowed with purpose. Therefore,
intentionality (in the sense of acting with purpose) is a constitutive property
that is immanent to all living organisms and is implicit in their operation. Nevertheless, it is very important not to assume that "purpose" here means conscious
reason: even in humans, collective behavior is often ruled by interactions that
are not consciously held (see Dyer et al. 2009).

According to Francisco Varela, the purposiveness of living organisms implies two complementary modes: *identity*, the maintenance of sameness before dynamic change; and *sense making*, the establishment of an organizational

perspective achieved through attraction or repulsion, that is, a scale of value (see Thompson 2007: 147, 154). Such are the roots of intentionality, out of which evolved the intentionality of more complex species and, eventually, after language emerged, human propositionality. In a very influential paper called "Biological foundations of individuality" (1968), the philosopher Hans Jonas characterizes this identity of living beings and the corresponding relation of self-isolation from the rest of reality as a form of "individuality" ("The realm of individuality, in all its grades, is coextensive with the biological realm as a whole"—ibid.: 233). In his view, to the extent that organisms enjoy "an independence from the same matter of which [they] nonetheless wholly consist" (ibid.: 237), one is entitled to speak of a "sort of freedom." Organisms are purposeful to the extent that they exercise this freedom: that is, they respond to a necessity, "namely, the need for constant self-renewal, and thus need for the matter required in that renewal, and thus need for 'world'." (ibid.: 241) One may, therefore, conclude that, in its more embracing aspect (i), world is a function of organic life.

Continuity in living organisms is no longer achieved by "the mere inertial persistence of substance," as in Heidegger's proverbial stone, but requires execution, that is, an effort to remain the same. World and its worlding are thus implicit in the very effort that organisms undertake to maintain their internal system when faced with their changing constitution. As Jonas puts it, the organism's being, "suspended in possibility, is to be actualized by the *use* of the world" (ibid.: 242, original emphasis). The roots of the simplest forms of transcendence, therefore, lie in this kind of being-projected-beyond-oneself of intentionality as mental directedness (see Thompson 2007: 156–57).

This process, however, is importantly qualified when multicellular organisms emerge, as they depend on "a partial obliteration of that degree of individuality which had been achieved already in the original, protozoic units of life" (Jonas 1968: 244). Thus, sociality involves importantly the qualification of the unicity of the organism, and, in particular, it involves the need for information. Note, information here is meant in the sense of what is conveyed by a particular arrangement or sequence of things, not in the sense of an item of propositional knowledge.

In Jonas' formulation, individuality is defined as "discontinuity with the world." Thus, he believes that the early multicellular condition is an interruption of a process of growing "individuality" in evolution. He argues, however, that individuality imposes itself again in more organized forms of life and eventually achieves itself in humans. As a matter of fact, he formulates the passage from vegetable to animal life in such terms. It is principally in this insistence on the unitariness of individualism that we must part ways with his proposal. Although he agrees that the organism cannot be seen as a monad, he then fails to address the ambivalent and complex nature of interaction involved in cell constitution and reproduction (see Kirschner, Gerhart, and Mitchison 2000).

When people choose to use the language of individuality, they are forced to play down how, in living processes, singularity and plurality constitute correlated modes, not separate conditions. In assuming individuality, we are then obliged to see sociality as a process that does not simply supervene upon but actually exists beyond the emergence of life. This, however, creates more problems than it solves. The identity and sense making of living organisms does involve a process of boundary maintenance, but organisms (and particularly multicellular organisms) cannot be conceived as separate or closed onto themselves, otherwise how would they reproduce? That means that the existence of organisms hovers between singularity and plurality, in an unstable dynamic that is better qualified as dividuality than individuality.

In this way, one is bound to agree with Jonas and Varela that life implies sense making; which, in turn, implies world. The problem is, again, if this sense making is seen in individualist terms, we are stuck with a formalist definition of life ("an island of form amidst a sea of matter and energy"—Thompson 2007: 152) that runs counter to what we know about evolution. It would seem, then, that the widespread adoption of the concept of "individual" in recent biological debates is less innocuous than it may at first seem. As we have seen, in the case of human beings, the concept fails to describe the essential constitutive dynamics of personhood. But, once transposed to debates about other organisms, it is no more satisfactory and it carries with itself profound anthropocentric implications.[4]

Keeping in mind Davidson's warning about the dangers of the scheme/content opposition (1974), life's dependence on self-identity and sense making is best seen in terms of in-formation—a process of response to world that relies on symmetry, the reproduction of sameness, an original feature of all matter

---

4.   As when, for example, one moves seamlessly from discussions of collective movement in animals to considerations concerning American-style electoral democracy—see Iain Couzin's lecture on democratic consensus:
https://www.youtube.com/watch?v=YzvTMwBD0ZA&nohtml5=False (accessed January 12, 2017).

(Lederman and Hill 2004).[5] "In many biological systems the first step in generating spatial complexity is the breakdown of a symmetrical into a more organized asymmetric or polarized structure" (Kirschner, Gerhart, and Mitchison 2000: 80). Thus, the primitive type of self which Varela proposes should not be interpreted in terms of an opposition of individual versus collective, for that would have closed us in a mechanical process of symmetric alterity, where identity and alterity alternate and the units become isolated monads. Rather, the primitive selfhood of life's sense making is better qualified as a dynamic dividuality which is stochastically moved (the result of world's worlding, that is, the constant production of broken symmetry leading to asymmetric alterity). I believe this is the ultimate drive of Lévi-Strauss' lesson in that beautifully evocative note, one of the last things he ever wrote, that he calls "An apology of amoebas" (2000).

In sum, as a disposition to act jointly for a shared purpose, that is, to act collectively for survival, sociality should be seen as the way dividuality operates in intentionality. It requires the passing of information between the singular members of the species by relation to that purpose. The world into which each member of a species enters is already marked by the modes of communication of that species. To that extent, when a new member emerges to life, the pathways of sociality are already outlined in the world and in the behavior of other members of the species. So much applies to all forms of life, as Lévi-Strauss argued. In humans, sociality occurs because intentionality potentiates worlding. The whole edifice of personhood and propositionality, as described in chapter 4 above, is only possible owing to the dynamics of life.

Sociality, therefore, antedates historically the emergence of the human species and, through intentionality, it remains active in humans beyond the emergence of conscious thought. By refusing to polarize the individual v. group opposition, the focus of our analysis shifts from *essence and identity* to *transformation and alterity*. We reject a symmetric, essence-driven view of the human condition. As we move back away from essence, human existence comes to be seen as one among many manifestations of life. Following on this path, mind reveals itself as an embodied, indeterminate, and underdetermined process that reaches beyond the boundaries of the organic person and, therefore, is

---

5.   "Metazoan multicellular development, as it has evolved in the past billion years, is an accomplishment in the informational realm, that is, of organizing cellular processes spatially and temporally" (Kirschner, Gerhart, and Mitchison 2000: 83).

constantly moved by the anterior alterity of worlding. Emphasis is given to the way thought is embodied and how it must be understood as a form of action (see Prinz and Clark 2004).

Kant's three original questions in the *Critiques* (What can I know? What must I do? And what can I hope for?—Foucault [1961] 2008) are decentered by such a view of sociality; one that fully owns up to an ambivalent response to a fourth question that integrates the former three (What is man?). From a post-structuralist perspective such as espoused in this book, "person" not "man" is the relevant level. Yet personhood lacks essentiality. So, even though it is ambivalent and indeterminate, the subject does not simply vanish. Rather, as person, he/she turns out to be metaphysically plural.

THE SCAFFOLDING OF MIND

Human mind is extended in that mental operations are not closed within the brain. Rather, recently, we have come to accept that, to the extent that it is embodied, cognition "seeps out onto the world" (Clark and Chalmers 1998; Clark 2010). By that, we mean that, on the one hand, the brain is not the exclusive seat of cognition and, on the other hand, mind's operation depends crucially on a whole realm of nonconscious processes and forms of long-term stored information (see Chemero 2009). Once we realize that mind is an interactive process with world that occurs in the brain, in the body, and beyond the body in the affordances of world that constitute vital information to live beings, the very meaning of cognition is radically decentered. This has an important implication, which is that Lévy-Bruhl's insight that persons *participate* in each other and in the objects around them ([1949] 1998) is to be seen no longer as some sort of symbolic or metaphoric event of consciousness, but instead as rooted in the process of constitution of information that founds our very embodiment. If mind seeps out onto the world, it is not only the prostheses of modernity (the mobile phone, the computer, the spoon, the pen) that come to extend it, but also the seepages, so to speak, that have always been part of our personal ontogeny. This makes participation a far less mysterious occurrence, but it also goes a long way in helping us see how complex is the scaffolding of mind.

As outlined above, during early personal ontogeny, the child discovers itself as other—that is, anterior alterity launches presence by means of a process of triangulation. The person is distanced from him- or herself, not internally—as a self-contained process—but by relation to world. It is a structuring of scales. As arenas of presence and action (β), persons approach themselves from the outside, as if they had been other. Propositionality implies an inscription of mind in the world. This scaffolding of mind involves both a closing in on the arena of presence and action and a distancing from it. This statement may seem paradoxical, but the impression vanishes once (a) we realize that ontogeny is a temporally complex process and (b) we abandon the all-or-nothing fallacy and accept that α, β, and γ occur stochastically, not mechanically (i.e., in terms of greater or smaller recurrence rather than in terms of dualistically formulated oppositions).

What this means is that, in ontogeny, the person acquires the means to store meaning in objects, and thus the world is invested with meaning. It is no longer only the person addressing world, but world now that addresses the person. This is why presence is world forming, as Heidegger insisted. The access to symbolic signification (as opposed to iconic or indexical signification—as per Peirce; cf. Short 2007) involves a scaffolding of mind, of which language is the principal but not the only tool. A hole in the wall of a grotto is an affordance of passage, quite as much as a door is. But, for the person who confronts it, the door also affords meaning by relation to who built it, for what purpose, and with what implications concerning the social use of space.

In short, the scaffolding of mind in propositionality is the process through which human meaning comes to humans as essence, that is, as existing outside themselves. Scaffolding is a way of investing intention (the purposive facet of sociality) with an existence that is separate from the immediate act of intending, and it can only be achieved by virtue of the distancing that presence institutes. The emergence of presence and the entry into propositionality are, therefore, codependent and occur coevally during early personal ontogeny. That is probably the principal lesson that we can take today from Saint Anselm's Ontological Proof.

Thus, in the case of humans, *pastness* (the impact of γ on α via the world) affirms itself through the process of worlding, even after the person enters into propositional thinking (β). But so does the investment in the future that the shared purpose of sociality necessarily entails. As a mode of imagination, *futurity* is as limiting as pastness. Indeed, as we have already shown, primary factors, synthetic images, paradigmatic scenes, are limits to the imagination as much in pastness as in futurity. They are central facets of the scaffolding of mind.

Each one of us, as we become persons, emerges to a dynamic social world that is a given to the extent that it is already marked as a space-time of purposeful action. Therefore, all human experience is imbued with collective inherence (γ). But humans, as opposed to other species, do something more than other animals: they are world forming. To that extent, human life is both given and built upon. In the case of humans, owing to the achievement of propositionality, the world-forming disposition alters the nature of what is given. Entering into personhood (the emergence of β) is concurrent with entering into language and that involves the sharing of forms of life. As the meaning of a person's words is dependent upon the objects and events "that have caused the person to hold the words to be applicable" (Davidson 2001: 37), people who dwell in close proximity share a form of life. This is how I understand what Wittgenstein meant when he declared that "what has to be accepted, the given, is—so one could say—forms of life." He then defined forms of life as "the use that gives life to signs" ([1953] 1967, II xi: 226; § 432: 128), which approximates it to Mauss' notion of *habitus* ([1935] 2007) or to Bateson's notion that there is an "economics of adaptability" associated to "habit formation" (1972: 257).

A stochastic process occurs within each one of us whereby some associations turn out to be favored over others. Forms of life, then, correspond to recurrent pathways of retention of associations; they are traditions of interpretation. Each historically located sociocultural environment provides evidence to the ethnographer of internal features of figuration that reflect the fact that world is a habitable environment where persons are cared for during early ontogeny and remain exercising choices over time. It is the ethnographer's main task to attempt to characterize which associations are more recurrently retained, that is, to postulate a *worldview*.

The emergence of a form of life, however, is marked by the very constraints of achieving collective action that are implicit in our intentional engagement with world. Since mutuality is constitutive of the person, all of us carry solidarities that mark our presence and that shape our choices within a world that is always already marked by modes of sociality—including continued identities. Value emerges out of the choices of intentionality. Implicit in that is an uneven distribution among persons of the capacity to influence the actions of others. As configurations emerge, therefore, a structure of domination is shaped. In sum, because scaffolding means that meanings are imposed on the person, in delineating worldview, ethnographers are bound to deal with the way in which each social environment is configured in terms of power.

WORLDVIEW BESIEGED

In characterizing world, anthropologists and philosophers are prone to using visual or tactile metaphors: you *approach* world, you have the world *at hand,* you see the world from a certain *angle,* you have a world*view,* you assume a *perspective.* Over and beyond the debate as to whether the centrality of vision is a modern European fixation or not (cf. Bloch 2008), the fact is that these metaphors carry three central features that are related to the way the world worlds.

The first is that people are prone to think in terms of combined environments (scapes)—with the implication of mental holism. The second is the perspectival nature of people's sense of situatedness. Now, situatedness (a feature of "basic minds") is not only a momentary thing, for (a) it implies dwelling, both for humans and animals,[6] and (b) there is purposefulness in it. Intentionality as an engagement with world is future-directed, it bears purpose (Short 2007: 44). The third feature is that space-time is marked by boundaries: containment and categorical differentiation are at work from the very beginning, as they are written into the physical environment where the person emerges.

This chapter will outline the principal features that make *worldview* a useful methodological tool for ethnographic comparison. Much has been written in anthropology about worldview, but, like Michael Kearney in his *Annual Review* article of 1975, I have to admit that, paradoxically, very little has been made of it. My suggestion is that the reason why that is the case is the same that explains why Kearney's contribution too leaves one disappointed. He defines worldview as "culturally specific cognition" (1975: 247), which strikes one as an attempt to state that people have worldviews to the extent that they think of the world in culturally standardized manners. The same problem is present in the use that anthropologists have given to Foucault's "episteme" or to Mary Douglas' "cosmologies." They all depend on the Durkheimian category of collective representation and on representationalist models of mind.

But there is also an empirical problem here. As Kearney himself acknowledges, the issue of the worldview's integration is a thorny one (1975: 249); the more you look for it, the less apparent it becomes. The indeterminacy of meaning precisely implies that cognition is always personal and, thus, worldviews will always be approximate things, subject to the vagaries of the negotiation

---

6.   As ethologists have long argued, "home" is centrally constituted by two processes: a "goal of flight" and a "place of maximal security" (Ingold 1995: 73).

of interpersonal power. Whilst it is possible to think of a worldview that com-
pounds other worldviews, it is nonsense to hope to achieve an ultimate, atem-
poral worldview. But does that mean "world does not exist," as Markus Gabriel
proposes?

Many philosophers are known to disparage of worldview. Gabriel, for example, exclaims "all worldviews are equally misguided insofar as they ground
our beliefs in a commitment to an overall world that already settles all big questions behind our back" (2015: 13). Derrida would agree (Garrison 1999; Gaston
2013), yet this position ails from two serious, albeit separate, problems. Firstly,
the commitment to the ultimate existence of world does not mean that we can
dispense with the indeterminacy of meaning; that we can somehow imagine
that it is possible to move outside of the human condition. Because something
remains indeterminate, it does not mean it does not exist. Gabriel's proposal
that we should impose artificial limits to the project of science by separating
"world" from "universe" is unwarranted, as it is based on a populist application
of the all-or-nothing fallacy to the basic metaphysical challenge.[7]

Secondly, in any case, our concern as anthropologists is not to validate the
"objectivity" of worldviews. The ethnographer (or the anthropologist, for that
matter) does not need to validate or invalidate worldview, that is, the proneness of humans in sociality to produce and reproduce *habitus* and to agree to a
large extent concerning a scaffolding of world. Rather, we only aim to understand how *they* do it. Incomplete and ambivalent as worldviews always are, for
anthropologists, they are central facets of the evidence we are called upon to
interpret as ethnographers and social scientists. We have all learned too little
from Malinowski's comments about how his informants did not produce whole
pictures of what they believed and how he was forced to piece together his ethnography not only from what they said but also from what they did and how
they reacted to his prodding.

Personally, I have found the concept of worldview very useful in the various
ethnographies I have undertaken over the years (see 1986; 2002a; Pina-Cabral
and Silva 2013) and, in this final chapter, I want to suggest that there are ways
of mobilizing it that relate it usefully to the notion of "forms of life" presented
above. A worldview, in this sense, would be an ethnographer's presentation of

---

7.   His defense of the irreducible essence of the German concept of *Geist*, whilst calling
      itself "realism," is in fact a politically disturbing example of a contemporary trend
      that opens the path to unwarranted forms of ontological pluralism (2015: 142).

the major figurations that she found to be recurrent in a particular form of life that she has explored ethnographically. The concept can be usefully interpreted in a way that avoids the sociocentric pitfalls that beset the more traditional notions of "culture" or "society."

Before that, however, we must briefly address the attacks on the notion of worldview that have recently been produced by both Tim Ingold (2010) and Eduardo Viveiros de Castro (2010). They go at it together, but funnily enough from almost opposite directions. Viveiros de Castro's attack is based on a framing of his opponents' views that, on the whole, denies the wealth and complexity of present-day anthropological consensus. He attributes excessively unsophisticated views to those who do not agree with him. He concludes his argument by claiming that

> No one denies that there are culturally specific phenomena (however one wants to define culture), nor that there are some cognitive tendencies and dispositions that characterize our species as a whole (and some others all primates, some others still all mammals, and so on). . . . To me the question seems to be if such commonalities and particularities are deployed in a unidimensional continuum or if, instead, there exists a *radical* heterogeneity in what we call cognition, as seems to be the case as much on the phenomenal or objective plane . . . as in that of styles of investigation. (Viveiros de Castro 2010: 331, my emphasis)

His argument stands or falls on a polarization between two alternatives that cannot possibly be seen as alternative. Firstly, the belief that the anthropological notion of worldview (and its associated single-world thesis) implies that all "communalities and particularities" will have to be placed in a "unidimensional continuum" is unwarranted—metaphysical pluralism has been recognized by many in anthropology for a very long time. If the argument, however, is that it is not only the content that changes between what he calls "cultures" but also the scheme, one is bound to respond, then, that the very scheme–content opposition must be cast aside (see Davidson 1974).

Secondly, "a radical heterogeneity in cognition" is not a necessary alternative. Radical surely is a matter of quantity (how radical?). If by radical we mean absolutely radical (i.e., no similarity in cognition whatsoever), then Viveiros de Castro would not be able to write the first part of his sentence, nor would he be able to have obtained any knowledge of the Araweté form of life. But if by radical we mean a whole lot, than there is little argument to be had, since we all agree on the complexity of metaphysical pluralism in the human world—we are all precisely, much like him, trying to establish the limits of human imagination.

To the contrary, according to Tim Ingold, the principal problem with the concept of worldview is that it assumes that those who view different things do the viewing in just the same form. He does have a point here that deserves to be noted. The drawback, however, will be significantly reduced if we remember that, in the first place, as he puts it, "difference is a function of positionality, within a continuous universe of relations" (2010: 353) and, in the second place, this is once again the product of a modern proclivity to presume that world is outside and view is inside. If we consider that world is everything that exists, we must conclude that it includes the embodied cognitive dispositions that make humans differ. Again, worldview is only a problem for so long as one continues (willingly or by lack of attention) to entertain a representationalist view of mind.

The configuring of world happens within historical human sociality as a fuzzy process that remains ever incomplete—that is what gives rise both to the freedom of transcendence that Levinas (1961) thematized and to the instability of presence that Ernesto de Martino observed ([1959] 2001). As a constant process of error correction (orientation and disorientation), the figuration of world is the result of the operation of indeterminacy and underdetermination, not the contrary. Furthermore, the material roots of more complex forms of propositional structuration (the sort of thing that anthropologists have called "cosmologies") never wrench themselves free of basic cognition, of the embodied organic dispositions of human beings. Humans build the world of content-bearing propositions in language and symbolic behavior by means of processes of imagination that are themselves embodied dispositions (namely, opposition, containment, reification). I repeat: behind scaffolded minds there always remain basic minds, as their absolute condition of possibility. The "poor" world of animals, as Heidegger would have it, is the ground upon which worlding in humans is based. In short, the worldviews that ethnographers postulate cannot possibly be described in representational fashion (as if they were "emic," that is). This is why we need not worry about the fact that the Kiriwina never managed to explain to Malinowski a theory of human reproduction that they manifestly possessed. He had to work it out on the basis of a multiplicity of observations of a varied nature: his abstraction, their structuration of the world.

In their monographs, ethnographers are primarily engaged in capturing the trends that result from numberless processes of fuzzy adjustment (error correction) within actual historically shaped contexts of human sociality. A "tribe" does not "have" a "culture"; rather, humans are constantly configuring their world and struggling with each other within it. And they do not do so necessarily only in conscious forms, by means of linguistically shared concepts. Intentionality as a future-directed engagement with world is going on all the time. As Peirce would note, "Any act of attention interprets an index; [but] it does not have to be an act that is a component of a thought" (Short 2007: 52).

The epistemological status of a worldview, therefore, is that of a hypothesis built by the ethnographer; a worldview is the way the ethnographer found of identifying the central structuring elements in a historically delimited form of life. Ethnographers are not representing people's thoughts, as the representationalist vulgate would have it; they are outlining the pathways within which persons are prone to move in the world. Many methodological discussions over the past two decades might have been avoided if it had been clearly understood that (a) what the ethnographer describes is part of world, but (b) it exists as stochastic recurrence, not as mental content ("knowledge," "ideas"). Worldviews are hypotheses, not anatomies, as David Maybury-Lewis brilliantly put it so long ago (1974: 295).

THE GOALPOSTS OF PRESENCE

Let us now return to the idea that ethnographers are expected to clarify not only what beings there are for the people they study (their ontology) but also how these beings constitute meaningful relations within a world (their metaphysics). Owing to the centrality of personhood, it cannot be a surprise that its modes of variation and its diverse forms of constitution should be one of the central topics of the ethnographic tradition.

World as "the manifestness of beings . . ." (Heidegger [1929/30] 1995: 304) arises in worlding, but it is through triangulation with other persons who are already persons in specific ways that presence emerges, thus opening ego to propositional thinking.[8] The process of ontogeny is one where the modes of

---

8.   Just to allay a justified possible confusion, it is worth clarifying that, therefore, mine is *not* a "metaphysics of presence" in the sense that Derrida gives to the word: "the doctrine of eternal, immutable presence that conceals and denies temporality, contingency, and change supposedly yielding objects of indubitable knowledge" (Garrison 1999: 3).

being person that are predominant in a particular social environment (γ) mobilize the organic person who is already engaged in worlding (α) to develop an arena of presence and action (β). This latter, therefore, is a bridge, a necessary mediator, between a being for whom the world manifests itself intentionally and a being for whom the world manifests itself propositionally. Personal presence (β)—uncertain and evanescent as this presence may be—is nevertheless the condition for a full engagement in human sociality. As such, one of the central tasks confronting the ethnographer is to outline the parameters of personhood that characterize the specific "form of life" that she is studying.

We are bound, therefore, to focus on the notion of *presence* before we proceed, particularly in its association with action and transcendence. Whilst persons are everywhere endowed with presence and attributable action, the manner in which this is done differs profoundly from social context to social context. Modes of presence and of attribution of action can differ considerably across the ethnographic register (cf. Pina-Cabral 2002a: 105–27). Furthermore, examples of pluralized (and serial) presence, as in the case of spirit possession in São Tomé Island (cf. Valverde 2000) or in Brazilian Umbanda (cf. Maggie 1975), demonstrate clearly that a unified continuous presence (a self), as naturalized by contemporary Anglo-American individualist ideology, should not be accepted as a valid description of personhood anywhere. And then again, the relation between presence and the attribution of action cannot also be assumed as simple. Personal dividuality and mutuality have historically evinced very diverse modalities. We will return to this idea below.

However, once again, the principal risk here for the comparativist is to succumb to the all-or-nothing fallacy. For, in spite of the diversity, the constitution of an arena of presence and action and the perceived need to safeguard it in the face of death, enslavement, or oppression are general features of human sociality—they are primary factors of experience. In the following discussion, I am particularly indebted to two totally unrelated accounts: Ernesto de Martino's ethnography of southern Italian magical formulas ([1959] 2015) and Mark Johnston's theological treatment of personhood and death (2010). What brings them together is that they both share a preoccupation with transcendence in their descriptions of personhood. Their aim is to show how personhood in sociality necessarily transcends its bodily conditionings. They both share a refusal to grant empirical validity to any form of supernaturalism (de Martino [1959] 2015: 93; Johnston 2010: 16) whilst, at the same time, aiming to capture the sense of personal transcendence that most ethnographers encounter when they carry out fieldwork, and which we discussed in chapter 2 above. We now have the means to move the argument further.

In his study of Lucanian magic formulas, de Martino situates his findings within a deep and complex local intellectual and political history but, at the same time, he proposes a framework of analysis that has a broader human reach. He sees the practice of magic as a response to situations of "crisis," which he characterizes as "the risk that the individual presence itself gets lost as a center of decision and choice, and drowns in a negation that strikes the very possibility of any cultural action at all" ([1959] 2015: 86–87). He sees these crises as corresponding to "experiences of emptiness and depersonalization" (ibid.: 98), that is, the users of magic take recourse to magical means as a response to situations of "loss of authenticity of self and the world" (ibid.: 97). And whilst it is not likely that magic is effective organically, there is no doubt that it is highly effective in what de Martino calls "a psychological-protective sense" (ibid.: 20).

A particularly valuable characteristic of his analysis[9] is that he relates presence with action throughout his study and thus, much in the same way that the evidence examined in this book suggests, treats person and world as coconstituted. Much like Mark Johnston (2010), when he examines the fear of death as a fear of loss of presence manifested in the incapacity to act, de Martino emphasizes the importance of "being-there" and the need of the person to safeguard the loss of presence that results from "being-acted-upon." Thus, he outlines a mode of existence of personhood which is dynamic, in that it is not ever a finished product, a permanent existence. Rather, personhood is a condition that is in constant affirmation through action and, thus, in permanent danger of being lost.

The notion of "presence and action" encapsulates brilliantly this view of personal ontogeny as a menaced activity; one which is menaced in all three aspects of personhood. In this way, self-consciousness is no longer seen in representationalist manner as a settled affair, and bodily health is no longer approached as the absolute boundary condition of personhood. To the contrary, person becomes a dynamic of constitution of the three aspects. It subsequently achieves a form of structural transcendence in its hypostatization in the world of the living—and this, as we have learned from so many studies in medical anthropology, applies to the whole person ($\alpha + \beta + \gamma$). Much in the same way that Johnston (2010) insists that one's personhood can outlive one's body, so one's "presence" (the awareness of self that launches reflexive consciousness, β) cannot

---

9.   Perhaps resulting from a reading of Heidegger, as his translator notes (ibid.: 15–16).

ever be an achieved presence, but it is always an ongoing task—thus, both immanent and transcendental. In this view of person and world, as the personal condition expands its reach, it becomes more unstable.

Following this insight, we can now postulate two boundary conditions (goalposts) for personhood as arena of presence and action. The first is *being-in-company*, the second *being-acted-upon*. We return again to Davidson's notion of company: since a process of triangulation is what launches personal ontogeny, and since ontogeny proceeds throughout the person's life, the immersion in complex social encounters (company) is a condition for presence. Without company, the conditions for survival of the arena of presence and action quickly fade away; a crisis of presence typically arises, leading to a reduction in the capacity for action. This is the reason why solitary confinement is one of the cruellest tortures that humans have devised for each other, as it leads to the erosion of personhood (cf. Gallagher 2014).

Perhaps the best study of company in the anthropological record is Monica Wilson's study of the Nyakyusa/Ngonde of Lake Nyassa, and, in particular, of the concept of *ukwangala*—"good company," that is, the enjoyment of the company of one's equals (Wilson 1951, 1957, 1959). For the Nyakyusa, wisdom and company go together with cleanliness and the affirming of personal presence. A chief's councillor once told the Wilsons:

> It is by conversing with our friends . . . that one gains wisdom (*amahala*); it is bad to sit quite still in men's company. A man who does this is a fool; he learns no wisdom, he only has his own thought. Moreover, a man who does not spend time with other people is always dirty, he does not compare himself with any friends. For we learn cleanliness of the body in company. . . . Wisdom and cleanliness are the two great things to be learnt in company. . . . It is better to live with other people. (Wilson 1951: 66)

There is, however, an aporetic side to company, since it is both the producer of presence and its destroyer. The Nyakyusa call the disapproval of one's fellows "the chilling breath of men," for it produces personal dissolution, confusion of mind, and ill-health. The principal lesson we take from the Nyakyusa, therefore, concerns the double-facedness of company; the way it constantly hovers between the two goalposts of presence.

> The value of good fellowship with equals is constantly talked about by the Nyakyusa, and it is dinned into boys from childhood that enjoyment and

morality alike consist in eating and drinking, in talking and learning, in the
company of contemporaries. . . . Now, this very emphasis . . . is doubtless a
reflection of the difficulty of achieving it. The frequent accusations of witchcraft
and movement from one village to another are evidence of friction between fellow villagers. (Wilson 1951: 163)

Thus, the "python in the belly" of the defenders of company is the same as the
one that lives in the bellies of the "destroyers of men" (the witches); the python
both causes death and protects life. Monica Wilson (1957) spends a considerable amount of effort showing how person and kinship emerge from the ritual
manipulation of this complexity: "Witches are dangerous, but the very power
which makes them dangerous also makes them valuable as 'defenders', for no
distinction between the power of attack and defence is consistently maintained"
(1951: 120).

One of the fascinating features of her studies is the way in which she shows
how company is qualified by gender and how its manifestations bear forms of
hegemony that oppress women by systemically reducing their presence. Her
study of the change to Christianity and the way in which this affected Nyakyusa
modes of company is especially valuable, for it shows how forms of life change
and how they change by relation to the very constitutive processes of personhood (Wilson 1959).

Thus, when approaching company, we must always contemplate the other
boundary condition of personhood: what de Martino calls being-acted-upon,
that is, "the experience of an individual presence that cannot manage to make
itself present, and for this reason it flounders and externalizes in various forms
both the attack and the resistance to it" ([1959] 2015: 62). To the extent that
humans achieve presence, they do so in company and by intervening in world
(see Gallagher 2014). This is the case from the beginning, as Colwyn Trevarthen
has noted: "Children from the age of six months onwards . . . are starting to
be part of culture. They want a rich environment, with lots of different kinds
of people doing different things, not totally unfamiliar. It is to build a kind of
working community, with jobs."[10]

---

10. Extract of oral communication in
    http://www.educationscotland.gov.uk/earlyyears/prebirthtothree/
    nationalguidance/conversations/colwyntrevarthen.asp (accessed 30 November
    2014—no longer available; cf. Trevarthen 1990).

The importance of exercising action for developing and sustaining personhood cannot be sufficiently emphasized, as it is through engagement with world that people confirm presence, and presence is a condition for propositional thinking, because it is a condition for reflexivity. And the notion that world is out there beyond the person and that cognition is enclosed within the person's mind is radically mistaken. To the contrary, if "meaning something is like going up to someone"—as Wittgenstein insisted ([1953] 1967: § 457) and radical embodied cognition confirmed (e.g., Chemero 2009)—then thinking is a form of acting, and presence and action merge in important ways. The paradox of free will is no longer so difficult to contemplate; it becomes the always-uncertain negotiation of the transcendental space opened up between the two goalposts of presence.

For the Nyakyusa, as much as for the Lucanian peasants, being-in-company and being-acted-upon are constants of personhood; they are not contradictory, as they are part of the same process. They merely push in opposite directions, thus revealing once again how personhood is always emotionally challenged (traumatic) in its condition as presence, for personhood affirms itself to the extent that it transcends itself.

THE CRADLE OF ETHICS

The historical origins of personhood lie outside of it, in person γ, that is, the instantiations of personhood present in those who surround the organic person (α) in the original context of cohabitation. In turn, the origins of γ are ultimately based in the evolutionary history of our species. Somewhere along the line humans developed a very sophisticated mode of communication, language, which was based on symbolic thinking and opened the door to presence (person β). Gesturing and the fabrication of tools were evidently an integral part of that process of evolution. Since then, from person to person, the chain has never been broken and the effects on our world that this innovation has brought about (the enriching of the world, so to speak) cannot possibly be doubted. In fact, at this point, what we have to ask ourselves is whether the evolutionary success of our species is not threatening the survival of world.

Thus, the process of transmission of frameworks of personhood (γ) demands that personal ontogeny be launched for each one of us; a process that is not inevitable and can be significantly reverted (as solitary confinement exemplifies—Gallagher 2014). This means that, in order to share a world with proximate others, the infant has to be docile to their meanings, to their forms of occupation of world. Should the infant resist the specificities of their use of signs (as in certain kinds of psychological deviance—see Tomasello 2008: 142–43), it will never become a full partner in their language games (and, by extension, their forms of life). There is great loss in that. Interpretive charity, therefore, is a condition for personhood and, prospectively, it is what opens the door of ethics to the new person.

As it approaches personhood, in primary intersubjectivity, the infant already experiences personhood in a basic manner via its participation (*à la* Lévy-Bruhl) in the carers and the joint worlding that occurs in shared intentionality with them. Participation is made possible by the extended nature of the human mind, as we have increasingly become aware with recent developments in neuroscience—contrary to traditional belief, cognition is hardly limited to the brain: "We rely on the properties of the external medium to bear some of the problem-solving load" (Clark 2014: 37). More than a semiotic disposition (a feature of propositional thought), mutuality of being is a cognitive condition.

The world that surrounds the child is formatted in ways that will eventually afford certain paths of meaning as the child develops its own personhood. The original disposition to accept the world one is brought into involves an inescapable docility ("charity," Quine called it). The child can only create an arena of presence and action to the extent that it has accepted the meanings of others: that is, of more than one other and, characteristically, in a gender-plural context of cohabitation, as we have seen. One's presence (one's existence to oneself) is predicated upon an experience of coresponsibility with those with whom one is solidary—our copresents, who coincide in our constitution of ourselves as a perspective upon world. As Marilyn Strathern put it: "Being parts of others carries its own responsibility" (2005: 28). Thus, presence and copresence exist in continuity, as not only is copresence anterior to presence, but singularity and plurality are constantly relating dynamically, so that presence is inhabited by copresence at all times. In sum, the futurity of others, as much as their pastness, is permanently part of one's own condition before world.

In the launching of personhood, the original mutualities become solidarities, that is, perspectives upon world that the person cannot simply cast away. Coresponsibility, thus, is compelling. But there is an emotional tone in all of this (as Heidegger and Sartre so often insisted) to the extent that presence emerges not from a confirmation of the arena of presence and action, but from a challenge to the child's earlier identifications. As we saw in the previous chapter, the original theater of ontogeny is such that the child's identification with its primary carer and its identification with other carers come into conflict, giving rise to a traumatic sense of differentiation, out of which the new person emerges. This triangulation is emotional because it involves a challenge to the shared intentionality the child continues to experience. Thus, the personal discovery of self through cross-participation is traumatic. This is the cradle of ethics.

In short, as it never allows the person fully to unmoor him- or herself from the meanings of others, all personhood is marked *ab initio* by domination to the extent that it involves an emotionally heavy dynamic of incomplete partition. As the person emerges from triangulation, its co-responsibilities produce an ambivalent condition: I experience my proximate other as one with me but, by relation to a third person, I find that he or she becomes my competitor. Sociality depends on sharing common purposes leading to joint action—the constitution of value. But, once presence (β) has come about, sociality becomes a context of uncertainty. In this way, I come to be framed by the two goalposts of presence: I must be in company, yet I must resist being acted upon. There is danger in that condition, for personhood is an unsteady construction. This means that trust and betrayal emerge in humanity at the same time; they are corollaries of each other. Because the process of arousal of personhood is one of triangulation, presence cannot ever rid itself of the distance produced by the third party and of the emotional challenge thus constituted.

The ambivalence of presence is something that Baroque thinkers elaborated upon in their day with great gusto; the aporias it opens up pleased their aesthetic sensibilities. The following quote from a sermon delivered by Padre António Vieira in 1640 in Brazil shines a bright (albeit metaphoric) light on what I have tried to capture in the paragraphs above. Speculating as to what the Virgin Mary might have felt after the Annunciation, when she had the presence of God growing in her womb, he explains that she felt very ambivalent about it; it confused her emotionally, since

> a presence in order for it to be a presence must have something of an absence. The object of sight, in order for it to be seen, must be present; but if it is glued and united to same potency, it is as if it were absent; in order to be seen, it must be distant from the eyes. Thus, presence in order to be a presence must not be intimate, nor totally united, but to the contrary a little distant. (Vieira [1640] 1959: 224)

The paradoxical nature of personal presence that Father Vieira captures so vividly is due to the fact that it arises in the precise moment that separation comes about. It involves both proximity and distance; it involves surrendering to the other whilst resisting the pressures of others. To that extent presence is ambivalent: that is, it is capable of profound entwinement as much as of schismatic eruption. Human proximity is a gradual phenomenon on a scale that goes from one's twin to the foreigner one meets by the side of the road, but our destiny for human collaboration bears an ever-present possibility of destruction. This is the moral of the story of Abel and Cain and it is the message that the Nyakyusa python has to teach us.

Each one of us as a person, therefore, has emerged onto a world where domination is always already instituted. We arise as persons to a set of responsibilities, but these go way beyond our immediate environing fellows, for they are "written into" the surrounding world: they are part of a form of life. We have these responsibilities, not because we agree to have them, but because we cannot help having them. In engaging socially with each other, persons are accepting configurations of power that, over time, institute themselves into hegemonies (see Pina-Cabral 1997 and 2002a). These are recurrent uses of signs that correspond to figurations of legitimate authority and that come to configure the form of life as a field of symbolic power (cf. Bourdieu 1991). One of the ethnographer's most challenging tasks in proposing a worldview is to create a model of that.

This is not the place to develop at length this matter of power and domination, as it would require at least another book. But it is indispensable to note that the institution of presence occurs by relation to a set of solidarities, which I have called *primary solidarities* (2002b) to the extent that they are foundational of the person's positioning within a form of life, that is, a hegemonically structured field. Therefore, the person emerges in ontogeny from a set of participations—not only with persons but also with socially marked features of his or her dwelling environment.[11] These mark the person's position by relation to the more broadly shared categories of collective belonging. The primary solidarities graft the person onto a set of continued identities in terms of filiation and alliance but also in things like class, race, religion, ethnicity, nationality, and so on. They do so in terms of modes of filiation and alliance, modes of dwelling,

---

11. I follow here Mauss' lesson concerning how the thing given is personified (see Mauss [1938] 1985 and Strathern 1984).

modes of authority, modes of obtaining subsistence. All of these are central facets of what the ethnographer will have to take into account when proposing a worldview.

METAPHYSICAL PLURALISM

As we proceed in attempting to characterize the way in which forms of life are configured, and namely how power relations pervade them systemically, the danger is to succumb to sociocentrism, that is, the disposition "according to which, in human multiplicity, the ego would be reduced to a part of a Whole, which reconstitutes itself in the image of an organism—or a concept—whose unity is the coherence of its members, or a comprehensive structure" (Levinas 1996: 165).

From the preceding discussion, we can confirm that, indeed, Levinas is right: the ontology and metaphysics which the ethnographer identifies within a form of life will always be (a) a constantly unachieved process, (b) manifested stochastically by the operation of complex processes of hegemony, and (c) subject to the modes of communication that characterize persons in their daily encounters: indeterminacy and underdetermination; polythetic association; and fuzzy structuration (see chapter 3). Therefore, in determining what exists and how it exists for a person who is immersed in a particular form of life, the ethnographer has to abdicate from the certainties resulting from the operation of the Aristotelian laws of logic.[12]

Moreover, different times, different societies, and different persons live in a world that is differently configured, with different entities, that interrelate in different ways, but also a diversity of modes of figuration is available to each one of us at all times. In any single social context, one can observe the coexistence of different modes of figuration that can come into contrast, contradiction, and conflict. Humans are metaphysically dynamic. There are even well-established, traditional ways of living with ontological diversity and instability. The very notion of rite of passage and the long tradition of anthropological examination of instituted marginality is an acknowledgment of the workings of ontological instability within human sociality (see Pina-Cabral 1997).

---

12. This was in fact Lévy-Bruhl's initial challenge that led him to propose the "law of participation" (see Keck 2008: 129–203).

Furthermore, as dividuality is an inescapable feature of personhood, meta-physical pluralism is a function of personal constitution. This is even more evident once we take on board the notion that the arena of presence and action is capable of, and indeed prone to, compartmentalization.[13] What this means is that metaphysical pluralism is not originally based on the confrontation of "cultures" (as the radical relativists would have it), or the confrontation of persons with different configurations of world based on different personal histories. The root of metaphysical pluralism is in the singular person itself—in the person's capacity to isolate parts of his or her world from other parts.

While we observe that there is a drive to create meaning by making the world cohere, it is not possible, nor indeed desirable, for it to go too far, since new participations are constantly emerging in a person's life that enter into conflict with former or concomitant participations (not only with persons, but more broadly with aspects of world). Full metaphysical integration is not necessary for the establishment of presence, nor is it functionally advantageous in terms of the very process through which person is constituted. Our reasons do not all add up, nor indeed should they if we are going to adapt to the challenges posed to us by the world that surrounds us. Ultimate rational integration is not a characteristic of socially viable persons.

However, we can now go one step further and state quite clearly that *all ontology is predicated upon ontogeny*. This is no game of words. Rather, it is an important principle if we are to observe Levinas' warning and still safeguard the possibility of the ethnographic gesture. Presence is the human door to transcendence; it illuminates the world, making it richer. Within propositional (symbolic) thought, therefore, the presence of other entities in world—persons, things, beings, patterns of action—is a function of my own presence. Essentially what is at stake here is that the institution of being-in-the-world can only be made by an agent who is already a being for him- or herself, possessing an arena of presence and action. This does not mean that all beings share the same condition of being as my own personal presence—metaphysical pluralism is the rule. But it does mean that they all interact with it as the sine qua non of human ontology.

At this point, I must clarify that consciousness does not emerge in humans out of nothing. Again, the error is the assumption that we have an all-or-nothing situation. To the contrary, it has been clear to many for a very long time

---

13. See Davidson's suggestions in the wake of Freud (Davidson 2004: 181)

that all life contains elements of interiority that result from life's effort to stay alive, its purposiveness (what Spinoza called *conatus*: "Everything, in so far as it is in itself, endeavours to persist in its own being"—[1677] 2013: part III, prop. VI). To that extent, inspired by Varela and Damásio, Evan Thompson argues that "the interiority of life is the interiority of selfhood, which is a precursor to the interiority of consciousness" (2007: 225). However (contra Kohn 2013), to identify this type of "minimal autopoietic selfhood" (Thompson 2007: 162), as manifested by nonhuman forms of life, with the kind of selfhood which we associate with personal presence is a serious error, for it is a failure to see that the ontology of the world that we assume and operate with in our normal human linguistic exchanges is transcendent. In turn, this transcendence is only open to persons in ontogeny because they have, so to speak, moved out of themselves by means of the scaffolding that symbolic (propositional) thinking permits. It is in this sense (not in one where we would reconstitute Descartes' *summa divisio*) that we mean that ontology is a function of ontogeny. To give Kohn's example, if the forest is transcendent for his Kuna friends, it is because the Kuna are persons endowed with presence.

But there is yet another important angle to consider. For each one of us, the world vanishes the moment our own arena of presence and action succumbs at death. Nevertheless, whilst *my* world vanishes, I do not vanish from the world, since my presence and capacity for action remain to the extent that they are inscribed in other participations all around me. And, of course, we do not mean here exclusively participation in other persons (my proximate others whose presences are penetrated by mine), but also through other parts of world into which my presence has been inscribed. Plato, Confucius, and Christ remain among the living all these many years later, for their actions continue to be felt in our world. But so do the presences of other no longer living persons of much more restricted import.[14]

In order to clarify the notion of worldview it is important to note that, within a single form of life, there can be different modes of apportioning presence and that these have a structuring effect upon that form of life. Two modes of metaphysical pluralism will be exemplified here, as they have a foundational

---

14. Mark Johnston's fascinating argument that personhood survives death but only to the extent that one was "good" in life is interesting and does require attention, but it involves a limitation to "goodness" that, unfortunately, cannot immediately be taken on board (2010).

role, but one cannot exclude the possibility of there being yet other possible angles to metaphysical pluralism.

Ontological weight

As a form of life is reproduced from generation to generation as a *habitus*, certain entities and certain configurations acquire greater centrality in its economies of meaning. These are facets of the world that, for those who share that form of life, create a framework around which other facets of the world can arrange themselves meaningfully; thus, as meaning is favored by retentivity (see chapter 2), the centrality of these entities is instituted over time by the very process of constitution of meaning.

Fortes ([1973] 1987) has shown how this works for personhood among the Tallensi, when he argued that their notion of personhood was a variable to the extent that it is only after they die that some people (not all people) attain the full condition of personhood. It is not that other persons (women, young people, men who die away from home, etc.) fail to exist as persons; it is rather that certain men exist more, they exist in a fuller way. But this applies also to other entities of our world that maximize meaning (and, to that extent, prop up figuration). Certain facets of the person or facets of the world come to "be" more than others; they assume greater *ontological weight*. It is not a matter of questioning the existence of other aspects, but rather a matter of confirmation; a greater readiness to affirm the existence of these facets. Certain parts of person or world are less prone to being silenced, they are more present. This notion came to my attention for the first time, when I was studying the way in which personhood is manifested in naming practices. I came to the conclusion that certain facets of personhood were attributed greater ontological weight than others and that this was structurally significant in terms of the general configuration of the naming systems and their relation to the forms of life to which they corresponded (see Pina-Cabral 2010c). For the ethnographer, it is immensely important to identify these, since they constitute central landmarks in the configuration of worldview.

In order to exemplify what is meant here, I will recall a moment of epiphany during my work in rural Alto Minho (NW Portugal). By the time it came to pass, the main period of fieldwork was over and the thesis had already been examined. As I was now living in Portugal, however, I could go back for shorter visits to see my friends in Paço. I was preparing the version of the ethnography that was soon to be published (Pina-Cabral 1986).

My closest companion in Paço was a man everyone knew as Morgado who was a passionate supporter of the "old ways," that is to say, the peasant modes of living that were by then becoming obsolete and which were the central theme of my work. This was a fascination we both shared and our sincere friendship was rooted in it. He was a relatively wealthy peasant who bossed over a large, traditional-style household (*casa*) and who had never been tempted to migrate, unlike the majority of his coevals in Minho. Although he was politically agnostic (being prone toward distrusting human nature in general), he had been the parish president for the last decades of the fascist regime. This meant that, by the time I met him, after the 1974 Democratic Revolution, he was in a sort of forced retirement from public life; his cousin's husband had become the new president. Still, he remained the undisputed authority on all that had to do with rural life.

Many of the people who had migrated in the late 1950s and 1960s were now returning home and investing their hard-earned savings in buying back the land that the wealthier townspeople had accumulated in the 1930s and 1940s, when conditions in rural regions in Portugal had been dire. The dream of the returned migrant was to become a landed peasant with a large and colorful house facing the road. That was their idea of the worthy life, even after all those decades living and working in Paris, Lille, Newark, or Vancouver.

What they wanted to buy were not large tracts of land, but small plots growing maize, beans, and wine (*vinho verde*) in what is a hilly, well-irrigated region (Wateau 2000). Still, their parents had lost the land they had owned to the urban moneylenders or, alternatively, had had to endure hunger and misery in order not to sell it. This meant that their children who went away to France or the United States, upon their return, were desperate to show that they were not *cabaneiros* (lit. hut dwellers), people of no concern, who did not own land and, therefore, did not have a *casa* (house) worthy of the name. The land, not the building, turned out to be the central defining factor in deciding whether one truly had a "house" and, thus, whether one was truly a member of the commune (the *freguesia*).

As a result, by the early 1980s, on the morning that I went out to the fields down by the river with Morgado, there were lots of people buying land and he was being regularly asked by the registry office in town to work as a land assessor. Throughout the whole district, he was officially and unofficially recognized as the person who could give the last word on such matters. We arrived at the designated plot—a reasonably good one, with a well-tended pergola all round it and a small stretch of forest with chestnut trees uphill from it. A canal that passed halfway through it irrigated the land. In this case, as I seem to remember, the plot was a disputed heritage.

This was not the first time I went out with him, and I had quickly learned his basic moves. He would start by dividing the land in easily measurable right-angled triangles and thus, with three or four measures with his long string meter, he would ascertain its size in square meters. Then comes the part that constituted an epiphany to me. He would mentally reduce the land, whatever there was of it, to basic maize production and ascertain, from the quality of the soil and the nature of the irrigation, how many carts of maize such a piece of land might yield. (*Carros de milho*, the traditional land measure, refers to the old oxcarts that were by then no longer in use, assuming that they were filled with sheathed maize cobs.) Then he would add some value for the likely wine crop; then he would subtract the value of things like bad walls or delapidated pergolas; then he would subtract some for the part that was forested; then he would add more or less depending on the nature of the trees and whether they were above the main point of access to the plot or below it; then he would count in the fruit trees that might exist; then he would take into account the ease of reach from the main road; and so on.

What struck me was that the land was essentially valued by how much maize it might produce, whether it was best suited for that purpose or not. This seemed extraordinary, since in fact the likelihood was that this particular plot, when sold, would be used for building a house. But, at that point, he had been asked to ascertain "the value of the land" and there was no doubt for him or for anybody else around (much as they certainly had not thought about it like I am putting it here) that the essential value of the land was what it would produce in terms of the staple food, maize bread (*broa*).

At that point, I understood all of a sudden something that I felt I already knew but that I had not known how to say: maize had greater ontological weight than other foods, other parts of the world, and most other entities in general. I now understood why the central marker of value for a peasant "house" was the visible granary standing elegantly on its tall granite legs (figure 2). Morgado's one, standing proudly in the hillside in front of the door to his kitchen, had its woodwork painted in red, even although, these days, it no longer made any sense to store grain there, and it was mostly being used as a toolshed.

Figure 2. A proud granary in Paço (Ruth Rosengarten, in Pina-Cabral [1993]2008).

This actually illuminated much of what I had already written in the thesis. And, in fact, retrospectively, I understood why I had felt it necessary to go through the trouble of researching certain things: to unearth the history of maize in the region; the details of the ritual of bread making and its implications for gender relations and household constitution; the central importance of female fertility in a region where marriage was essentially uxorilocal; the meaning of not having land, not eating one's own bread, and therefore being morally suspicious; how people claimed (against all likelihood) that they could taste with certainty whether or not a portion of maize bread was made in their "house"; why, in all the years I was there, I never managed to get anyone to provide me regularly with *broa* for a weekly price; and so on. I suddenly found a nexus between all of these things and many more.

In rural Alto Minho, by the mid-twentieth century, this crop that had arrived in the last decades of the eighteenth century had become the staple food and the mainstay of peasant living. Their world, contrary to that of the people in the towns and cities, was dependent on the notion that the good life was one where one produced one's own food in one's own land—and that was *broa*; all other foods were seen as additions to it. Thus *broa* became the central mode of distinguishing those who had value, and therefore had a right to be there, from those who did not, and were therefore mere passing residents. Their persons, their houses, their community, existed more or less to the extent that they were capable of ensuring their own subsistence from their own land by means of *broa*.

I should note here that this did not mean that the region was ever demonetarized. To the contrary, there has been money circulating in these hills since the Pax Romana brought the population down from the hilltops to the riverside plots. Later, *minhoto* peasants were in the forefront of Portuguese empire building at the onset of the Modern Era and, later still, in the nineteenth century, of economic migration to Brazil, Europe, or North America. Ever since the fifteenth century, therefore, there had been men (and also, to a lesser extent, women) returning to these houses from all sorts of very distant places around the world (India, China, Africa, Brazil, Australia, North America). Therefore, what was being celebrated with maize bread was not sustenance as such—for many of the returned migrants over the centuries had eaten plenty of very diverse foods throughout their travels or as sailors in the cod fisheries off Newfoundland.

What was being celebrated by attributing greater ontological weight to maize and maize bread was its centrality in a certain form of life; the role it played in configuring who each one of these persons was and desired to be. What surprised me, in a way, was how I suddenly was confronted with the presence of the past (the pastness) in a social situation where, indeed, the centrality of maize was no longer what it had been. I was surprised not by how things changed, but by how they survived.

For each one of those people, maize did not "represent" anything; rather, it condensed a nexus of meanings that, in being shared and in acquiring hegemonic implications over a long period, became more present, more visible, more likely to be retained by each person in his or her daily dealings. No wonder that, after each meal, Morgado's wife would carefully gather the breadcrumbs left on the table top and spread them around the house outside the walls. This way the souls of the dead would eat them and be grateful, and thus leave the residents of the house alone, granting it prosperity.

The way in which world is marked not only by the presence of entities but also by their relative ontological weight might equally well be exemplified by recourse to images such as the statues of the Virgin, the Nativity Scene, or the Crucifixion that one encounters all over Europe. These icons (and the stories that are told about them) facilitate access to a set of meanings; they constitute paradigmatic scenes (Needham 1985: 67–69) to the extent that they trigger off retentivity. They are modes of apportioning ontological weight, of reminding people what entities and actions are *more present* in the world.

Ontological plurality

The second type of metaphysical pluralism is ontological plurality as exemplified by Göran Aijmer's discussion of the matter: as he puts it, "life is a modal narration telling many alternate stories" (2001: 69). What concerns us here is the way in which forms of life need not cohere and, quite the contrary, generally seem to be based on modes of condensing signs that open more than one pathway of constitution of presence. In light of the emphasis on personal ontogeny in this book, it seems relevant to show how the very mode of presence of the person can be constructed in plural ways in any one specific social environment. Thus, the examples we will now examine all have to do with personhood and forms of defining continued identity by the manipulation of personal dividuality.

The principal aim here is to show how diverse can be the forms of ontological plurality: in the first example, one type of continued identity hides but does not efface the other; in the second example, two types of continued identity cohabit in a formally diversified manner, producing a complex panoply of figurations; in a third ethnographic example, two modes of constructing the person enter into conflict, leading to creative equivocation. In this last case, metaphysical pluralism is manifested both in ontological weight and in ontological plurality.

1. Taking recourse to two classical ethnographies (Fei 1939; Hsu [1948]; 1967), Aijmer (2013, 2015) examines Chinese attitudes to personhood in terms of childhood and of ancestry in order to highlight the ways in which the constitution of continued identities is subject to a form of ontological pluralism. He argues that two ontological registers coexist in these ethnographic examples: one, more closely related to discursive processes, that emphasizes paternal filiation and agnatic group belonging—here the ancestral cult comes to the fore; the other, more closely related to iconic manifestations, where the person's connection to the mother is silently but strongly emphasized—here the context of the kitchen and the Stove God is especially relevant.

I have in the past written about the analytical challenges posed by the presence of the Stove God in Han kitchens, concluding that the contradiction that arises from the confrontation of the two asymmetrically related forms of continued identity that Aijmer identifies (the patriarchal and the uxorilateral) is actually constitutive of the Chinese forms of being a person (Pina-Cabral 1997: 38). There are different versions of the myth, but they mostly correspond to the tale of a man who, having betrayed and repudiated his good wife, wasted away his fortune in loose living. Reduced to hunger, he is one day saved from sure death by a wealthy woman who turns out to be his former wife. She takes him back into her home, for she considers that she never stopped being his wife. Coming to his senses, and seeing how shamefully he has behaved, he throws himself into the hearth, committing suicide. The Emperor of Heaven, seeing that he has truly repented, makes him the Stove God. Since then, he has been placed above all stoves and, at New Year, he goes back to visit heaven for a few days to report on the way in which each particular household is being run.

There is a central ambiguity to this myth, for it is the man who repents who is made into a god and not his brave and faithful wife. So, we might be led to assume that the story reinforces the spirit of Han patriarchalism. And yet from within the story comes a strong reminder that, although women are marginal to the family, they are the very source of fertility and prosperity, as demonstrated by the ethnographic material described by Hsu and Fei that Aijmer revisits. The story enshrines meanings and messages that run counter to the everyday assumptions but which cohabit with them in a penumbral, subdued condition. Outwardly, the Stove God seems to reinforce patriarchalist assumptions, but inwardly he reveals the complexity of the family's dependence on women. We see here, therefore, a clash between two continued identities that are foundational of personal presence and yet imply a structure of domination. They are expressed mostly in different contexts and times (discursive v. iconic, hall v. kitchen) and are left to produce their different modes of condensation in an ontologically pluralist fashion. But they are markers of the continued identities that go into forming the arenas of presence and action of the persons raised in these households.

If, indeed, regular social living depends on the acceptance of legitimated forms of domination (hegemony), the mere presence in everyday social intercourse of those who are not favored by that hegemonic order implies necessarily that the possibility of an alternative order is never fully eradicated. Ontological pluralism must, then, be seen as a constant challenge to a form of life, and it is up to the ethnographer in her account of worldview to capture how that possibility is characteristically configured.

2. A further interesting example can be found in the innovative work of Klaus Hamberger (2011) on kinship in the Ouatchi Plateau (Togo). There the author shows how everyday kinship depends on two kinds of continued identities that are conceived and manipulated by recourse to two different modes of association. Contrary to the Chinese example above, he argues that there is no particular repression of one form of association over the other. In fact, he

demonstrates how complex and rich can be the modes of ontological plurality to which the simultaneous recourse to these two forms of institution of personal presence give rise.

A correlation is established between agnatic participation and metonymy, and another between uterine participation and metaphor. They are two modes of understanding continued identity. Over and above mere difference, the two regimes of personal participation are elaborated in different manners, according to whether contiguity or similarity, respectively, are emphasized. Thus, male-related people are in contiguity with each other in the household; while female-related people stand for each other before the gods. System emerges from the combination of the two principles, so that agnatic kin turn out to be coresident and exercise outward control over the political system; while uterine kin reside separately but share with each other greater spiritual identification and mutual support.

A significant level of complexity is achieved as the two principles are combined and explored in different facets of the world, particularly as the religious and political components interpenetrate. What Hamberger argues is that, whilst previously the attention of ethnographers had focused on the visibility of the coresident agnatic kin group, this led them to see only part of the picture and to fail to see the nexus in much of what was going on in ritual life. He sustains that the worldview should not be formulated as a bilineal system of descent; rather, it is a worldview where ontological plurality is being explored systematically at all points in the constitution of person and world. As they use one or another of the two analogical modes of association (metaphor or metonymy), each person is drawing on different parts of being. As this is done by everyone over time, a complex system emerges that is not essentially about kinship per se but about world: a world where two registers of apportioning presence are systematically being engaged.

3. The third example is taken from fieldwork carried out in Macau in the 1990s in the hope of showing how metaphysical pluralism can manifest itself jointly in terms of ontological weight *and* ontological plurality. This small territory in southern China was administered by the Portuguese from the mid-sixteenth century to December 1999. Whilst the majority of the population throughout the city's long history was always Cantonese (both the wealthier and the poorer), the top administrators were high officials sent from Goa and later Lisbon to secure Portuguese rule. In practical terms, however, the city was run by a Eurasian administrative middle class whose fortunes waxed and waned repeatedly during the past five centuries. They originated in the mid-fifteenth century in the Creole

population which was formed around Portuguese Malacca and which remained in place after the Portuguese lost the control of naval commerce, playing the role of mediators and compradores throughout the coastal regions of South and Southeast Asia. Some of the central evil figures in Conrad's Eastern novels, for example, are "Portuguese of the Orient" (e.g., *Almayer's Folly* or *Lord Jim*).

I was asked to study this Eurasian administrative class in Macau during the Transition Period (1987–99), as they anxiously prepared for what would be a major political and economic change of condition. They were to lose the monopoly over the city's administrative structure ("their privilege," as they called it) to the hands of the local Cantonese middle class (cf. Pina-Cabral 2002a). As it happens, today, they remain an important presence, although the city that has emerged from the new geopolitical order, in which the Chinese state has a world-dominant position, has totally changed. They adapted well to the new conditions of extreme wealth, as the city became the world's largest casino and a global money-laundering den of major proportions.

One of the first characteristics that came to my attention as I studied their presence in the city in the 1990s was the matter of personal naming. Most of the Eurasian population lived in an ambiguous linguistic world in which Cantonese, Portuguese, and English mixed freely. The vocal allegiance to European ways that had characterized the Colonial Period had come to an end in 1976, when the new democratic Portuguese state withdrew its military presence from the territory, thus signaling that its rule would eventually come to an end. Furthermore, as China opened itself in the 1980s and 1990s to global consumer and media trends, young Eurasians were increasingly drawn to Chinese forms of sociability (particularly with the media of Taiwan and Hong Kong as dominant references). The result was a population that constantly had to negotiate their cultural abilities and allegiances.

Chinese and Portuguese naming practices differ very significantly, and I soon came to realize that the ubiquitous visiting cards that one was constantly exchanging as one was introduced to new people and negotiated one's way through the city's administrative and commercial spaces were far less straightforward than they seemed. One side was written in alphabetic form, and whether one's name was originally Portuguese, English, or Filipino, it was written in such a way as to be clearly readable to a Portuguese- or English-speaking audience. The other side was written in Chinese characters and, again, whatever one's original name, it was adapted to be read by a Chinese person. So far, so good. The problem was that, when one started trying to compare the two sides of the same card, one found that, whilst they corresponded to each other, they did not correspond in the same way.[15]

The principal difference was in the actual name. Apart from the order of the names being different (the surname coming first on the Chinese side), the names of Chinese people were translated on the alphabetic side differently from how Portuguese names were translated on the other side, in the case of both proper names and surnames. Most Chinese people have adopted a European-style first name (Mike, John, Miguel, Irene, Stella, etc.) that they readily use on the alphabetic side of their card. To the contrary, European names were presented in Chinese characters in metonymic continuity with the original Portuguese name (it could be either one of the person's surnames or one of their proper names, depending on the translator's fancy). This was done, however, in such a way as the first syllable was always made to correspond to a recognizable Cantonese patronymic (e.g., Lourenço ⇒ Lo Len-So; Cabral ⇒ Ka Pak-Lo). This was a way of facilitating recognition for Chinese people, whilst making the European person in question appear a little more respectable to Chinese eyes. Indeed, if the surname were not recognizable to a Cantonese ear as a patronymic, this would make the person sound comic.

Chinese patronymics were phonetically recognizable and integral on the alphabetic side; to the contrary, Portuguese surnames were being metonymically transformed to correspond to Chinese traditional patronymics. In fact, it turns out that—once one goes past superficial appearances—Portuguese surnames are not entities of the same nature, with the same properties, as Chinese patronymics, and that was the reason for the asymmetry. But neither are proper names, since the centrality of baptism and the person's spiritual name that is an important facet of Western European traditions is totally absent from the Chinese cultural universe. Moreover, on the visiting cards, Chinese proper names were never translated literally or adapted to sound European, as their connotations would sound ridiculous to a Portuguese subject.

The ontological weight of the distinct parts of personal names is very different in Portuguese and Chinese. Whilst, in the Portuguese case, the proper name has a decisive priority over the surname and describes the person more

---

15. For discussions of naming practices in Macau, see Pina-Cabral (2002a, 2010b). A further feature deserving of attention which will not be dealt with here is that, in Macau, Chinese toponymy and Portuguese toponymy very seldom correspond, so that very often the addresses on each side of the card were not direct translations of each other.

fundamentally (being the baptismal name—cf. Pina-Cabral 2012b), the contrary is the case in the Chinese system, where agnatic descent is emphasized. The option of using the mother's surname instead of the father's, or of combining them in creative ways, as is so characteristic of Portuguese naming systems, was utterly repellent to a traditional Chinese person.[16] As it turns out, the different order of the names was significant: diverse ontological weights were being granted to distinct parts of the name, reflecting the way in which persons are constituted differently in the two traditions (Pina-Cabral 2002a).

The interesting characteristic of Macau, of the Eurasians, and of these cards that were such an integral part of the daily life of this town is that both traditions were constantly present. Whether we understood the differences in naming systems or whether we manipulated the differences without being aware of them, which was mostly the case, the fact is that we were all navigating an environment where the different implications of the different uses had specific relevance to each and every one of us. The derisive laughter that I heard from my Portuguese companions about the Chinese use of names was the same as I heard from my Chinese companions about the Portuguese.

Ethnic grit and personal pride were being negotiated through name use, which is something that is relevant to each and every person who is living in the city. Ontological pluralism, in fact, permeated the daily negotiations of name use for everyone. For the younger Eurasians, however, whose Portuguese name was no longer really as important as it had been for their parents; whose knowledge of Cantonese had improved tremendously; and who were using patronymics on the Chinese side of their cards that their ancestors had already been using for generations, the equivocations present in the naming systems constituted both a source of weakness and a useful tool for negotiating the intercultural gap. They navigated the border of ontological pluralism in such a way as to make those equivocations compatible (see Pina-Cabral 2010b).

To sum up, the world of persons is metaphysically unstable owing to its ontological dependence on personal presence and, in turn, personal presence is ever incomplete and dynamic owing to personal partibility: the world of humans is one and it is many.

---

16. It seems that new forms of naming are emerging today, as a result of an adaptation to the one-child policy. It is too early, however, to know how this will eventually alter traditional Chinese family practices.

CONCLUSION: ON RELATION[17]

In conclusion, I propose that the discovery that ontological weight and ontological pluralism are inescapable features of worldviews can help us open up the
way toward clarifying one of the thornier issues in anthropology: What is the
nature of *relation* (as in a relation, social relations, relatedness, relationality)?
Ever since that strange and provocative inaugural lecture delivered by Marilyn
Strathern in Cambridge in 1994 (Strathern 1995), we have known that the
matter is not pacific, as had been assumed by all up until then. She returns to it
in *Partial connections* (2004), but without proposing a more decisive answer. Finally, in *Kinship, law and the unexpected*, she advances the debate significantly by
stressing the "embeddedness of relational thinking in the way Euro-Americans
come to know the world" (2005: viii).

Strathern defines relationality in terms of "relationships," following Alfred
Gell in using the concepts of relation and relationship interchangeably and then
in understanding the *relata* as social agents (ibid.: 170, n. 11). She points out
that, at the time of the Enlightenment, scientists developed a "special tool" of
knowledge that operates by analogically encompassing a distinction—she calls
it a "duplex." These duplexes are instances of analogical mediation to the extent
that they are semiotic tools the aim of which is to overcome (or bypass) a distinction. She concludes that "the duplexes mentioned here . . . that belong to
no single logical order, and appear to summon diverse materials, are all tools
for grasping facets of one world. That world is *known* not only from different
viewpoints but also from specifically divergent, that is, related, ones. Any of
the divergences . . . produces the 'relation'." (ibid.: 13, my emphasis) Thus, for
example, anthropology uses relations in order to study relations. Strathern's own
analysis would then be a case of raising this duplex to the power of two.

Unfortunately, I worry that her highly sophisticated historical exegesis may
fail to respond to one of the principal challenges that confronts ethnographic
theory today: namely, the need to overcome the primitivist polarization between the West and the Rest, freeing ethnography from ethnic/nationalist
identity politics, and opening it ecumenically to all. That is, Strathern's analysis remains enclosed within the cosmological divide between, to one side, the

---

17. This section expounds an approach that is ethnographically tested in the final
    section of Pina-Cabral and Silva (2013).

Euro-Americans[18] and, to the other side, the Melanesians (the Strathernian prototype of the Other). In this sense, and as we saw above, like many of our contemporary theorists, her approach is a form of metaphysical agnosticism, in that she places her own analysis squarely within the very polarizations that she critiques.

It is well beyond the scope of this book to discuss "relation" from either a logical or a physical point of view, so we will limit ourselves to our central concern: how persons come to relate to each other and to world. But we must do this in a nonanthropocentric fashion, for humans are also animals and they live in a physical world (i.e., with its own "agencies," if you wish). That is, we cannot assume that all relations are social relations or that social relations are exclusively facts of consciousness and therefore that their existence depends on their essence as "knowledge" (i.e., as ideas in the mind of propositionally reflex- ive persons). In adopting a theory of affordances—relations between animals and world—we vow to overcome the semiotic reduction that treats all rela- tions as forms of knowledge. As relations, affordances are indeed tools (*zeug*, in Heidegger's original sense) in the in-formation of world (by that, as we saw above, we mean a purposeful engagement with world). But their essence de- pends on their existence and their existence is not uniquely a matter of propo- sitionally constituted minds.

In characteristic fashion, Strathern is well aware of this and of the problems it raises: "Positivism and its critiques develop together. They are both—overtly or not—an outcome of scientific thinking insofar as they put 'knowledge' at the forefront of relational endeavour and can imagine different approaches to it" (2005: 42). But the problem is that, if we continue to rely on "knowledge" as our central analytical category, we are constrained to treat information as the prod- uct of knowledge (e.g., ibid.: 35). This brings about two main unwanted results. Firstly, we objectify the pathways of human imagination as representations, that is, we deal with the modes of processing and communicating information as

---

18. Apologetically typified by her by the English (ibid.: 43), but with the notable exception of Portuguese-speakers (ibid.: 180). Ever since her Inaugural Lecture in 1994, I and my Portuguese colleagues have failed to understand precisely what she has in mind in reproducing this strangely unsubstantiated claim. As Spanish is grammatically and lexically so akin to Portuguese (the major difference being in pronounciation), does this also include her own Spanish-speaking disciples? Does it include French-trained Brazilians, such as Viveiros de Castro? A truly puzzling matter.

objects of the mind (concepts). Secondly, we conjoin sociocentrically a collectively held disposition with the actual processes occurring in persons' minds. In this dual way, the role of basic mind is obscured, and as Alberto Corsín would put it, we fail to account for "the residues that [reflexive] thought proportions *out* of itself" (2004: 17, original emphasis).

If, then, we are to avoid these hurdles, we must not start our discussions, in characteristic ethnographic fashion, by reference to categories. For example, in this present argument, I might have started by attempting to define a relation mathematically as an association, correspondence, or connection between two or more terms. But if I had done this, I would have immediately raised the duplex connection/disconnection that Strathern identifies. This is the old quandary that constituted the hub of the classical debate between structural functionalists and structuralists: To what extent does the relation affect the terms? And, by implication, to what extent are the terms constituted by the relation?

More generally, as Strathern demonstrates, this is a quandary that has accompanied Anglo-American philosophical approaches to relation ever since the Enlightenment. We need not go as far back as Locke. For instance, in a classical essay on the notion of relation, Russell's colleague G.E. Moore (1919) distinguishes between two types of relation: *internal*—those where the relation changes the nature of the terms; and *external*—those where the relation does not affect the nature of the terms, that is, where the terms remain essentially the same as they would be if the relation had not been the case. This distinction is aimed at validating the view that entities have an existence beyond relations, which characterized the positivist and sociocentric preferences of many during the early part of the twentieth century.

At midcentury again, George Van Sant writes a paper where he proposes the notion of constitutive relations, which he exemplifies as "a is *the* father of b" (1959: 28, his emphasis). According to him, a constitutive relation would be "one in which the relation itself conditions the referent" (there is only *one* father of a, he claims) (ibid.: 29). This example turns out to be especially interesting in light of Strathern's recent work. We do in fact dispute that all relations of paternity are necessarily constitutive in this way, for relations of paternity need no longer be unique (both in terms of artificial reproduction and in social terms).

At the end of his paper, however, Van Sant wonders whether constitutive relations, such as he defined them, should be considered relations at all, since they are not simple. This means that, half a century after Moore's paper, the issue seems to have remained a source of perplexity. Indeed, already Moore had felt obliged to acknowledge that "no relational facts are *completely* analysable" (ibid.: 44, his emphasis). He safeguarded his view that entities in the world are essentially nonrelational by differentiating between relations and relational properties. But if relations are distinct from relational properties, then they are objects of the mind, categories, ideas. And if that is the case, where do we place the relation between relations and relational properties? This only postpones the problem, of course (i.e., it is a version of the *homunculus* paradox). Strathern calls this the "connection/disconnection duplex": an analogical mediation (or imaginative equivocation) that allows for the analytical survival of the very notion of relation. Unfortunately, in order to dispel the equivocation, we would have had to (a) avoid defining relation in the received "Euro-American" way as prototypically characterized by a "relationship" and (b) we would have had to refuse to reify information as "knowledge" (2005: 35). It would seem, then, that roughly fifty years after Van Sant, the paradox has not been clarified in a significant way.

In fact, as one looks back on philosophical discussions about relation, one observes that, somehow, filiation presents itself to Anglo-American philosophers as the prototype of all relations. This is no recent matter. As Strathern points out, "We know that nineteenth-century evolutionists looked to the connection between individuals (genealogies) to talk about connections (classifications) between nonhuman creatures and things" (ibid.: 46). But the analogy has continued to prosper to this day. A century ago, Moore (1919) chose as the prototype of relation the paternity of kings, no less; at midcentury, Van Sant gave as his first example of relation "that the music of Beethoven fathered that of Brahms" (1959: 27); more recently, however, maternity seems to have become the favored choice (Bar-Yam 2016). Even an author like John Ryder, who treats all relations as intrinsically constitutive, goes on to exemplify relations in general by human relations in particular (2013: 70). Nevertheless, for him, all relations imply an element of interaction, which does suggest a path out of the original quandary.

This sociocentric proclivity to typify relation by means of filiation turns out to raise yet another problem: as it happens, "Euro-American" anthropologists *do not* agree at all concerning the meaning of the concept "filiation" (e.g., Bonte, Porqueres and Wilgaux 2011). Now, one suspects that, from a Lévi-Straussian (French) perspective on filiation, the problem of relations would pose itself in a rather distinct fashion than to the Anglo-Americans, since Lévi-Strauss adopts an explicitly interactionist approach to relations.[19]

---

19. Which again points to a large field of equivocation in the reading of Deleuze or Derrida by many of the so-called ontologists.

In any case, relations among persons (or between persons and the socially salient features of their surrounding environment) are constitutive in a particular way that does not apply to all relations in general, such as those between the sun and the moon, between the fork and the dish, or between two letters of the alphabet. Again, the reason I differentiate these two kinds of relations is not to do with agency versus inertness, as the followers of Latour would be sure to critique; neither is it because I contemplate the existence of nonrelational entities, as Ryder would protest. Rather, relations that involve personal ontogeny are a bad analogy for the more generic condition of being relational in world because ontogenetically constitutive relations are propositionally scaffolded in ways that other relations are not. Persons are not only particular, they also are possessed of an immanent transcendence. While it can be argued that there is an emergent form of transcendence associated to the purposiveness of all forms of sociality (as Peirce would have it), it must nevertheless be acknowledged that the emergence of personhood potentiates transcendence in a powerful way. To use social relations (relationships) as the prototype of relations is to facilitate the works of the *cogito* disposition, which splits mind away from world.

As we have seen, for persons, being-in-the-world is being-with-others; place is always marked by sociality, since alterity is anterior. Filiation, in particular, implies a very specific attribution of causality leading to participation between the persons involved. Before the recent days of paternity testing, paternal filiation in particular was legally and socially defined as an unverifiable (thus classificatory) assumption, a matter of "knowledge" rather than "observation." By treating all relations as being akin to paternal filiation, Anglo-American philosophers succumbed to the sociocentric proneness to situate relations as propositional facts, suggesting that things may exist in some essential way independently of their relations. Thus, by analogically generalizing transcendence, they adopted a position where essence and existence drifted apart. Moreover, in so doing, they silently and indirectly validated the ontological differentiation between organic and moral filiation—the old paradox of nature/nurture that continues to befuddle kinship theorists to this day. This is a serious problem with the notion of "relatedness" that has played such a significant role in kinship studies over the past decade (see Carsten 2004: 82).

An alternative route emerges from our earlier discussions. Humans engage relationally with world in varied ways. The affordances that surround us are relations that provide us with invitations to act. Thus, I have a relation with the sound of the fireman's bell in my village, with the tree that stands out at the top of the hill behind my home, with the size of the door of the café, with the person next to me in the suburban train, with the key to my office, and so on. These, however, are relations that in the normal run of things do not affect me constitutively as a person. They may or not come to be elaborated propositionally, but they are not constitutive of my arena of presence and action. This does not mean that they are "external" in the sense defined by Moore, for indeed I find Ryder's approach more appealing, as it implies that all relations possess an element of interaction (the theory that Moore had meant to disprove).

Now, contrary to the examples I gave above, the signet ring my grandfather left me in his will, the Aborigines' totem animal, my mother's wedding dress, the consecrated Host, my own sister, Edward VII for George V, to use Moore's example—all of these are relations that (a) have been propositionally elaborated in very significant ways and (b) bear deep implications for the intrinsic nature of the arena of presence and action of the persons involved in the relation. To define all relations by reference to ontogenetically constitutive relations of this kind is to forget both that all affordances can be recognized as relations in an intentional sense and that personhood as an emergent property is constituted propositionally through participation in secondary intersubjectivity.

Thus, ontogenetically constitutive relations operate in a very different way to other relations. In a study about ova donors and recipients in contexts of assisted reproduction in Great Britain, Monica Konrad, a disciple of Marilyn Strathern, manages to advance this discussion by exploring her own ethnographic material (Konrad 2005). Her analytic challenge is simple to state: English law at the time was very insistent on the need to keep absolute anonymity between ova donors and their recipients (and the eventual child who is born of the exchange). However, donors made the gift because they knew they were going to help somebody become fertile—symbolically, a heavy life-giving gesture. In turn, the recipients—and the people who ultimately result from their assisted pregnancies—knew that there was somebody who gave them the ova and with whom they were . . . related? The very biologistic tone of the activity of assisted reproduction alerts people to the fact that they are physically constituted by connections that are not "relations." Furthermore, the Maussian kind of sociocentric reading of reciprocity does not work here either, since the eggs circulate only in one direction and there is no payment or expression of relatedness that could move in the contrary direction.

Konrad speculates on how a person would feel who knows that their mother, before conceiving them, had already donated gametes that would have given rise to persons who may be living in one's proximate environment. She claims, "The knowledge is instantly 'relational' since it exposes the existence 'somewhere' of a genetic half-sibling. It is relational, and specifically transilient in nature, because it sets up irrelational kinship" (ibid.: 118). Unfortunately, this concept of transilience, which Konrad devises, does not advance us at all since it bears no other meaning apart from the one she gives it. The problem is that the meaning she gives it depends integrally on the concept of "irrelationality," and that is precisely what we are trying to understand.

The issue she is trying to address is far more common in the ethnographic register than may at first seem. One of the central aporias that Vanda Silva and I attempted to respond to in our study of kinship relations among the poor periurban population of coastal Bahia is a manifestation of it (Pina-Cabral and Silva 2013). People were very explicit to us that the roots of kinship/house relations were in *consideração*, a very heavily weighed concept in their daily life that implied mutual attention, continued support, and long-term reciprocity. Thus, a person who did not give "consideration" to a relative was denying that relation. The relation was as good as nonexistent, except that it did not fade away: it merely became dormant, it became a possibility, an emotionally disturbing repressed engagement. These bad fathers, bad mothers, bad siblings, bad husbands, bad friends, who fell out of the relational circle of a person never stopped being there in a latent condition, an irrelational condition, to use Konrad's term. This is the quandary that we had to address.

The problem is that the very language of social anthropology does not facilitate our task, as we are constantly called to speak of "relating," "by relation to," "establish relationships with," and so on, as if these were patently obvious things to characterize. The fact is that all relational language transports with itself an analytical trap: precisely because it is a "duplex," the concept of relation produces a caesurist effect. I mean, it assumes (a) that we are speaking of something that occurs between two or more separate entities and (b) that the path between them is symmetric (see Viveiros de Castro 2007). Plainly, neither of these is the case in the two examples we detailed above. There, we are faced with forms of . . . relating . . . that are not relational, because they involve a questioning of the very processes of generation of the entities related. Being fusional but not symmetric, they mobilize anterior alterity, as they place the one and the many in dynamic engagement (persons are dividual).

As Konrad discovered, we are here at the limit of what is possible to say in scientific speak, as we are confronted with such analytic monstrosities as the notion of an "irrelational relation." In both of the examples above, what is at stake is less who the persons involved think they are and more the traces of their generation in world. Relations without *consideração*, much as relations subject to the schism of anonymity, never stop existing as a possibility because they were never only a matter of the management of categories; they were always something that emerged from the person's intentional positioning in the world. Whoever has been in a certain place can never stop the fact of having been there, even if that positioning does not come to be propositionally formulated into an instituted relation (see Pina-Cabral 2011). Personal ontogeny is deeply historical and the relational practices that persons engage in within propositional communication are constantly being undermined, altered, and made subject to the becoming of people's intentional engagement with world—which is fusional and not dualist.

I conclude, therefore, that we must swap round the focus of our analysis. If we are to follow Alberto Corsín's advice (2004) and remain within the language of relatedness we must turn things around and, instead of treating personally constitutive relations as the prototype of all relations in sociocentric fashion, treat them as a very special case of relation. The acknowledgment of such a relation is a propositional occurrence based on an experienced affordance, not the actual affordance. The nature of the affordance can be very diverse: people are related to each other, the sun and the moon relate with each other, ants relate with humans, the letters of the alphabet are related, and so on. All of these are relations, but they are of very diverse nature. By propositionally *instituting* a relation (e.g., "This is my cat" or "The postman comes at 7 a.m."), I place it within another field of relatedness; I transform it into a recurrent occurrence within a form of life. It becomes a feature of the scaffolding of mind. As persons live in a world that they construct propositionally, that they configure, the instituting of these relations (i.e., their existence as recognizable occurrences independent of the specific nature of the affordance at stake) is the process through which world is configured but also through which persons are formed.

This allows us to resolve the quandary posed by "irrelational relations." Social relations exist insofar as they have been propositionally instituted, otherwise they are merely affordances, links in a world formed of millions and trillions and more of effective causal ties that are not deserving of reaching human conscience or of playing a role in human social life, but which do not, for all that, cease to exist.

A social relation, therefore, is a function of the attribution of ontological weight to an association that is recognized by persons. There can be more and less relation, and there are even social relations that, because their ontological weight is denied, can lay dormant as mere potentialities. Certain social relations are personally constitutive in an ontogenetic way, since they involve constitutive participation between the persons or the persons and the parts of world that they specify. Filiation is a special way of being related that engages persons transcendentally in their relation with world. Philosophers and anthropologists would be advised not to choose filiation as the prototypical example of relation, for transcendence is a function of personhood but not of all relational occurrences.

In turn, what ethnographers must attend to when they propose a worldview is how relations are instituted within a form of life, and that results not from there having been causal associations (affordances, such as a gamete donation or an unwanted pregnancy) but from the fact that ontological weight (more or less of it) was placed on them. I may choose to identify an affordance propositionally: for example, the relation between the tree and the wall in my garden. But when I identify a social relation between two or more persons, I am doing more than that, for I am stating that the relational properties of these persons have interacted constitutively in a transcendental manner. To conclude, all acknowledged relations carry within them the processes of their propositional constitution, but some of them are constitutive of the persons involved.

Epilogue

Long ago, Friedrich Waisman commented that "you may confute and kill a scientific theory; a philosophy dies only of old age" (1968: 66). This observation applies much more broadly than he might have imagined: in the case of anthropology, we have been profoundly resistant to abandoning the analytical underpinnings of twentieth-century sociocentrism.

I entered into anthropology in the early 1970s, at a time when it was bravely responding to the challenges posed by decolonization and the emergence of new and very brutal forms of imperialism. We knew we wanted to purge our discipline of its political and theoretical drawbacks, but we did not know what that involved. The sociocentric consensus of the Classical Period had never been total, but it was comfortable to the point of being irresistible. Every time you chipped off a piece of it, you thought you had done the job, but the hegemonic hulk continued to exercise its silent magnetic influence. The political implications of anthropology's engagement with imperialism seemed easy to deconstruct, whilst, in fact, they remained to this day more opaque than we are keen to admit. But the epistemological implications of neo-Kantian sociocentrism took a long time to unravel. And the principal reason for that is that the Cartesian epistemological framework provided great security.

We wanted order and, when we found it no longer, like spoilt children, we succumbed to analytical dissolution. Instead of finding new paths for analysis, we gave up on analysis; instead of searching for new modes of comparison, we gave up on comparison. But, worse still, instead of looking for new ways to engage human transcendence, we simply succumbed to anthropological agnosticism, taking recourse to the weak-kneed solution of postulating a transcendental unreachable Other. Most of us did hold on to ethnography, however, as a perennial source of fascination, even as many of us wrongly abandoned the history of our discipline as a source of authority; we stopped being able to grasp the profound value of the humanist legacy that the anthropological tradition constitutes. Anthropology had its long moment of self-doubt.

Over the decades I have come to be convinced that the principal reason for this sorry state of affairs is our distaste for messy thinking. We find it hard to accept the complexity, ambivalence, and equivocation of real-life processes: the messiness of it all. Still, it is only in that direction that a new and more satisfactory theoretical pathway may be pursued. The arena of presence and action is a mediating platform; therefore, it will ever hover in thin air. Yet it is upon such an unsteady scaffold that human propositional worlds are built. The price humans pay in order to transcend their intentional (animal) condition and achieve reflexive (symbolic) thinking is to remain ever incomplete, ever uncertain, ever underdetermined, and decidedly indeterminate. Fuzzy logic (based on error correction) was developed to reproduce in machines the way humans control their everyday environment, and it was incredibly successful at doing just that, but, surprisingly, anthropologists never used it as a form of modeling how humans engage their environment. The notions of polythetic thinking, stochasticism, participation, partibility, dividuality, mutuality, equivocation, have met with extreme resistance in anthropological circles. Social scientists find it safer to stick to the underpinning certitudes that representationalist models provide, even after having encountered their limits more than a quarter-century ago.

ALTERITY AND TRANSCENDENCE

It is not enough to stay with agnostic debunking; we have had too much of that over the years. Anthropology has to start working at reconstructing itself so as to be able to satisfy the needs of ethnographic theory. In particular, we have to abdicate decisively from the sort of primitivist fascination with the symmetric Other that has defined our discipline for far too long. Note, however, this should not be understood as an argument in favor of refocusing the study of humans on sameness as opposed to difference. The issue here is not the substitution of a focus on the Other by a focus on the Same, but rather how sameness and difference are to be conceived. We must move away from the sociocentric emphasis on group-to-group, symmetric alterity (particularly when presented in the format of "us" v. "Other"). Rather, we must place the emphasis on the sort of anterior, asymmetric alterity that is foundational of all levels of human sociality (intrapersonal, interpersonal, and all the many collective levels).

As it happens, we might have taken lessons from Kant on this topic:

> What concerns anthropology is always already there and never entirely given; what comes first for anthropology is bound up with a time which in any case envelops it from a distance. It is not that the problem of the origin is unknown to it; on the contrary, it gives the problem back its true meaning, which is not to reveal and to isolate the first time in a single instant, but to recover the temporal framework that, having already begun, is no less radical. The originary is not the really primitive, it is the truly temporal. (Foucault [1961] 2008: 92)

As anthropologists, alterity is our challenge. But not symmetric alterity—the epitome of which is the "West v. Rest" polarity that drives rhetorically so many of our contemporary arguments. In time, all duality is ultimately unstable and, in any case, our capacity to grasp it is nothing but an embodied intuition. Alterity is always already universally present and we have to explore it ethnographically everywhere. Our guiding purpose, therefore, must be the examination of the *anterior alterity* that inheres in each and every one of us; the founding historicity as persons that endows us with world *but* an ambiguous world. Paternalist primitivism—with its mesmerizing promise of radically alternative worlds and its fascination with mimetic difference—turns out to be an abdication from anthropology's basic ethical responsibility as science. Anthropologists are practitioners of a discipline that is not a Western one, but that must and does belong to all of humankind. This has to be seen both as an ethical and as an analytical injunction.

If we look over this past century of anthropological history, we have to conclude that the troubled fascination of Tylor, Frazer, Durkheim, and Lévy-Bruhl with magic, religion, and spirituality remains central to our discipline. It would seem that there is some reason why transcendence challenges directly the anthropological project of studying the human condition. The quandaries it poses remain central to our present-day anthropological debates (e.g., Engelke 2002).

This book attempts to demonstrate that those who, from within anthropology, continue to engage the perplexities caused by the false polarization of mind and matter are laboring in a losing battle. Transcendence is an inevitable and ever-present characteristic of the human condition, and we would be better advised to search for it where it can readily be found: within ourselves as persons as well as in worlds afar. In so doing, we can then embrace the charms of our contemporary polydivinistic condition; we can come to terms with our own proneness to "superstition" (see Pina-Cabral 2014a). Metaphysical pluralism in humans is not to be approached as a limitation, a flaw, a vicious recidivism. Quine's lesson about human communication was that, once we give up on an all-or-nothing posture toward truth, these uncertainties and doubts stop being impediments and become tools for grappling with our uniquely human presence in world. Rather than being forced to square the circle by denying our indeterminacy and underdetermination, thus being left to bemoan our loss of eternity, we are better off in accepting that our limitations as live embodied humans are our door to a more ecumenical and decidedly more humane polydivinistic acceptance of our immanent transcendence.

THE ETHNOGRAPHIC GESTURE

Ethnographic engagement is the lifeline of the anthropological undertaking, for it is what gives it an active connection with world. As an analytical engagement, it explores the human condition in ever-renewed light and, in this way, it pushes through the task of de-ethnocentrification, that is, the process of constant questioning of our limitations concerning what we know about human sociality and how it engages world. It is by its very nature a messy task that will never be exhausted, since the metaphysical dynamism of the human condition means that we will ever waver between different and new views of the world and the person; we will never settle to a final truth. There is no defeatism in this position, nor is there a distrust of the possibility of engaging truth in our path through earth. To the contrary, the aim of this book was to demonstrate that veridicality is a condition of human thinking and, therefore, of the scientific enterprise. Humans will always search for and find truth; what they will not find is *the* final truth, as that is an absurd chimera.

Ethnography is intrinsically a comparative activity—what makes a worldview is not what it is per se but how it differs from other worldviews. The notion that there could be such a thing as "a straightforward ethnographic description" is part of naïve ontology; it should have been worked out of any anthropological student by the second year of his or her degree. Ethnography is comparative in at least three senses: (a) by relation to the general anthropological discourse of the day and the debates that are in fashion; (b) by relation to what has already been written concerning the particular object of description (geographically and thematically); and (c) by relation to the private leanings, inclinations, and interests of the ethnographer.

For this reason I have always preferred to avoid the concept of anthropology at home, since it promotes a simplistic reification of the ethnographer's home culture (the imperial "we" that continues to dominate the less sophisticated versions of the anthropological discourse—cf. Pina-Cabral 1992). Now, this is absurd as some of us have an interest in, for example, matters of fertility, whilst others have an interest in, say, death and grieving. Others, still, have read a lot of Malinowski or Monica Wilson, but not enough Bateson, and will always have their inspirations marked by that background. Still others have political or ethical issues to address and respond to: feminism, racism, socialism, homophobia, human rights, and so on.

The notion that, in writing ethnography, an ethnographer is necessarily comparing her "home" assumptions with those of the natives is an imperialist artifact, every year more absurd. It is up to us today to invent modes of carrying out our ethnography that correspond better to our postimperial, globalized condition. This can only be done by working at an anthropology that is accessible to all, not by pretending that there can be many anthropologies, for the idea that each culture has its own anthropology is a dangerous truism. It is a false play on the meaning of the word *anthropology* that ends up serving the interests of those who are sitting in a position of global hegemony and for whom cultural incommensurability is a useful ploy for avoiding the ethical challenges of comparison.

The ethnographic gesture, therefore, may be defined as the movement of a trained social scientist who goes somewhere in order to attempt to identify the central figurations and recurrent modes of engagement with world that inform a certain form of life. The aim of the ethnographer's work is to propose a worldview or to clarify an aspect thereof. It is not a discourse on discourses, for that would be to presume that one can separate understanding from world—both as far as the analyst and as far as the analyzed are concerned.

As a methodology of research, ethnography depends more directly than other less qualitative methods on the personal encounter of the ethnographer with the persons she studies. Its dependence on the achievement of mutual understanding based on the intersubjectivity that results from sharing a lived environment gives ethnography a particular empirical richness and qualifies it ideally for its main aim: the de-ethnocentrification of our scientific understanding of social life. This concept, borrowed from Pitt-Rivers (1992), is of a piece with the minimalist realism espoused in this book. It assumes that our socioscientific task is never achieved and, like science, is ecumenical, in the sense that it corresponds to a process of ever-expanding human relevance.

For this reason it seems adequate to designate as a "gesture" the disposition that moves the ethnographer. It is, indeed, a gesture to the extent that it necessarily involves an ethical engagement in world with the particular form of life it aims to analyze and comparatively qualify. This is not only the strength of the ethnographer's work, it is also her main challenge, for the personal nature of the understanding she achieves also means that readers cannot easily verify the veracity of what they are being told. Ultimately, the reader's interpretive charity and the writer's capacity to produce a verisimilitudinous impression (outlandish as what we are told may at first seem) are the principal tools of our trade. They have served us well over the decades, and we are fully justified in trusting that they will continue to do so for a long time to come.

WORLD FORMING

Human immersion in space/time is unavoidable, for the affordances persons meet with are constantly evolving. There is no final resting point in humanity's course, no end to history. In fact, after the last human has died, human history will not come to an end for quite a while still, for humans fire up the world with the constant reifications that characterize their communicational endeavors. Human action moves the world and is moved by world in processes that constantly reflect our social condition as live beings.

Because it emerges traumatically, personhood is ethically challenged. Each one of us has to struggle permanently with the limits of his or her own coresponsibility because personal presence allows us to dissociate from our fellow humans. Although this dissociation cannot ever be complete, its effects are continuously felt in human social life; evil emerges in our propositional engagement with world. As Levinas has noted, "It is the ethical claim upon me not to kill that persecutes me, and it persecutes me precisely because I may well be moved to kill or I may well have to resist my will at the moment the commandment not to kill is addressed to me" (in Butler 2012: 62). We all bear the mark of Cain. But domination is anterior to that, as it is a function of sociality, a condition for collective action. Owing to our capacity to dissociate from our fellow humans (a byproduct of presence, our capacity to dissociate from ourselves), we can take it to extremes of self-destruction that no other species could ever contemplate. Every year we remember the horror of the nuclear bombs in Nagasaki and Hiroshima, and yet every year, by paying our taxes, we contribute toward keeping those bombs alive.

As opposed to other species, humans are world forming. Not because other species fail to act on the world, but because, with the emergence of propositional thinking, we succeed in accessing world as if we were apart from it—we transcend our immediate world. Thus, we achieve forms of action that depend on highly complex systems of communication and that transcend our own personal reach very considerably. The scaffolded world that results from our propositional engagements is richer than that of animals. I need hardly insist on this point by depositing further words into my iMac.

Over time, the distribution of legitimate power among humans gives rise to hegemonies: that is, reasonably stable configurations of power. Each one of us enters a world that is both given and constructed; sociality constitutes forms of life by establishing a *habitus*. We are only free to question the configurations of power to a point, and we are never free to move out of them, for they are a function of human sociality. Yet we are ethically bound to ever query them, for whilst we are the bearers and reproducers of hegemony, we are also mutually engaged with those humans who are reduced by the tragically brutal ways in which human power can come to be instituted. Personal presence is conditioned on an anterior alterity; we are defined by the burden of the suffering of others.

Once personhood emerges, personal participation is ever reconstituting itself. However, although we have our primordial solidarities and they remain with us way beyond the ends of our organic lives, the process of triangulation is constant. As it results from triangulation, personhood as an emergent property is first experienced by each one of us as a lack, not a completion. This means that space is always available for generic alterity to affirm itself; place is always open to be shared, whether we want it or not. Therefore, the anterior presence of others in the caring environment turns early personal ontogeny into a sharing of place. Cohabiting is a foundational condition of personhood and, therefore, of humanity. Thus, in personhood, place sharing (participation) is not an option; it is rather an imposed condition. The place of personhood will always also be someone else's place. And, furthermore, it is *not* a specific (individual) condition but a generic one, for it opens us up to future participations.

This sharing of place is the basis for the universality of hospitality, as the other who arrives finds a space of occupation that is owed to them not through some sort of contract but because of the gap that anterior alterity always leaves open in sociality. As it occurs in time, containment, like opposition, always remains incomplete. The condition of being a neighbor, therefore, is anterior to the condition of being a person. Yet, once personhood is established, the presence of the other turns into an imposition. This means that the place of the neighbor is always ambivalent, for it is at one and the same time both a responsibility one cherishes (a charity) and a responsibility that impinges upon one (a drudgery). This space-for-the-other affords both a charity one cannot deny and a drudgery one cannot avoid. Everyone who has had a guest knows of the ambiguity of hospitality; everyone who has had a sibling knows of the ambivalence of sharing place (participation).

And here we turn again to the deep wisdom of Anselm's insight. When he used the words of Isaiah to argue that belief is a condition for understanding, he took recourse to the sharing of space (to dwelling) as his dominant metaphor. Place and understanding are linked because reason only exists within communication and all communication occurs in spaces previously marked by our social historicity, providing all kinds of affordances. This is the case with all everyday environments, where the objects that surround us provide paths to meaning that are not, strictly speaking, semiotic and where things and locales that we are bound to use implicitly afford possibilities of action that are not propositionally transmitted.

Hospitality is a general human proclivity, because the place of the other can never be closed, as the Warlpiri ethnography that we recalled above exemplifies. Ethnography has relied on hospitality from the beginning as an affordance that provides it with one of its conditions of possibility, and if there is something that ethnography has demonstrated over the last century and a half in which it has been systematically practiced, it is that hospitality very rarely fails us. Outside momentary situations of crisis, ethnographers have been able to rely on it ever since the discipline started. In fact, from the days in the sixteenth century when people like Tomé Pires or Hans Staden wrote their visionary protoethnographies that so inspired Montaigne, it has been clear that anthropology is a direct product of the more basic dispositions of humans, and in particular their proneness for interpretive charity.

Anthropology, thus, is a part of that ever-unfinished effort that humans undertake in history to move out of their own conditionings, to rise above the limits of their environment. The possibility of transcendence with which personal presence has endowed us is the central drive through which we can achieve this. By engaging in ethnography (whether we do it around the corner or in some place we did not know before), we are placing ourselves in others' shoes and exercising the limits of our imagination by entering a place that others cannot but have left open for us. Anthropology's aim of de-ethnocentrification is dependent upon these basic human processes: shared intentionality leading to intersubjectivity; the capacity to transcend partially one's condition through imagination; hospitality leading to human survival and social participation.

Bibliography

Aijmer, Göran. 2001. "The symbological project." *Cultural Dynamics* 13 (1): 66–69.

———. 2013. "Counterpoint and social belonging: Creator and creatrix in Southwestern China." *Journal of Ritual Studies* 27 (2): 65–81.

———. 2015. "Erasing the dead in Kaixiangong: Ancestry and cultural transforms in Southern China." *Cambridge Journal of Chinese Studies* 10 (2): 39–52.

Anderson, Michael L., Michael J. Richardson, and Anthony Chemero. 2012. "Eroding the boundaries of cognition: Implications of embodiment." *Topics in Cognitive Science* 4: 717–30.

Anselm, Saint. 1998. *The major works.* Oxford: Oxford University Press.

Ardener, Edwin. 2007. "Comprehending others." In *The voice of prophecy and other essays*, 159–85. Oxford: Berghahn.

Arendt, Hannah. 1958. *The human condition.* Chicago: University of Chicago Press.

Bar-Yam, Yaneer. 2016. "Relational properties in objective science." *Complexity science, society and (beyond) big data analysis.* https://medium.com/complex-systems-channel/relational-properties-in-objective-science-d723ddb-4fac4#.dvrivdbkh.

Bateson, Gregory. 1972. *Steps to an ecology of mind: Collected essays in anthropology, psychiatry, evolution, and epistemology.* Chicago: University of Chicago Press.

―――. 1979. *Mind and nature: A necessary unity.* New York: Dutton.

Beidelman, T. O., ed. 1971. *The translation of culture: Essays to Evans-Pritchard.* London: Tavistock Press.

Belland, Brian, and Joel Drake. 2013. "Toward a framework on how affordances and motives can drive different uses of scaffolds: theory, evidence, and design implications." *Educational Technology Research Development* 61: 903–25.

Bennett, Jane. 2010. *Vibrant matter: A political ecology of things.* Durham, NC: Duke University Press.

Benveniste, Émile. 1966. *Problèmes de linguistique générale, I.* Paris: NRF, Gallimard. (Available in English: *Problems in general linguistics, I.* Translated by Mary Elizabeth Meek. Coral Gables, FL: University of Miami Press, 1971.)

Bloch, Maurice. 2008. "Truth and sight: Generalizing without universalizing." *Journal of the Royal Anthropological Institute* (N.S.) (Special Issue): S22–32.

―――. 2012. *Anthropology and the cognitive challenge.* Cambridge: Cambridge University Press.

Bonte, Pierre, Enric Porqueres i Gené, and J. Wilgaux, eds. 2011. *L'argument de la filiation.* Paris: Maison des Sciences de l'Homme.

Boon, James A., and David M. Schneider. 1974. "Kinship vis-à-vis myth contrasts in Lévi-Strauss' approaches to cross-cultural comparison." *American Anthropologist* (N.S.) 76 (4): 799–817.

Bourdieu, Pierre. 1991. *Language and symbolic power.* Translated by Gino Raymond and Matthew Adamson. Cambridge, MA: Harvard University Press.

Bowman, Glenn. 1991. "Christian ideology and the image of a Holy Land: The place of Jerusalem pilgrimage in the various Christianities." In *Contesting the sacred: The anthropology of Christian pilgrimage,* edited by Michael Sallnow and John Eade, 98–121. London: Routledge.

Bråten, Stein, ed. (1998) 2006. *Intersubjective communication and emotion in early ontogeny.* Cambridge: Maison des Sciences de l'Homme/Cambridge University Press.

Butler, Judith. 2012. *Parting ways: Jewishness and the critique of Zionism.* New York: Columbia University Press.

Candea, Matei. 2011. "Endo/exo." *Common Knowledge* 17 (1): 146–50.

Carsten, Janet. 2004. *After kinship.* Cambridge: University Press.

Caygill, Howard. 2002. *Levinas and the political.* London: Routledge.

Chemero, Anthony. 2003. "An outline of a theory of affordances." *Ecological Psychology* 15 (2): 181–95.

―――. 2009. *Radical embodied cognitive science.* Cambridge, MA: MIT Press.

Cicero, Marcus Tullius. 1884. *Laelius de amicitia*, edited by C. F. W. Müller. Leipzig: Teubner (cf. http://www.forumromanum.org/literature/cicero/amic.html).

Clark, Andy. 2010. "Memento's revenge: The extended mind extended." In *The extended mind*, edited by Richard Menary, 43–66. Cambridge, MA: MIT Press.

———. 2014. "Busting out: Predictive brains, embodied minds, and the puzzle of the evidentiary veil." *Noûs.* doi: 10.1111/nous.12140.

Clark, Andy, and David J. Chalmers. 1998. "The extended mind." *Analysis* 58: 10–23.

Cole, Sally. 2003. *Ruth Landes: A life in anthropology.* New York: University of Nebraska Press.

Collingwood, R. G. (1933) 2005. *An essay on philosophical method.* Revision and introduction by James Connelly and Giuseppina D'Oro. Oxford: Clarendon Press.

——— (1946) 1994. *The idea of history.* Edited by Jan van der Dussen. Oxford: Oxford University Press.

Connolly, William E. 2001. "Spinoza and Us." *Political Theory* 29 (4): 583–94.

———. 2011. *A world of becoming.* Durham, NC: Duke University Press.

Corsín Jiménez, Alberto. 2004. "The form of the relation, or anthropology's enchantment with the algebraic imagination." http://digital.csic.es/bitstream/10261/98307/1/the%20form%20of%20the%20relation.pdf.

Damásio, António. 1999. *The feeling of what happens: Body, emotion and the making of consciousness.* London: Vintage.

Davidson, Donald. 1974. "On the very idea of a conceptual scheme." *Proceedings and Addresses of the American Philosophical Association* 47: 5–20.

———. 1984. *Inquiries into truth and interpretation.* Oxford: Oxford University Press.

———. 2001. *Subjective, intersubjective, objective.* Oxford: Oxford University Press.

———. 2004. *Problems of rationality.* Oxford: Oxford University Press.

———. 2005. *Truth, language and history.* Oxford: Oxford University Press.

de Martino, Ernesto. (1959) 2001. *Magic: A theory from the South.* Translated by D. L. Zinn. Chicago: Hau Books.

Deleuze, Gilles. 2001. "Immanence: A life." In *Pure immanence: Essays of a life,* 25–33. New York: Zone Books.

Descola, Philippe. 2005. *Par-delà nature et culture*. Paris: Gallimard. (Available in English: *Beyond nature and culture*. Translated by Janet Lloyd. Chicago: University of Chicago Press, 2013.)

———. 2010. "Cognition, perception and worlding." *Interdisciplinary Science Reviews* 35 (3–4): 334–40.

———. 2014. "Modes of being and forms of predication." *HAU: Journal of Ethnographic Theory* 4 (1): 271–80.

Douglas, Mary. 1970. "Introduction: Thirty years after *Witchcraft, oracles, and magic*." In *Witchcraft confessions and accusations*, edited by Mary Douglas, xiii–xxxviii. London: Routledge.

———. 1980. *Evans-Pritchard: His life, work, writings, and ideas*. New York: Viking Press.

Duranti, Alessandro. 2015. *The anthropology of intentions: Language in a world of others*. Cambridge: Cambridge University Press.

Durkheim, Émile, and Marcel Mauss. (1903) 1963. *Primitive classification*. Translated and introduced by Rodney Needham. Chicago: University of Chicago Press.

Dyer, John R. G., Anders Johansson, Dirk Helbing, Iain D. Couzin, and Jens Krause. 2009. "Leadership, consensus decision making and collective behaviour in humans." *Philosophical Transactions: Biological Sciences* 364: 781–89.

Edelman, Gerald M. 1992. *Bright air, brilliant fire: On the matter of the mind*. New York: Basic Books.

Edwards, Jeanette, and Carles Salazar. 2009. *European kinship in the age of biotechnology*. Oxford: Berghahn.

Elden, Stuart. 2004. *Understanding Henri Lefebvre*. London: Bloomsbury Publishers.

Elster, Jon. 1983. *Sour grapes: Studies in the subversion of rationality*. Cambridge: Cambridge University Press.

Engelke, Mathew. 2002. "The problem of belief: Evans-Pritchard and Victor Turner on 'the inner life'." *Anthropology Today* 18 (6): 3–8.

Evans, G. R. 1989. *Anselm*. Canterbury, UK: Morehouse-Barlow.

Evans-Pritchard, E. E. 1933. "The intellectualist (English) interpretation of magic." *Bulletin of the Faculty of Arts* 1 (2) (Cairo, Egypt: Farouk University): 282–311.

———. (1934) 1970. "Lévy-Bruhl's theory of primitive mentality." *Journal of the Anthropological Society of Oxford* 1 (2): 39–60.

———. 1936. "Science and sentiment: An exposition and criticism of the writings of Pareto." *Bulletin of the Faculty of Arts* 3 (2) (Cairo, Egypt: Farouk University): 163–92.

———. (1937) 1976. *Witchcraft, oracles and magic among the Azande.* Abbreviated by Eva Gillies. Oxford: Clarendon Press.

———. 1962. *Essays in social anthropology.* London: Faber and Faber.

———. 1963. *The comparative method in social anthropology.* London: Athlone Press.

———. (1973) 1976. "Some reminiscences and reflections on fieldwork." In *Witchcraft, oracles and magic among the Azande,* 240–54. Oxford: Clarendon Press.

Fei Hsiao-tung. 1939. *Peasant life in China: A field study of country life in the Yangtze Valley.* London: Routledge & Kegan Paul.

Feleppa, Robert. 1988. *Convention, translation, and understanding: Philosophical problems in the comparative study of culture.* New York: State University of New York Press.

Fernandez, James. 1991. *Beyond metaphor: Theory of tropes in anthropology.* Stanford: Stanford University Press.

Finkielkraut, Alain. (1984) 1997. *The wisdom of love.* Translated by Kevin O'Neill and David Suchoff. Lincoln: University of Nebraska Press.

Foot, Philippa. 2001. *Natural goodness.* Oxford: Clarendon Press.

Fortes, Meyer. 1969. *Kinship and social order.* Chicago: Aldine.

Fortes, Meyer. (1973) 1987. "The concept of the person." In *Religion, morality and the person: Essays on Tallensi religion,* 247–86. Cambridge: Cambridge: University Press.

Foucault, Michel. (1961) 2008. *Introduction to Kant's anthropology.* Translated by Kate Briggs and Roberto Nigro. Los Angeles: Semiotext(e).

Frankfurt, Harry G. 2009. *On bullshit.* Princeton, NJ: Princeton University Press.

Gabriel, Markus. 2015. *Why the world does not exist.* London: Wiley & Sons.

Gallagher, Shaun. 2014. "The cruel and unusual phenomenology of solitary confinement." *Frontiers in Psychology.* https://doi.org/10.3389/fpsyg.2014.00585.

Gallagher, Shaun, and Rebecca Seté Jacobson. 2012. "Heidegger and social cognition." In *Heidegger and cognitive science,* edited by Julian Kiverstein and Michael Wheeler, 213–45. London: Palgrave Macmillan.

Garrison, Jim. 1999. "John Dewey, Jacques Derrida, and the metaphysics of presence." *Transactions of the Charles S. Peirce Society* 35 (2): 346–72.

Gaston, Sean. 2013. *The concept of world from Kant to Derrida.* London: Rowman & Littlefield.

Gellner, Ernest, 1974. *Legitimation of belief.* Cambridge: Cambridge University Press.

Gettler, Leo. 2010. "Direct male care and hominin evolution: Why the male–child interaction is more than a nice social idea." *American Anthropologist* 112 (1): 7–21.

Gibson, James J. 1979. *The ecological approach to visual perception.* Boston: Houghton Mifflin.

Givens, Terry. 2009. *When souls had wings: Pre-mortal existence in Western thought.* Oxford: Oxford University Press.

Gluckman, Max. 1962. "Les rites de passage." In *Essays on the ritual of social relations,* edited by Max Gluckman, 1–52. Manchester: Manchester University Press.

Godlove, Terry F. 1996. *Religion, interpretation, and diversity of belief: The framework model from Kant to Durkheim and to Davidson.* Macon, GA: Mercer University Press.

Goldman, Márcio. 2003. "Os tambores dos mortos e os tambores dos vivos: Etnografia, antropologia e política em Ilhéus, Bahia." *Revista de Antropologia* 46 (2): 423–444.

Goodwin, Charles, and Marjorie Harness. 2004. "Participation." In *A companion to linguistic anthropology,* edited by Alessandro Duranti, 222–44. Oxford: Blackwell.

Gutman, Bruno. 1926. *Das Recht der Dschagga.* Munich: C. H. Beck.

Hamberger, Klaus. 2011. *La parenté vodou: Organisation sociale et logique symbolique en pays ouatchi (Togo).* Paris: Éditions de la Maison des Sciences de L'Homme.

Hammel, Eugen. 1984. "On the *** of studying household form and function." In *Households: Comparative and historical studies of the domestic group,* edited by Robert Netting, Richard Wilk, and Eric Arnould, 29–43. Berkeley: University of California Press.

Hann, Chris. 2005. "Foreword." In *One discipline, four ways: British, German, French, and American anthropology,* edited by Chris Hann, vii–ix. Chicago: University of Chicago Press.

Hannerz, Ulf. 2010. *Anthropology's world: Life in a twenty-first-century discipline.* London: Pluto Press.

Hattiangadi, Jagdish. 2005. "The emergence of minds in space and time." In *The mind as a scientific object: Between brain and culture*, edited by in Christina E. Erneling and David Martel Johnson, 79–100. New York: Oxford University Press.

Heidegger, Martin. (1929/30) 1995. *The fundamental concepts of metaphysics: World, finitude, solitude.* Translated by William McNeill and Nicholas Walker. Bloomington: Indiana University Press.

———. (1950) 2002. *Off the beaten track.* Edited and translated by Julian Young and Kenneth Haynes. Cambridge: University Press.

———. (1953) 2010. *Being and time.* Translated by Joan Stambaugh. Albany: SUNY Press.

———. 1998. *Pathmarks.* Edited by William McNeill. Cambridge: University Press.

———. 1988. *The basic problems of phenomenology.* Translated by Albert Hofstadter. Bloomington: Indiana University Press.

———. 1999. *Contributions to philosophy (from Enowning).* Translated by Parvis Emad and Kenneth Maly. Bloomington: Indiana University Press.

Holbraad, Martin. 2010. "Ontology is just another word for culture." *Critique of Anthropology* 30 (2): 152–200.

Hsu, Francis. (1948) 1967. *Under the ancestors' shadow: Kinship, personality, and social mobility in village China.* Garden City, NY: Doubleday.

Hurston, Zora Neale. (1935) 1990. *Mules and men.* New York: Harper Perennial.

Hutto, Daniel. 2008. *Folk psychological narratives.* Cambridge, MA: MIT Press.

Hutto, Daniel, Michael D. Kirchhoff, and Erik Myin. 2014. "Extensive enactivism: Why keep it all in?" *Frontiers of Human Neuroscience* 8: art. 706.

Hutto, Daniel, and Erik Myin. 2013. *Radicalizing enactivism: Basic minds without content.* Cambridge, MA: MIT Press.

Ingold, Tim. 1995. "Building, dwelling, living: How animals and people make themselves at home in the world." In *Shifting contexts: Transformations in anthropological knowledge*, edited by Marilyn Strathern, 57–80. London: Routledge.

———, ed. 1996. *Key debates in anthropology.* London: Routledge.

———. 2000. *The perception of the environment: Essays on livelihood, dwelling and skill.* London: Routledge.

———. 2010. "The man in the machine and the self-builder." *Interdisciplinary Science Review* 35 (3–4): 353–64.

Jackson, Michael. 1995. *At home in the world*. Durham, NC: Duke University Press.

Jahoda, Gustav. 1970. *The psychology of superstition*. Harmondsworth, UK: Penguin.

James, Deborah, Evelyn Plaice, and Christina Toren, eds. 2013. *Culture wars: Context, models, and anthropologists' accounts*. Oxford: Berghahn.

James, William. 1918. *Principles of psychology, 1*. New York: Henry Holt.

Jenkins, Richard. 2000. "Disenchantment, enchantment and re-enchantment: Max Weber at the millennium". *Max Weber Studies* 1: 11–32.

Johnston, Mark. 2010. *Surviving death*. Princeton, NJ: Princeton University Press.

Jonas, Hans. 1968. "Biological foundations of individuality." *International Philosophical Quarterly* 8 (2): 231–51.

Kaehler, Steven D. 2015. "Fuzzy logic—An introduction." *Seattle Robotics*. http://www.seattlerobotics.org/encoder/mar98/fuz/fl_part1.html.

Kan, Sergei. 2001. *Strangers to relatives: The adoption and naming of anthropologists in Native North America*. New York: University of Nebraska Press.

Kandel, Eric R. 2006. *In search of memory: The emergence of a new science of mind*. New York: W. W. Norton & Company.

Karsenti, Bruno. 1998. "Présentation." In *Les carnets de Lucien Lévy-Bruhl*. Edited by Bruno Karsenti, i-xxxvii. Paris: Presses Universitaires de France.

Kearney, Michael. 1975. "World view theory and study." *Annual Review of Anthropology* 4: 247–70.

Keck, Frédéric. 2008. *Lévy-Bruhl: Entre philosophie et anthropologie*. Paris: Éditions CNRS.

Kirschner, Marc, John Gerhart, and Tim Mitchison. 2000. "Molecular 'Vitalism'." *Cell* 100 (1): 79–88.

Kitcher, Philip. 1982. "Implications of incommensurability." *Proceedings of the Biennial Meeting of the Philosophy of Science Association* 2: 689–703.

Kohn, Eduardo. 2013. *How forests think: Toward an anthropology beyond the human*. Berkeley: University of California Press.

Konrad, Monica. 2005. *Nameless relations: Anonymity, Melanesia and reproductive gift exchange between British ova donors and recipients*. Oxford: Berghahn.

Koterski, Joseph W., S.J. 1992. "The doctrine of participation in Thomistic metaphysics." In *The future of Thomism*, edited by Deal W. Hudson and Dennis W. Moran, 185–96. Notre Dame, IN: University of Notre Dame Press.

Krige, Eileen J., and Jacob Krige. 1965. *The realm of the Rain-Queen: A study of the pattern of Lovedu society.* Oxford: Oxford University Press for the International African Institute.

Kuhn, Thomas S. 1962. *The structure of scientific revolutions.* Chicago: University of Chicago Press.

———. 1983. "Commensurability, comparability, communicability." In *PSA: Proceedings of the biennial meeting of the Philosophy of Science Association, 2: Symposia and invited papers*, edited by Peter D. Asquith and Thomas Nickles, 669–88. East Lansing, MI: Philosophy of Science Association.

Lakoff, George, and Mark Johnson. 1980. *Metaphors we live by.* Chicago: University of Chicago Press.

———. 1999. *The philosophy in the flesh: The embodied mind and its challenge to the Western thought.* New York: Basic Books.

Landes, Ruth. (1947) 1994. *The city of women.* Albuquerque: University of New Merxico Press.

Larsen, Timothy. 2014. *The slain god.* Oxford: Oxford University Press.

Latour, Bruno, 1991. *Nous n'avons jamais été modernes.* Paris: Découverte. (Available in English: *We have never been modern.* Translated by Catherine Porter. Cambridge, MA: Harvard University Press, 1993.)

———. 1996. "On interobjectivity." *Mind, Culture, and Activity: An International Journal* 3: 228–45.

Lederman, Leon M. and Christopher Hill. 2004. *Symmetry and the beautiful universe.* New York: Prometheus Books.

Lenarčič, Adam, and Michael Winter. 2013. "Affordances in situation theory." *Ecological Psychology* 25 (2): 155–81.

Levinas, Emmanuel. 1961. *Totalité et infini: Essai sur l'extériorité.* Paris: Livre de Poche/Kluwer Academic. (Available in English: *Totality and infinity: An essay on exteriority.* Translated by Alphonso Lingis. Dordrecht: Kluwer Academic, 1991.)

———. 1996. *Emmanuel Levinas: Basic philosophical writings.* Edited by Adriaan T. Peperzak, Simon Critchley, and Robert Bernasconi. Bloomington: Indiana University Press.

———. 1998. *Discovering existence with Husserl.* Translated by Richard L. Cohen and Michael B. Smith, Evanston, IL: Northwestern University Press.

Lévi-Strauss, Claude. (1958) 1963. "Do dual organizations exist?" In *Structural anthropology.* Translated by Claire Jacobson and Brooke Grundfest Schoepft, 132–63. New York: Basic Books.

————. 1966. *The savage mind.* Chicago: University of Chicago Press.

————. 1973. "Réflexions sur l'atome de parenté." In *Anthropologie structurale deux,* 103–35. Paris: Plon.

————. 1998. "Entrevista. Lévi-Strauss nos 90: A antropologia de cabeça para baixo." Interview by Eduardo Viveiros de Castro. *Mana* 4 (2): 119–26.

————. 2000. "Apologie des amibes." In *En substance: Textes pour Françoise Héritier,* edited by Jean-Luc Jamard, Emmanuel Terray, and Margarita Xanthakou, 493–96. Paris: Fayard.

Lévy-Bruhl, Lucien. (1949) 1998. *Les carnets de Lucien Lévy-Bruhl.* Edited by Bruno Karsenti Paris: Presses Universitaires de France.

————. 1952. "A letter to E. E. Evans-Pritchard." *British Journal of Sociology* 3 (2): 117–23.

Lienhardt, Godfrey. 1985. "Self: Public, private: Some African representations." In *The category of the person: Anthropology, philosophy, history,* edited by Michael Carrithers, Steven Collins, and Steven Lukes, 141–47. Cambridge: Cambridge University Press.

Lloyd, G. E. R. 2014. "On the very possibility of mutual intelligibility." *HAU: Journal of Ethnography* 4 (2): 221–35.

Lupton, Julia Reinhard. 2015. "The affordances of hospitality: Shakespearean drama between history and phenomenology" *Poetics Today* 35 (4): 615–33.

Lynch, Michael P. 1998. *Truth in context: An essay on pluralism and objectivity.* Cambridge, MA: MIT Press.

Maggie, Ivonne. 1975. *Guerra de Orixá: Um estudo de ritual e conflito.* Rio de Janeiro: Zahar.

Malinowski, Bronislaw. 1932. *Argonauts of the Western Pacific.* London: Routledge & Sons.

Mariott, McKim. 1976. "Hindu transactions: Diversity without dualism." In *Transaction and meaning,* edited by Bruce Kapferer, 109–42 (ASA Essays in Anthropology 1). Philadelphia: ISHI Publications.

Mauss, Marcel. (1925) 2016. *The gift: Expanded edition.* Edited and translated by Jane I. Guyer. Chicago: HAU Books.

————. (1935) 2007. "Techniques of the body." In *Beyond the body proper: Reading the anthropology of material life,* edited by Margaret Lock and Judith Farquhar, 271–93. New York: Duke University Press.

————. (1938) 1985. "A category of the human mind: The notion of person; the notion of self." Translated by W. D. Halls. In *The category of the person:*

Anthropology, philosophy, history, edited by Michael Carrithers, Steven Collins, and Steven Lukes, 1–25. Cambridge: University Press.

Maybury-Lewis, David. 1974. *Akwe-Shavante society*. Oxford: Oxford University Press.

Mills, Martin A. 2013. "The opposite of witchcraft: Evans-Pritchard and the problem of the person." *Journal of the Royal Anthropological Institute* (N.S.) 19: 18–33.

Moore, George E. 1919. "External and internal relations." *Proceedings of the Aristotelian Society* (N.S.) 20: 40–62.

Moss, Lawrence S. 2014. "Non-wellfounded set theory". *The Stanford Encyclopedia of Philosophy* (Winter Edition), edited by Edward N. Zalta. http://plato.stanford.edu/archives/win2014/entries/nonwellfounded-set-theory/.

Needham, Rodney. 1962. *Structure and sentiment: A test case in social anthropology*. Chicago: University of Chicago Press.

———. 1963. "Introduction." In *Primitive classification*, Émile Durkheim and Marcel Mauss, vii–xlviii. Chicago: University of Chicago Press.

———. 1967. "Percussion and transition." *Man* (N.S.) 2: 606–14.

———. 1972. *Belief, language, and experience*. Oxford: Basil Blackwell.

———, ed. (1973) 1978. *Right and left: Essays on dual symbolic classification*. Chicago: University of Chicago Press.

———. 1975. "Polythetic classification: Convergence and consequences." *Man* (N.S.) 10: 349–69.

———. 1976. "Skulls and causality." *Man* (N.S.) 11 (1): 71–88.

———. 1978. *Primordial characters*. Charlottesville: University Press of Virginia.

———. 1980. *Reconnaissances*. Toronto: University of Toronto Press.

———. 1981. *Circumstantial deliveries*. Berkeley: University of California Press.

———. 1983. *Against the tranquility of axioms*. Berkeley: University of California Press.

———. 1985. *Exemplars*. Berkeley: University of California Press.

———. 1987. *Counterpoints*. Berkeley: University of California Press.

Newton, Michael. 2002. *Savage girls and wild boys: A history of feral children*. London: Faber & Faber.

Paleček, Martin, and Mark Risjord. 2013. "Relativism and the ontological turn within anthropology. *Philosophy of the Social Sciences* 43 (1): 3–23.

Parkin, Robert. 2013. "Relatedness as transcendence: On the renewed debate over the meaning of kinship." http://www.isca.ox.ac.uk/fileadmin/ISCA/JASO/2013/Parkin_JASO_5_1_2013.pdf.

Pedersen, Morten Axel. 2012. "Common sense: A review of certain reviews of the 'ontological turn'." *Anthropology of This Century* 5. http://aotcpress.com/articles/common_nonsense/#sthash.1yvGKe2k.dpufPedersen.

Pina-Cabral, João de. 1986. *Sons of Adam, daughters of Eve: The peasant worldview of the Alto Minho (NW Portugal)*. Oxford: Clarendon Press. http://pina-cabral.org/PDFs/001_Adam.pdf.

————. 1989. "L'Héritage de Maine: L'érosion des categories d'analyse dans l'étude des phénomènes familiaux en Europe." *Ethnologie Française* 19: 329–40.

————. 1992. "Against translation." In *Europeans observed*, edited by João de Pina-Cabral and John Campbell, 1–23. London: Macmillan/St. Antony's.

————. 1993. "Tamed violence: Genital symbolism in Portuguese popular culture." *Man* (N.S.) 28: 101–20.

————. (1993) 2008. *Aromas de Urze e de Lama*. Illustrated by Ruth Rosengarten. Lisbon: ICS.

————. 1997. "The threshold diffused: Margins, hegemonies and contradictions in contemporary anthropology." *African Studies* 56 (2): 31–51.

————. 2002a. *Between China and Europe: Person, culture and emotion in Macao* (LSE Monographs in Social Anthropology 74). London: Berg.

————. 2002b. "Dona Berta's garden: Reaching across the colonial boundary." *Etnográfica* VI (1): 77–91.

————. 2005. "The future of social anthropology." *Social Anthropology/Anthropologie Sociale* 13 (2): 119–28.

————. 2006. "Anthropology challenged: Notes for a debate." *Journal of the Royal Anthropological Institute* (N.S.) 12 (3): 663–73.

————. 2009. "The all-or-nothing syndrome and the human condition." *Social Analysis* 53 (2): 163–76.

————. 2010a. "The door in the middle: Six conditions for anthropology." In *Culture wars: Context, models and anthropologists' accounts*, edited by Deborah James, Evelyn Plaice, and Christina Toren, 152–69. New York: Berghahn.

————. 2010b. "The dynamism of plurals: An essay on equivocal compatibility." *Social Anthropology/Anthropologie Sociale* 18 (2): 1–15.

————. 2010c. "The truth of personal names." *Journal of the Royal Anthropological Society* (N.S) 16 (2): 297–312.

————. 2010d. "Xará: Namesakes in Southern Mozambique and Bahia (Brazil)." *Ethnos* 73 (3): 323–45.

———. 2011. "Afterword: What is an institution?" *Social Anthropology/Anthropologie Sociale* 19 (4): 477–94.

———. 2012a. "The functional fallacy: On the supposed dangers of name repetition." *History and Anthropology* 23 (1): 17–36.

———. 2012b. "Les noms de famille lusophones: Une lecture anthropologique." In *Cum nomine patris: I cognomi italiani nell'ambito dell'antropologia dell'Europa Mediterranea*, edited by Roberto Bizzocchi, Andréa Addobbati, and Gregorio Salinero, 155–68. Pisa: Pub. Universitá di Pisa.

———. 2013a. "Albinos don't die: Belief and ethnicity in Mozambique." In *Philosophy and anthropology*, edited by Ananta Giri and John Clammer, 305–21. London: Anthem Press.

———. 2013b. "The core of affects: Namer and named in Bahia (NE Brazil)." *Journal of the Royal Anthropological Institute* (N.S.) 19 (1): 75–101.

———. 2013c. "The two faces of mutuality: Contemporary themes in anthropology." *Anthropological Quarterly* 86 (1): 257–74.

———. 2014a. "On the resilience of superstition." In *Religion and science as forms of life: Anthropological insights into reason and unreason*, edited by Carles Salazar and Joan Bestard, 264–85. Oxford: Berghahn.

———. 2014b. "World: An anthropological examination (part 1)." *HAU: Journal of Ethnography* 4 (1): 49–73.

———. 2014c. "World: An anthropological examination (part 2)" *HAU: Journal of Ethnography* 4 (3): 149–194.

———. 2016. "Brazilian serialities: Personhood and radical embodied cognition." *Current Anthropology* 57 (3): 247–60.

Pina-Cabral, João, and Vanda Aparecida da Silva. 2013. *Gente livre: Consideração e pessoa no Baixo Sul da Bahia*. São Paulo: Terceiro Nome.

Pitt-Rivers, Julian. 1992. "The personal factors in fieldwork." In *Europe observed*, edited by João de Pina-Cabral and John K. Campbell, 133–47. London: Macmillan/St. Antony's.

Porqueres i Gené, Enric, ed. 2009. *Défis contemporains de la parenté*. Paris: Éditions de l'EHESS.

Pouillon, Jean, 1982. "Remarks on the verb 'to believe'." In *Between religion and transgression: Structuralist essays in religion, history and myth*, edited by Michel Izard and Pierre Smith, 1–8. Translated by John Leavitt. Chicago: University of Chicago Press.

Praet, Istvan. 2015. "La lune de Saturne et les 'nous' oecuméniques: Entre astrobiologie et anthropologie." *Gradhiva* 22: 137–66.

Prinz, Jesse, and Andy Clark. 2004. "Putting concepts to work: Some thoughts for the twenty-first century." *Mind & Language* 19 (1): 57–69.

Quine, W. V. (1960) 2013. *Word and object*. Cambridge, MA: MIT Press.

Quine, W. V., and J. S. Ullian. 1978. *The web of belief.* Second edition. New York: McGraw-Hill.

Radcliffe-Brown, A. R. (1940) 1952. *Structure and function in primitive society.* Edited by E. Evans-Pritchard and Fred Eggan. London: Cohen and West.

Radcliffe-Brown, A. R., and Daryll Forde. 1950. *African systems of kinship and marriage.* London: Oxford University Press for the International African Institute.

Rapport, N. J. 2001. "The anthropology of personhood." In *The international encyclopedia of the social and behavioral sciences*, edited by N. J. Smelser and P. B. Baltes, 11339–43. Amsterdam: Elsevier.

Ricoeur, Paul. (1997) 2004. "Otherwise: A reading of Emmanuel Levinas' 'Otherwise than being or beyond essence'." Translated by Matthew Escobar. *Yale French Studies* 104: 82–99.

Rivière, Peter. (1971) 2004. "Marriage: A reassessment." In *Rethinking kinship and marriage*, edited by Rodney Needham, 57–74 (ASA series). London: Routledge.

Robbins, Joel. 2007. "Continuity thinking and the problem of Christian culture: Belief, time and the anthropology of Christianity." *Current Anthropology* 48 (1): 5–38.

Ross, Timothy J. 2010. *Fuzzy logic with engineering applications.* Third edition. Chichester, UK: Wiley.

Ruel, Malcolm. (1982) 2002. "Christians as believers." In *A reader in the anthropology of religion*, edited by Michael Lambek, 99–113. Oxford: Blackwell.

Ryder, John. 2013. *The things in heaven and earth: An essay in pragmatic naturalism.* New York: Fordham University Press.

Sabbatucci, Dario. 2000. *La prospettiva storico-religiosa.* Rome: Seam.

Sahlins, Marshall. 2011a. "What is kinship (part one)." *Journal of the Royal Anthropological Institute* (N.S.) 17 (1): 2–19.

———. 2011b. "What is kinship (part two)." *Journal of the Royal Anthropological Institute* (N.S.) 17 (2): 227–42.

Sartre, Jean-Paul. 1936. *L'imagination.* Paris: Pressed Universitaires de France. (Available in English: *The imagination.* Translated by Kenneth Williford and David Rudrauf. Abingdon, UK: Routledge, 2012.)

Schaeffer, Jean-Marie. 2007. *La fin de l'exception humaine.* Paris: NRF/Gallimard.

Shapiro, Warren. 2008. "What human kinship is primarily about: Toward a critique of the new kinship studies." *Social Anthropology/Anthropologie Sociale* 16 (2): 137–53.

Short, T. L. 2007. *Peirce's theory of signs.* Cambridge: University Press.

Siegel, Daniel. 2016. *Mind: A journey to the heart of being human.* New York: Newton and Co.

Siegel, Susanna. 2010. *The contents of visual experience.* Oxford: Oxford University Press.

Southern, R. W. 1990. *Saint Anselm: A portrait in a landscape.* Cambridge: University Press.

Spinoza, Benedict de. 2013. *The ethics (Ethica ordine geometrico demonstrata).* BookRix online.

Steiner, Franz Baermann. 1999a. *Selected writings, 1: Taboo, truth, and religion.* Edited by Jeremy Adler and Richard Fardon. Oxford: Berghahn.

———. 1999b. *Selected writings, 2: Orientpolitik, value, and civilisation.* Edited by Jeremy Adler and Richard Fardon. Oxford: Berghahn.

Strathern, Marilyn. 1984. "Subject or object? Women and the circulation of valuables in Highlands New Guinea." In *Women and property—Women as property*, edited by Renée Hirschon, 158–75. London: Croom Helm.

———. 1988. *The gender of the gift.* Berkeley: University of California Press.

———. 1995. *The relation: Issues in complexity and scale.* Cambridge: Prickly Pear Pamphlet. http://www.thememorybank.co.uk/pricklypear/6.pdf.

———. 2004. *Partial connections.* London: Rowman AltaMira.

———. 2005. *Kinship, law, and the unexpected. Relatives are always a surprise.* Cambridge: University Press.

Tambiah, Stanley J. 1990. *Magic, science, religion, and the scope of rationality* (Lewis Henry Morgan Lectures 1984). Cambridge: University Press.

Taussig, Michael. 1997. *The magic of the state.* London: Routledge.

Thomas, Keith. (1971) 1991. *Religion and the decline of magic.* London: Penguin.

Thompson, Evan. 2007. *Mind in life: Biology, phenomenology, and the sciences of mind.* Cambridge, MA: Belknap for Harvard University Press.

Tomasello, Michael. 2008. *Origins of human communication.* Cambridge, MA: MIT Press.

Toren, Christina. 1990. *Making sense of hierarchy: Cognition as social process in Fiji* (LSE Anthropology Series 61). London: Athlone.

———. 1993. "Making history: The significance of childhood cognition for a comparative anthropology of mind." *Man* (N.S.) 28 (3): 461–78.

————. 1999. *Mind, materiality and history: Explorations in Fijian ethnography*. London: Routledge.

————. 2002. "Anthropology as the whole science of what it is to be human." In *Anthropology beyond culture*, edited by Richard G. Fox and Barbara J. King, 105–24. London: Berg.

————. 2012. "Imagining the world that warrants our imagination—The revelation of ontogeny." *Cambridge Anthropology* 30 (1): 64–79.

Toren, Christina, and João de Pina-Cabral, eds. 2011. *The challenge of epistemology: Anthropological perspectives*. Oxford: Berghahn

Trevarthen, Colwyn. 1980. "The foundations of human intersubjectivity: Development of interpersonal and cooperative understanding in infants." In *The social foundations of language and thought: Essays in honour of J. S. Bruner*, edited by David R. Olson, 316–42. New York: Norton.

————. 1990. "Signs before speech." In *The semiotic web, 1989*, edited by Thomas A. Sebeok and Jean Umiker-Sebeok, 689–775. Berlin: Mouton de Gruyter.

————. 1993. "The self born in intersubjectivity: An infant communicating." In *The perceived self: Ecological and interpersonal sources of self-knowledge*, edited by Ulric Neisser, 121–73. Cambridge: Cambridge University Press.

————. 1998. "The concept and foundations of infant intersubjectivity." In *Intersubjective communication and emotion in early ontogeny*, edited by Stein Bråten, 15–46. Cambridge: Cambridge University Press.

Tsing, Anna. 2011. "Worlding the Matsutake diaspora: Or, can actor-network theory experiment with holism?" In *Experiments in holism*, edited by Ton Otto and Nils Bubandt, 47–66. Oxford: Blackwell.

Valverde, Paulo J. 2000. *Máscara, mato e morte*. Edited by João de Pina-Cabral. Lisbon: Celta.

Van Sant, George M. 1959. "A proposed property of relations." *The Journal of Philosophy* 56 (1): 25–31.

Varela, Francisco, Evan Thompson, and Eleanor Rosch. 1991. *The embodied mind: Cognitive science and human experience*. Cambridge, MA: MIT Press.

Veyne, Paul. (1983) 1988. *Did the Greeks believe in their myths? An essay on the constitutive imagination*. Translated by Paula Wissing. Chicago: University of Chicago Press.

Vieira, Pe. António. (1640) 1959. "Sermão da nossa Senhora do Ó." In *Sermões*, ed. Pe. Gonçalo Alves, Book X, 203–32. Porto: Lello.

Viveiros de Castro, Eduardo. 2007. "Intensive filiation and demonic alliance." http://amazon.wikia.com/wiki/Intensive_filiation_and_demonic_

alliance_-_E._Viveiros_de_Castro. (Original publication: "Filiação intensiva e aliança demoníaca." *Novos Estudos CEBRAP* 77: 91–126.)

———. 2009. *Métaphysiques cannibales.* Paris: Presses Universitaires de France. (Available in English: *Cannibal metaphysics.* Translated by Peter Skafish. Minneapolis: Univocal, 2014.)

———. 2010. "In some sense." *Interdisciplinary Science Review* 35 (3–4): 318–33.

———. 2011. "Zeno and the art of anthropology: Of lies, beliefs, paradoxes, and other truths." *Common Knowledge* 17 (1): 128–45.

Wagner, Roy. 1975. *The invention of culture.* Chicago: University of Chicago Press.

Waismann, Friedrich. 1968. *How I see philosophy.* Edited by Rom Harré. London: Macmillan.

Wateau, Fabienne. 2000. *Conflitos e água de rega: Ensaio sobre a organização social no vale de Melgaço.* Lisbon: D. Quixote.

Weber, Max. 1948. "Science as a vocation". In *From Max Weber: essays in sociology,* edited by H. H. Gerth, and C. W. Mills, 129–56. London: Routledge & Kegan Paul.

Wilson, Monica. 1951. *Good company: A study of Nyakyusa age-villages.* London: International African Institute.

———. 1957. *Rituals of kinship among the Nyakyusa.* London: Oxford University Press for the International African Institute.

———. 1959. *Communal rituals of the Nyakyusa.* London: Oxford University Press for the International African Institute.

Winch, Peter. (1958) 2008. *The idea of a social science and its relation to philosophy.* London: Routledge.

Winnicott, D. W. 1971. *Playing and reality.* London: Routledge.

Wittgenstein, Ludwig. (1953) 1967. *Philosophical investigations.* Translated by G. E. M. Anscombe. Third edition. Oxford: Blackwell.

Wood, David, Jerome S. Bruner, and Gail Ross. 1976. "The role of tutoring in problem solving." *Journal of Child Psychology and Psychiatry* 17: 89–100.

Wrathall, Mark, and Morganna Lambeth. 2011. "Heidegger's last god." *Inquiry* 54 (2): 160–82.

Zadeh, L. A. 1987. *Fuzzy sets and applications: Selected papers by L. A. Zadeh.* Edited by R. R. Yager et al. New York: John Wiley.

Index

HAU Books is committed to publishing the most distinguished texts in classic and advanced anthropological theory. The titles aim to situate ethnography as the prime heuristic of anthropology, and return it to the forefront of conceptual developments in the discipline. HAU Books is sponsored by some of the world's most distinguished anthropology departments and research institutions, and releases its titles in both print editions and open-access formats.

www.haubooks.com

Supported by

HAU-N. E. T.
Network of Ethnographic Theory

University of Aarhus – EPICENTER (DK)
University of Amsterdam (NL)
University of Bergen (NO)
Brown University (US)
California Institute of Integral Studies (US)
University of Campinas (BR)
University of Canterbury (NZ)
University of Chicago (US)
University College London (UK)
University of Colorado Boulder Libraries (US)
CNRS – Centre d'Études Himalayennes (FR)
Cornell University (US)
University of Edinburgh (UK)
The Graduate Institute, Geneva Library (CH)
University of Helsinki (FL)
The Higher School of Economics in St. Petersburg (RU)
Humboldt University of Berlin (DE)
Indiana University Library (US)
Johns Hopkins University (US)
University of Kent (UK)
Lafayette College Library (US)
London School of Economics and Political Science (UK)
Institute of Social Sciences of the University of Lisbon (PL)
University of Manchester (UK)
The University of Manchester Library (UK)
Max-Planck Institute for the Study of Religious and Ethnic
Diversity at Göttingen (DE)
Musée de Quai Branly (FR)
Museu Nacional – UFRJ (BR)
Norwegian Museum of Cultural History (NO)
University of Oslo (NO)
University of Oslo Library (NO)
Princeton University (US)
University of Rochester (US)
SOAS, University of London (UK)
University of Sydney (AU)
University of Toronto Libraries (CA)

www.haujournal.org/haunet